The Madrasa in Asia

The Madrasa in Asia

Political Activism and Transnational Linkages

Farish A. Noor, Yoginder Sikand
& Martin van Bruinessen (eds.)

MANOHAR
2009

First published by Amsterdam University Press in 2008
Reprinted 2009

ISBN 978-81-7304-837-1

Published by
Ajay Kumar Jain *for*
Manohar Publishers & Distributors
4753/23 Ansari Road, Daryaganj
New Delhi 110 002

Printed at
Salasar Imaging Systems
Delhi 110 035

Contents

Acknowledgement

Most of these essays are updated versions of papers that were first presented at the international conference 'The Madrasa in Asia: Transnational Linkages and Real or Alleged Political Roles', in May 2004 in Leiden and jointly organised by the International Institute for the Study of Islam in the Modern World (ISIM) and the Zentrum Moderner Orient (Centre for Modern Oriental Studies) of Berlin. Chapters 4 and 7 were commissioned especially for this volume.

Introduction

Behind the Walls: Re-Appraising the Role and Importance of Madrasas in the World Today

Farish A. Noor, Yoginder Sikand and Martin van Bruinessen

The term madrasa derives from the Arabic root *darasa*, which means 'to study,' and is related to the term for lesson, *dars*. Technically, a madrasa is an institution where lessons are imparted or, in other words, a school. In the Arabic-speaking world, the term applies to all sorts of schools, including both those that teach only the traditional Islamic subjects as well as those that are completely secularised and have no provision for religious education. In much of the non-Arabic speaking parts of Asia, however, the word is generally understood in a more restricted sense – as a school geared essentially to providing students with what is understood as Islamic education, although the ways in which this is conceived and its scope are widely divergent.

Madrasas, as understood in this sense – as schools for the imparting of Islamic knowledge – have for centuries served the crucial function of training Muslim religious specialists or ulama, besides imparting basic Islamic education to Muslim children who need not necessarily continue their training to become professional religious experts. They are instrumental in sustaining, preserving, promoting and transmitting the Islamic tradition over the generations. They are not a homogenous phenomenon, however, contrary to what the media generally presents them as. They differ widely in terms of curricula, teaching methods and approaches to the challenges of modernity, which makes any generalisations about them hazardous and untenable. They also differ in terms of the levels of religious education that they provide their students, from the small *maktab* or *kuttab* attached to a mosque and catering to small children, providing them with skills to read and recite the Quran and perform basic Islamic rituals, to university-size *jami'as* and *Dar al-'ulums*.

Despite the central importance that madrasas play in the lives of Muslim communities around the world, relatively little academic attention has been paid to them. Advocates of the 'modernisation' thesis had assumed that along with the economic and social 'development' of Muslim societies, which they saw as following the path adopted by Western countries, the influence of religion, including of the madrasas, would decline significantly, relegating the madrasas to the status of relics from a by-gone age. Consequently, scholars of contemporary Muslim societies devoted relatively little attention to the madrasas, focussing, instead, on groups such as 'modernists' and Islamists, who were thought to be the harbingers of a new age.[1]

However, the predictions made by advocates of the 'modernisation' thesis proved to be hollow. Despite the fact that in many predominantly Muslim countries authoritarian governments either forcibly closed down madrasas or merged them with the general or 'modern' educational stream in many other parts of the world, most notably in South and Southeast Asia, the number of madrasas increased substantially, a phenomenon that continues to the present day. The Islamic Revolution in Iran, the role of Western- and Saudi-funded madrasas in Pakistan in training the *mujahidin* to fight the Soviets, the coming to power of the Taliban in Afghanistan and so on, all helped propel the madrasas, particularly of Asia, into the limelight of the media.

This resulted in a sudden burst of writings on the madrasas, especially by journalists. These reports were often sensational, focussing on those madrasas or ulama that were depicted as 'radical', 'militant' and 'fundamentalist'. Broad generalisations were made about all madrasas based on these isolated instances. Consequently, madrasas, long forgotten by the media, suddenly received a lot of bad press. The word madrasa was used to conjure up lurid images of blood-thirsty mullahs, ranting and raving against the 'modern' world and against 'non-Muslims' to help establish the global hegemony of Islam. This was despite the fact that the vast majority of madrasas did not fit this description, being concerned mainly with the transmission of the Islamic scholarly tradition, and remaining aloof from overt political involvement, for which they are often derided by their radical Islamist critics.

In the wake of the 9/11 attacks in the United States and the bombings in Bali, madrasas came under even greater suspicion as alleged breeding grounds for 'terrorists'. From the Taliban to the Bali bombers, many radical Islamic movements appeared to be rooted in madrasas, or so it was alleged by many in the media as well as by many politicians. Al Qaeda's leaders and the men who carried out the 9/11 attacks had no madrasa backgrounds, but media coverage indicated that Osama bin Laden was very popular among many madrasa students across Asia. In the Western popular imagination, madrasas came to be seen as 'incubators for violent extremism' and 'jihad factories,' imprisoning Muslim youth in backwardness and indoctrinating them with a hatred for the West that was considered to be the root cause of all that was said to be 'wrong' with Islam.

Talk of madrasas today is thus often laced with suspicion if not outright contempt and an attitude that can best be described as adversarial. Living as we do in the age of the global 'War on Terror', where entire regions such as Central and Southeast Asia have been designated as 'front line conflict zones' by the dominant Western powers, madrasas are often seen and presented as sniping posts against the frontiers of the Occident, fortresses that occasionally send out armies of would-be martyrs to die in the name of Islam. In American deliberations on long-term strategies to prevent 'Islamic terrorism', the madrasa became a subject of primary concern. Consequently, there has been much pressure on regional governments, from Pakistan and India to Thailand and Indonesia, to bring madrasa education under closer control and monitor 'radical' tendencies. 'Experts' like the Brookings Institution's P.W. Singer have repeated the Huntingtonian thesis of the inevitable 'Clash of Civilisations' with a vengeance, talking of the *'new cultural war to be won'* – a campaign whose success can only be guaranteed with the taming of the madrasa beast.[2]

The madrasa was the first spearhead in the White House policy developed after 9/11 that attempted to change the face of Islam, with Pakistan being its most immediate target. When President Pervez Musharraf visited Washington, DC at the time of the offensive against Afghanistan, he was offered additional aid for educational reform and was told in no uncertain terms that there changes needed to be made in the madrasa curriculum to ensure that its students became 'integrated' into the modern world.[3] The Indian and Thai governments have, for reasons of their own, clamped down on the madrasas and *pondoks* (the traditional Malay equivalent of the madrasa), blaming them, without proper justification, for a string of violent incidents and the widespread disaffection among the Muslims of Kashmir and Southern Thailand. The governments of Malaysia and Indonesia were pressured to place their *pondoks* and *pesantrens* under close surveillance. In fact, however, the Bali bombings of October 2002 were the only major terrorist attack in which a number of the participants had a madrasa background. Even in this case, the planners of the attack were – not unlike most other acts of terrorism – men with modern college or university educations, and who had never studied in madrasas. There is, therefore, good reason to question the policy makers and media's obsession with the madrasa.

This is not to deny, however, that *some* madrasas in Pakistan have indeed been engaged in providing armed training to their students. Other madrasas elsewhere may not do so directly, but may encourage their students to see the world in starkly dualistic, almost Manichaean terms, exhorting them to wage war against 'unbelievers' in order to protect Muslims, whom they see as under grave threat from the West or other non-Muslim powers, or in order to establish global Islamic supremacy. The mistake that is often made, however, is to regard these madrasas as representative of all madrasas as such, a generalisation that is quite unwarranted. Further, these 'radical' madrasas also need to be understood in the particular contexts in which they are located. The militancy that they espouse may have less to do with any tendency inherent in the madrasa system as such than with local and international political factors.

Increasing economic inequality, which is especially conspicuous in a country like Pakistan but which has accompanied the neo-liberal remaking of the world everywhere, has contributed significantly to the rise of radical and anti-Western protest movements, as have the growing cultural contradictions between Westernised urban elites and rural masses. Competition between different claimants to religious authority has also often tended to strengthen radical tendencies. But it would be naïve to the point of inanity to deny that Muslim radicalism is at least to some extent a response to Western policies. Without taking into account such factors as the heavy-handed military interventions in defence of Western and more specifically American interests (most recently the invasion and occupation of Iraq), the consistent Western support of dictatorships in the Muslim world, Western connivance in Israeli aggression in Palestine, the phenomenon of militancy in certain madrasas cannot be properly understood.

In the case of Pakistan, the only country where there has been any significant involvement by selected madrasas in providing mental and physical training for armed *jihad*, this connection goes back to the 1980s international campaign to support the Afghan *mujahidin*, bankrolled by the US and Saudi Arabia and co-ordinated by Pakistan's military intelligence organisation ISI. The later Taliban movement as well as the various armed groups fighting in Indian Kashmir since the 1990s were largely the creations of ISI.[4]

Seen in a sociological vacuum, radicalism is often projected as simply an ideological problem or phenomenon, somehow inherent in Islam. Based on this conclusion, the solution that is proffered to combat it is often through measures that entail harsh physical control or even elimination, which, in the long-run, only further compounds the problem rather than resolving it. Clearly, in seeking to understand this sort of radicalism, the root causes must be kept in mind.

It is unfortunate, but true, that today discussions about madrasa education are generally framed in terms of their real or alleged security and political implications. In the process, the valuable functions that many madrasas play in providing free or highly subsidised education, along with boarding and lodging, for vast numbers of Muslim children from impoverished families, is readily forgotten. The expansion of the madrasa network must be appreciated in the context of abysmal levels of poverty in many Muslim communities, with governments, often under pressure from international, Western-dominated organisations such as the World Bank and the International Monetary Fund, being forced to cut back on welfare spending and 'opening' up their economies, and egged on by dominant Western powers to enter into a fierce arms race so as to oil the machines of the international weapons industry, thereby reducing resources for public education. Obviously, if governments were encouraged and enabled to spend much more on quality education for the Muslim poor than they are presently doing, many Muslim families would prefer to send their children to general schools rather than to madrasas. By situating the madrasa debate securely within a security-driven paradigm, without appreciating the crucial socio-economic roles that madrasas play in the lives of poor Muslims, this obvious point is obscured.

Madrasas and Modernity

It is ironic that the *madrasa* system today is often criticised and even ridiculed for its supposedly antiquated ways and its alleged stubborn resistance to any form of modernisation. In many parts of Asia, particularly in Southeast Asia, the term '*madrasa*' itself carries connotations of modernity and development, because the earliest institutions thus called in Malaysia and Indonesia emerged as a reaction to what was then seen as an outmoded form of education provided by the traditional *pondok* or *pesantren* systems of British Malaya and the Dutch East Indies. These early madrasas represented a response to colonial rule and missionary activities but were also influenced by recent reforms in the traditional education system in India and the Middle East, known to Southeast Asian Muslims through the connection to Mecca. Mecca was not only the centre of the annual *hajj* pilgrimage but also a centre of learning that attracted scholars and students from all over the Muslim world, and where many who refused to live under colonial rule took up residence. Indian traders and scholars established a modern madrasa there in 1874, the Madrasa Sawlatiyya, which trained several generations of Indian as well as Southeast Asian scholars and played a part in the national awakening in both regions.[5] This school was part of the religious and national revival in North India that also gave rise to the famous madrasa at Deoband.

The emergence of a new type of madrasas in the nineteenth century on the Indian subcontinent, which was modelled in part on the new Western-style schools introduced by the British, was not devoid of polemics and internal debates within the Indian Muslim community. The Indian revolt of 1857 against the British represented the last major effort on the part of some Hindu as well as Muslim elites, faced with the rising might of the British, to retain their increasingly threatened privileges. It appears that leading ulama participated or even led the fighting in several places, considering this as a religious *jihad* against the infidels. After the British forcibly crushed the revolt, they embarked on a bloody campaign against Muslim elites whom they saw as primarily responsible for the uprising. Numerous ulama, accused of having participated in or instigated the revolt, were sent to the gallows.[6] Scores more were dispatched to long spells of imprisonment in the Andaman islands.[7]

As a result of this evident loss of power, Muslims all over the subcontinent sought refuge in the modern madrasas of the late nineteenth century, which were meant to play the role of the last bastion of faded Mughal-Muslim glory. The most significant of the *madrasas* to emerge in the aftermath of the revolt of 1857 was the renowned Dar-ul-'Ulum, established in 1867 in the town of Deoband, in the Saharanpur district of the then United Provinces. The founders included leading ulama such as Qasim Nanotawi (1832-80) and Rashid Ahmad Gangohi (1828-1905), who were regarded as pioneers of the Indian freedom movement by subsequent generations of Indians. In setting up the *madrasa*, the founders of the Deoband school saw themselves as being engaged in an educational struggle, having now realised the futility of armed struggle against the country's new masters.[8]

Another prominent Indian *madrasa* to appear in the post-Mughal era was the Dar al-'Ulum Nadwat al-'Ulama (established in 1898). The Nadwa represented a pragmatic compromise of the ulama with the exigencies of colonial rule. The madrasa received generous financial support from rulers of various Muslim princely states, including Bhopal, Bahawalpur and Hyderabad, as well as from the Aga Khan, the leader of the Nizari Isma'ili Shi'as, in addition to donations from individual Muslim well-wishers. Over the years, the Nadwa managed to attract some of the leading Islamic scholars of northern India, such as the noted *'alim* Shibli Nu'mani (1857-1914), who joined the madrasa in 1905. In contrast to conservative ulama who saw the West as wholly evil, Shibli advocated a middle path, exhorting Muslims not to shun those aspects of 'modernity' that did not conflict with Islam. He pointed out that Muslims had not hesitated in the past to take advantage of the knowledge of people of other faiths, such as the Greeks, Romans, Persians and Hindus. Hence, he recommended that madrasas must also include modern subjects in their curricula, such as English, social and natural sciences and mathematics, without this affecting their religious character.[9] The Nadwa, and other such notable madrasas set up in India in the late colonial period, represented a certain Islamic approach to and appropriation of 'modernity'.

In Southeast Asia, we find the stirrings of similar educational reforms and political awakenings in the Straits Settlements, the cosmopolitan hubs connecting mainland and insular Southeast Asia with the wider world. Here, reform-minded Malay ulama such as Syed Sheikh al-Hadi and Sheikh Tahir Jalaluddin were among the first to introduce the madrasa as a modern alternative to the more traditional *pondok* school system. In the modern madrasas established in the British colonies of Singapore, Malacca and Penang such as the Madrasah al-Iqbal al-Islamiyyah (Singapore), Madrasah al-Hady (Malacca) and Madrasah al-Mashoor (Penang), new modes of teaching were employed for the first time in the Malay states. These madrasas were also the first Malay-Muslim institutions to pioneer the methods of the modern printing press, publishing not only religious texts but also journals and magazines that helped to create the fledgling imagined community of a literate public in the Malay Peninsula.

The point, therefore, is that the media's portrayal of madrasas as dens of unrepentant and incorrigible 'obscurantism' urgently needs to be re-examined and critiqued. Here, as elsewhere, such broad generalisations are quite unwarranted. It is true that certain madrasas are indeed hostile to any influence of 'modernity', but there are scores of others that today are pioneering their own Islamic ways to appropriate and express 'modernity'. Thus, for instance, the growing number of madrasas in many Asian countries that combine both secular and Islamic subjects, the many educational societies that run both madrasas and general schools, allowing madrasa students to enrol in the latter after finishing a basic course of study, and the large numbers of madrasas that have adjusted their timings in such a way as to allow their students to study in general schools simultaneously. For the ulama in the forefront of such reforms, this is not a deviation from Islam. Rather, they would argue that Islam is itself opposed to any rigid distinction between 'religious' and 'worldly' knowledge, and that, therefore, madrasa students should be encouraged to acquire different forms of 'useful' knowledge. This is a point that several essays in this volume address.

Unfortunately, given the way the grand madrasa debate has evolved in recent years, with sections of the media bent on presenting certain 'radical' madrasas, a small minority, as representative of all madrasas, these efforts of reformist ulama have hardly been given the attention they deserve. Highlighting these new ways of understanding and formulating Islamic education is, however, crucial, to opening up spaces for possible collaboration between madrasas, governments and non-governmental organisations to work on common goals. Obviously, efforts on the part of certain governments to force madrasas to 'reform' cannot bear any fruit in the face of the unwillingness of the ulama, and will only make them even more hostile and suspicious of talk of 'reform'. Surely, then, the way out is for governments to engage in serious dialogue with ulama proponents of madrasa 'reform', who, despite their invisibility in the media, are numerous. This requires intensive, field-based research in order to highlight these ulama voices, a task that the contributors to this book take upon themselves in their own ways.

Madrasas as Hubs in Transnational Networks

Besides the role of madrasas around the world as fountainheads of religious learning and guardians of tradition, and their increasingly important role in bringing a degree of general education to broad groups at the grassroots levels of society, another aspect that contributes to their societal importance is that they have long constituted nodes in extensive networks of communication. No madrasa stood alone; each was linked to other madrasas through a steady exchange of visiting scholars, teachers and students. Even in pre-modern times, ideas travelled across the Muslim world with surprising speed due to the madrasa network. In the nineteenth and twentieth centuries, when the number of madrasas expanded rapidly, the pattern of communications also became more complex, and madrasas provided the infrastructure to various religious and political movements, reformist, anti-colonial, and nationalist. Whereas in the Ottoman Empire, the last great Muslim state, the major madrasas were all established and supervised by the state, throughout most of Asia the madrasas were established by private initiatives and they jealously guarded their autonomy vis-à-vis the state. In their own way they contributed to the integration of the Muslim world, bringing hitherto marginal localities within the orbit of a global system long before the term 'globalisation' became commonplace. This was a parallel globalisation driven not by the flow of capital but rather by the traffic and circulation of ideas – perhaps the most remarkable form of transnationalism from below.

Even at the lowest levels of education, the madrasa introduced its students to an awareness of the wider world. The students at the madrasa hail from different regions; the friendships moulded here, which are often for life, broaden their horizons and facilitate travel. The teachers have usually studied in various other madrasas, often completing their own education in one of the major centres of learning in the wider region or abroad, and the more ambitious students follow in their footsteps. For many Asian students, the great mosque schools of Mecca and Medina or the Azhar in Cairo long were considered highly desirable destinations, and most of the founders of new madrasas had in fact studied in one of these centres. The different regions of the Muslim world were connected with one another through these centres. The annual pilgrimage to Mecca and Cairo's privileged position in book printing consolidated and strengthened the communication networks emanating from these cities.

In the course of the nineteenth and twentieth centuries, however, several other centres of learning and dissemination of religious thought, often more 'modern' than the old centres, emerged. The seminary at Deoband and the Nadwat al-'Ulama seminary at Lucknow attract students not only from all over India but from neighbouring countries and Southeast Asia as well. A more recent madrasa that enjoys popularity among students from all over Asia and Africa is the Abu Nur institute in Damascus (established by the late Ahmad Kaftaru, Syria's mufti and a Sufi of the Naqshbandi order), and surprisingly, the seminaries of Qom in Iran attract not only students from Shi'i communities abroad but even from predominantly Sunni regions. Reformist, Islamist, pietistic and puritanical trends in Islam have established their own prestigious centres, and most of these centres have spawned their own networks of secondary and even tertiary centres.

The madrasa networks have become considerably denser and less centralised over the past century, and the movement of people and ideas through these networks has grown more complex. This has been due at least in part to the developments in communication and transportation technologies, as well more generally the increased demand for education and the proliferation of distinct sub-traditions of scholarship. The late-colonial and post-colonial migration of numerous Asians to parts of Europe, Africa and North America has added even more to the complexity of the networks and the range of ideas communicated in them. Contrary to widespread prejudice, the world of the madrasa is not a stagnant and backward relic of the past, isolated from and in opposition to the modern world; it is precisely the madrasa networks that connect geographically marginal and socially subaltern groups with other social circles and impart a more cosmopolitan outlook. The essays in this volume provide rare insights into the transnational dimension of madrasa education and communication, documenting not only transnational flows between Asia and the Middle East but also the increasingly significant exchanges of people and ideas between different parts of Asia.

Alleged links with Terror Networks and the Clampdown on the Madrasas

These transnational madrasa networks never received much attention, either scholarly or political, but that changed with the 'War on Terror,' when madrasas came under suspicion as being hotbeds of radicalism and the props of 'international terror networks.' With 'radical Islam' being cast as the adversary to American ideas and America's ambitions, the madrasa system was soon brought to the fore and re-presented as a major cause of concern for security and strategy analysts. American foreign policy outreach extends well beyond military-strategic objectives alone and American (as well as European) strategy analysts have already begun talking about the final battle for the 'hearts and minds' of Muslims via the proxy battle for control of the madrasas. At the heart of the matter is the belief that madrasas remain fundamentally anti-Western *in toto*; are profoundly anti-secular and bent on keeping Muslims separated from the rest of humanity. This impression was reinforced even more after the bombing attacks in London in June 2005, after which it was revealed that at least one of the bombers had travelled to Pakistan for his religious education in a madrasa.[10]

As the logic of the 'War on Terror' followed its inevitable course, America's political and military elite have tried their best to win the support of Muslim leaders and governments. The warming of America's frosty relationship with Pakistan came in the form of outright support for the military government of General Pervez Musharraf, despite the fact that Washington had initially condemned the *coup d'état* that brought the military leader to power. US involvement in the country has included not only the importation of surveillance technology, expertise and personnel, but also a sustained effort to help the Musharraf government crack down on 'errant' madrasas that are said to be linked to radical Islamist groups all over the country.

In neighbouring Southeast Asia – a region that was dubbed 'the second front in the global War on Terror' – US intervention in the domestic political affairs of the ASEAN states was equally evident. In Indonesia, great efforts were made to help promote 'moderate' Islam via US funding for a wide range of Muslim 'civil society' activism. Media coverage of the growing tensions and increasing religiously inspired violence in places such as southern Thailand and the southern Philippines also attempted to draw links between the escalation of bloodshed and the alleged 'militant activities' taking place in local madrasas there.

The madrasas of Southeast Asia have come under tremendous media and political scrutiny since 2001. The governments of countries like Singapore and Malaysia have attempted to control the development of local madrasas through a combination of inducements and restrictions, isolating important Muslim constituencies and risking further domestic political fall-out in the process. In Malaysia, the situation was further complicated due to the government's repeated claim that many of the country's unregistered madrasas were indirectly linked to the main Islamic opposition party PAS, and were thus being used as 'recruitment' and 'training centres' for future supporters and members of the Islamic opposition.

The net result of this concerted campaign to demonise, stigmatise and regulate the madrasa system has been the disruption of educational services for thousands of young Muslims throughout the world. In some cases, the governments concerned have attempted to shut down the madrasas altogether without tackling the fundamental root problem that explains their popularity and relevance in the first place: the near-total absence of a functioning state educational system. Pakistan's attempts to control its madrasas is a case in point; the country has a high illiteracy rate and a substantial proportion of its population has no access to basic education in state schools.[11]

In other cases, the attempts to reform the *madrasas* have been marred by ill-disguised political agendas that have nothing to do with the desire to 'modernise' Islamic education in the first place. In India, Thailand, Singapore and the Philippines for instance, talk of *madrasas* and the alleged threats that are contained within their walls is often laced with a profound and evident anti-Muslim bias. In India, in particular, attempts to start a sensible and rational discussion on *madrasa* reform have been tainted by the anti-Muslim sentiments of Hindu fascist parties. Under these kinds of circumstances it is easy to understand why many Muslims in these countries regard any attempt to reform the *madrasas* as part of a grander strategy against Islam and Muslim interests in general. In some Muslim-majority countries like Malaysia and Indonesia talk of controlling the menace of militant *madrasas* is equally coloured by domestic political concerns, based on the belief that these institutions serve as the bedrock of popular support for domestic Islamic opposition parties, movements and NGOs.

As a result of this growing climate of fear that is being actively stoked by the media, political ideologues and security analysts alike, one of the most expansive global networks that has emerged over the past few hundred years is being increasingly threatened. In August 2005, Pakistan's Pervez Musharraf announced that foreign students would henceforth no longer be allowed to study in the country's madrasas. The few foreign students who remain in the country have either gone into hiding or risk the danger of being arrested and deported for overstaying their visas. In neighbouring India, the flow of foreign students to the country's historically important and prestigious madrasas has fallen to a mere trickle. Across the Indian Ocean, the countries of Southeast Asia have reciprocated by denying their students the much needed 'Certificate of Approval' that would allow them to travel abroad to further their studies. Consequently, it can be predicted that in the coming years, this transnational network of itinerant students and scholars may cease to exist altogether, bringing to a graceless and untimely end a significant page of Muslim history: that of the global transfer of education and ideas across a global Muslim landscape that did not recognise the formal boundaries of the modern nation-state.

The Essays in this Volume

This volume brings together essays by scholars who have worked extensively on the issue of madrasa education in different Asian countries. They highlight some of the features and challenges that madrasas in these countries share, as well as the fact of their considerable diversity, which makes generalisations about madrasas hazardous and misleading.

Yoginder Sikand's account of the developments taking place in the Dar al-'Ulum in Deoband, widely regarded as one of the most important and influential madrasas on the Indian subcontinent and beyond, focuses on the debate surrounding the theme of educational reform in the madrasa itself. Sikand shows how the Deoband madrasa has from the outset dedicated itself to a singular mission: namely, to create a generation of morally-upright and independent Muslim scholars whose future role will be that of the religious leaders and scholars of their community. Yet, as Sikand demonstrates, even an institution as well-known as Deoband has not been able to escape the debate on reform due to internal and external pressures. Central to the question of reform is the challenge of upgrading and improving the curriculum of the madrasa without compromising its Muslim identity and standards of religious education. Here Sikand shows that the reluctance to expand the curriculum of the madrasas has less to do with a suspicion towards 'modernity', Western sciences or the outside world, but is rather motivated by the belief that the madrasa is a unique institution that serves the primary purpose of being the custodian and reproducer of authentic Islamic knowledge and instruction. Sikand also illustrates the difficulties of reforming the madrasas by setting the process in the wider context of an India that has witnessed an alarming rise of right-wing conservative Hindu politics, where Hindutva parties have been vocal in their demands to alter the teaching of the madrasas to make them conform to a 'national mainstream' that has increasingly been defined in Hindu-centric communitarian terms. Sikand argues that the reform process has been an embattled one thanks to these overbearing pressures on the madrasas as a whole, which in turn explains the slow pace of reform and resistance on the part of many Muslim schools in a country like India.

Moving on from Sikand, Dietrich Reetz's chapter on the Deoband madrasa sets the school in a broader regional and international context, showing how the Dar al-'Ulum at Deoband emerged from its historical role as a bastion of Indian Muslim identity to become a well-knit and integrated network of schools that foregrounds a specific and increasingly sectarian school of Muslim thought. While Sikand explains the madrasa's complicated relationship with the wider Indian Hindu social milieu of modern-day India, Reetz elaborates on Deoband's role in foregrounding its own reformist and puritanical interpretation of Islam before that of other schools of Muslim thought. Paying special attention to the role played by foreign students, the Deoband alumni network, and Deoband's numerous publications and organisational links, Reetz maps out the wider network of Deobandi-linked actors and agents that make up the increasingly expansive Deobandi universe today, that stretches from South Africa to Malaysia and beyond. While Sikand explains why the Deoband madrasa has been reluctant to embrace the process of change and reform wholesale, Reetz's account of the developments in the madrasa from the 1980s shows that significant developments and innovations have taken place there, although with the intention of further consolidating and streamlining a specific Deobandi approach and understanding of Islam that has become the normative standard for the Dar al-ʻUlum and its vast network of related alumni madrasas.

Mareike Winkelmann's chapter looks at the developments in one of the few girls' madrasas in India, a phenomenon that is seldom covered in the press, even though it marks a significant development in the area of Muslim education in particular. While Sikand's and Reetz's account of the changes that have taken place in the madrasa of Deoband point to the ways in which madrasa reform has often taken place due to the pressure imposed on the madrasas by external variable political factors, Winkelmann's account of the goings-on in this particular girls' madrasa demonstrates an even more complex intra-community debate taking place: namely the need for basic levels of religious education for Muslim girls in a Muslim-minority country like India as part of their search for a distinct identity. Winkelmann also elaborates upon the complex and inter-dependent relationship between this madrasa and other Muslim institutions such as the prestigious Nadwat al-ʻUlama madrasa of Lucknow and the Tablighi Jamaʻat movement in India. In her detailed exposition of the daily life of the madrasa, she demonstrates how Muslim notions of propriety, good conduct and the moral education of girls – epitomised by the concept of *purdah* or seclusion of women from the public eye – also helps to invert conventional gender hierarchies and opens up new spaces for identity politics; resistance to masculine dominance and creative individual agency; albeit against a backdrop of masculine power and religious authority.

From India we move on to Pakistan, where the madrasas of the country have attracted an inordinate amount of media attention over the past few years. Mariam Abou Zahab's account of the relatively recent phenomenon of Shiʻi women's madrasas offers interesting material for comparison with Winkelmann's contribution. More clearly than in the Indian case, these Shiʻi madrasas in Pakistan appear to provide women with channels for a modest degree of emancipation and empowerment – or at least to increase their value as spouses. The inauguration of these schools and the gradual growth of their number appears closely linked with the rise of the reformists in post-Khomeini Iran and with the opportunities for women to pursue advanced religious studies in Qom, one of the two major centres of Shi'i learning. The three madrasas on which Abou Zahab focuses, that serve very different social circles ranging from modern urban middle classes to rural populations steeped in peasant syncretism, have close connections with Qom, where several of the teachers studied and where many students hope to continue their studies. Reformist influences emanating from Iran, mediated by Iranian-funded cultural centres and madrasas, are transforming Pakistan's Shi'i communities, not without evoking angry defensive responses, however. Abou Zahab's observations among Pakistani students in the leading women's seminary in Qom offer a tantalising glimpse of the modalities of transnational communication and influence.

The theme of students' movements is raised once again in Farish A. Noor's chapter, although the focus here is on the movement of male students from Southeast Asia to pursue their studies in the madrasas of Pakistan. Noor begins by highlighting the media attention that has been paid to the role of foreign students in the madrasas of Pakistan, both real and imagined. Following the arrest and deportation of more than a dozen Malaysian and Indonesian students in two of the more notorious madrasas of Karachi, he proceeds to question the media stereotype of madrasas and madrasa students by looking at the process of enrolment and education that is given in the madrasas of the country. To balance the image of Pakistan's madrasas as 'jihadi training camps', Noor's chapter focuses on the activities of another madrasa – the Syed Maudoodi International Educational Institute (SMII) of Lahore – and its links to the Jama'at-i Islami party of Pakistan. Noor argues that while the SMII is indeed a conservative madrasa known for both its elite status and links to an Islamist political party, it is also a 'modern' educational institution that is well-managed, regulated and has a clear purpose. Noor emphasises the need to keep in mind that the madrasas of Pakistan, as well as the rest of the Muslim world, are not a homogenous phenomenon and that madrasas vary in terms of their size, reputation, religio-political orientation and long-term ambitions.

Moving east now, Jackie Armijo's paper looks at the revival of Islamic education in China and its linkages to international centres of Muslim learning abroad. Armijo notes that while an estimated twenty million Muslims live in China and Islam has had a presence in the country for centuries, little is known about the Muslims of China and their educational centres, which have features unique to the country, such as the relatively higher number of religious schools for girls. She shows that for a host of historical and political reasons, Chinese Muslim education has been deeply entwined with the politics of Muslim identity and nationalism in the country. For China's Muslims, Islamic education serves as a basis of their collective identity, a means to develop educational links abroad, as well as a means to gain status and respectability in their own communities. Of late, however, China's Muslims have been exposed to other currents of Muslim thought emanating from countries like Saudi Arabia and Iran, signs of which can be detected in changes in Chinese mosque architecture, modes of dress for Muslim women in particular, as well as their relations with non-Muslims in China. The opportunity to travel to countries like Pakistan and Malaysia also means that China's Muslims today are able to select alternatives in their search for knowledge, which will have an impact on the development of Muslim identity and education in the long run. Finally, the impact of the 'war on terror' has also been felt in China, with the Chinese government placing greater restrictions on the movement of Muslim scholars and students and increasing control over the curriculum and activities of the Chinese Muslim schools themselves.

The role of the *pondoks* and madrasas in the development of Malay-Muslim political consciousness and their relation to the Islamic Party of Malaysia (PAS) is examined in Farish A. Noor's next contribution. Noor looks at how the image of the *pondoks* in Malaysia have changed from the early 20th century to the present day; from once having been considered the bastions of early Malay-Muslim political consciousness during the early nationalist period, to how they are now seen and treated with some degree of suspicion by the Malaysian government, which considers many of them to be strongholds of Islamist support and recruitment centres for the PAS instead. In the course of a century, the trope of the *pondok* and madrasa has experienced many instances of semantic and semiotic slippage, as it was configured as progressive, radical, exotic and dangerous at different points in Malaysian history. The chapter also looks at the PAS's cultivation of the *pondoks* and madrasas that have come under the Islamic party's patronage, and how the Malaysian state in turn has sought to blunt the thrust of PAS by creating its own network of government-funded and controlled *pondoks* and madrasas in turn. Noor argues that the fate of the *pondoks* and madrasas in Malaysia will ultimately depend on the political contest between the Malaysian government and the Islamic opposition party, and how this contest in turn ensures that the image and perception of the entire *pondok* system will be shaped by other overriding political concerns as well.

The final two chapters take us to Indonesia. Martin van Bruinessen takes a closer look at various *pesantrens* considered as 'radical' and locates them in the context of the broader history and sociology of Islamic education and Islamic movements in the country. The vast majority of *pesantrens* are traditionalist and have generally sought forms of accommodation with the government in power while maintaining a certain distance from it. Though often said to be conservative and backward, their curricula and teaching methods have undergone considerable changes in response to reformist criticism and the government's education policies, even while resisting these. Social activism and critical thought flourished precisely among the students and graduates of traditionalist *pesantrens*, rather than the more 'modern' reformist schools. The various 'radical' *pesantrens* were established relatively recently, and Van Bruinessen shows that most of them share a historical connection to the Darul Islam movement, an indigenous movement to establish an Islamic state that first took shape during the struggle for independence and continued in the form of regional rebellions against the secular Republic. These schools have been more receptive to reformist and Islamist thought from the Middle East than other *pesantrens* have, and one of them served as a recruitment centre for hundreds of young men in the 1980s and early 1990s who joined the jihad in Afghanistan. More significant, however, has been the increasing volume of Indonesian *pesantren* graduates who pursued their studies in the Middle East, many of whom came under the influence of Arabic Islamist and Salafi thought.

Indonesia's Salafi movement is a recent phenomenon and is entirely the creation of a few men who studied in Saudi Arabia in the 1980s and 1990s and upon their return established a number of different madrasas than had hitherto existed. In the final chapter, Noorhaidi Hasan outlines the history of this movement and comments on the brief but important role the Afghan jihad played in it. He documents the emergence of two competing factions in the movement: one being favoured by wealthy sponsors in the Gulf region and with close ties to the Saudi religious establishment, while the other affiliated itself with Yemeni ulama and accordingly had much less foreign funding. The latter faction was for several years actively involved in the jihad in the Moluccas and seemed to be allied with certain factions within Indonesia's military but has since returned to a more placid, non-political stance. Noorhaidi's treatment clearly brings out the essentially transnational character of this movement as well as the local factors contributing to its successes among certain segments of the population (most remarkably the syncretistic peasantry!) as opposed to others.

Notes

1 There are some shining exceptions, however, notably the brilliant study by Muhammad Qasim Zaman, *The Ulama in Contemporary Islam: Custodians of Change*, Princeton, NJ: Princeton University Press, 2002 and Jamal Malik's *Colonialization of Islam: Dissolution of Traditional Institutions in Pakistan*, New Delhi: Manohar, 1998. Two recently edited volumes deserve mention as significant additions to the corpus of academic studies on the madrasa: Robert W. Hefner and Muhammad Qasim Zaman (eds.), *Schooling Islam: The Culture and Politics of Modern Muslim Education*, Princeton, NJ: Princeton University Press, 2007, and Jamal Malik (ed.), *Madrasas in South Asia: Teaching Terror?* London: Routledge, 2007.

2 P. W. Singer, 'Pakistan's Madrassahs: Ensuring a System of Education not Jihad' (Analysis Paper #14, Foreign Policy Studies, Brookings Institution, November 2001). Available online at: http://www.brookings.edu/views/papers/singer/20020103.pdf .

3 See the transcript of Bush and Musharraf's White House press conference on 13 February 2002, at http://www.whitehouse.gov/news/releases/2002/02/20020213-3.html. On the White House campaign to 'change the face of Islam,' as it developed in subsequent years, see: David E. Kaplan, 'Hearts, Minds, and Dollars', *US News and World Report*, 5 April 2005, online at: http://www.usnews.com/usnews/news/articles/050425/25roots.htm.

4 On the role of the ISI and madrasas in the rise of the Taliban, see Ahmed Rashid, *Taliban: Islam, oil and the New Great Game in Central Asia*, London: I.B. Tauris, 2000. The involvement of ISI in creating the various jihadist groups active in Kashmir is discussed in Zahid Hussain, *Frontline Pakistan: The Struggle with militant Islam*, London: I.B.Tauris, 2007, and the International Crisis Group report 'Pakistan: madrasas, extremism and the military', Asia Report no. 36, Islamabad and Brussels: International Crisis Group, 2002.

5 See Martin van Bruinessen's contribution in this volume.

6 Sayyed Asad Madani, *Jang-i Azadi Mai Jami'at ul-'Ulama-i Hind Ki Khidmat*, New Delhi: Jami'at ul-'Ulama-i Hind, n.d., p.6.

7 Sayyed Abul Hasan 'Ali Nadwi, *Madaris-i Islamiya Ka Muqam Aur Kam*, Khatauli: Mahad al-Imam Abul Hasan 'Ali Nadwi, 2002, pp.26-32.

8 Barbara Daly Metcalf, *Islamic Revival in British India: Deoband, 1860-1900*, Princeton, NJ: University Press, 1982.

9 Mehr Afroz Murad, *Intellectual Modernism of Shibli Nu'mani: An exhibition of His Religious and Socio-Political Ideas*, Lahore: Institute of Islamic Culture, 1976. On Nadwat al-'Ulama see also: Jamal Malik, *Islamische Gelehrtenkultur in Nordindien: Entwicklungsgeschichte und Tendenzen am Beispiel von Lucknow*, Leiden: Brill, 1997.

10 Samina Ahmed and Andrew Stroehlein, 'Pakistan: Still Schooling Extremists', *Washington Post*, 17 July 2005; see the analysis of available data by Juan Cole in his "Informed Comment" blog dated 22 July 2005, online at: http://www.juancole.com/2005/07/networks-of-london-bombing-shehzad.html.

11 On the failure of Pakistan's state education system, see the ICG report 'Pakistan: reforming the education sector', Islamabad and Brussels: International Crisis Group, 2004.

1 Voices for Reform in the Indian Madrasas

Yoginder Sikand

Introduction

Reforming the *madrasas* has today emerged as a major concern for many. Governments, such as those of India, Pakistan and countries in the West, particularly the US, are now eagerly seeking to bring about changes in the madrasa system, in the belief that 'unreformed' madrasas are rapidly emerging as major training grounds for 'terrorists'. In addition, many Muslims, including numerous ulama themselves, are also in the forefront of demands for change in the madrasa system. The different actors in this complex political game have widely different understandings of reform, each reflecting their own particular agendas. This article seeks to examine the different ways in which reform of the madrasas in contemporary India is imagined and advocated by a range of actors, including different sections of the ulama, Muslim social activists, Hindu nationalists and the Indian state. It also looks at state policies vis-à-vis the madrasas in recent years.

Imagining 'Reform'

While discussing the question of madrasa reform, it is pertinent to keep in mind the role that the ulama and many Muslims actually envisage for the madrasas. Arguments for madrasa reform often miss the point that, as many Muslims see it, the madrasa is not meant to be an institution for the general education of Muslims, training them for the job market. Rather, the madrasa is regarded as a specialised institution providing Muslims specifically with a 'religious' education and transmitting the Islamic scholarly tradition. This being the case, it would make sense to judge the performance of the madrasas not according to any external criterion, but, rather, in terms of the goals that the ulama of the madrasas and the students who study there set themselves. As the former head of the Deoband madrasa,[1] India's largest Islamic seminary, the late Qari Muhammad Tayyib, insisted:

> When people criticise the madrasa syllabus, they forget that the aim of the madrasa is different from that of a modern school ... The only way to pass judgement on the madrasas is to see how far they have been able to achieve their own aims, such as inculcating piety, promoting religious knowledge, control over the base self (*tahzib-i nafs*) and service of others. Therefore, no suggestion for reform of the syllabus which goes against these aims is acceptable.[2]

Critics of the madrasas tend to see them in stereotypical terms, often branding all madrasas as backward and reactionary. They are routinely described by their detractors, Muslims as well as others, as conservative and illiberal. They are seen as a major burden on Muslim society, consuming much of its meagre resources, and a stumbling block of the progress of the community.[3] Much of what they teach is said to be 'useless' in the contemporary context. This complaint reflects a view that 'useful' knowledge is that which helps equip a student to participate in the modern economy.

As one critic, Anwar 'Ali, who is himself a Muslim argues:

> The mushroom growth of madrasas has caused a great setback to the spread of modern education among Muslims. Madrasas preach hatred for worldly progress, and misinterpret the spirit of Islam and the teachings of the Prophet, who actually insisted on the need to acquire knowledge. They preach poverty to the Muslims by insisting that the only knowledge worth acquiring is that which is taught in the madrasas, and that the learning of science, technology and so on is un-Islamic and opposed to the *shari'a*.[4]

Such critiques, while not entirely bereft of truth, appear somewhat far-fetched and exaggerated. To claim that all madrasas are static and impervious to change is grossly misleading. Madrasas today are considerably different from their counterparts in pre-colonial and colonial India, although there are significant continuities as well. As for the argument that madrasas are conservative, this is to state the obvious, for, as the madrasas generally see themselves, they are indeed the guardians of Islamic 'orthodoxy', regarding their principal role as the conservation of the Islamic 'orthodox' tradition, which, although diversely understood, historically constructed and in a constant process of elaboration, is generally seen by the ulama as unchanging and fixed. Not surprisingly, therefore, many ulama regard the existing madrasa system as not in need of any major reform. They argue that since the madrasas in the past produced great Islamic scholars there is no need for any change even today. If the madrasas are not producing pious, God-fearing and socially engaged ulama today, the fault lies, so it is asserted, in the declining standards of piety and dedication, the increasing materialism and the consequent straying from the path set by the pious elders, and not in the madrasa system as such, which is considered as largely adequate and not in need of any major reform. As Maulana Sa'eed Ahmad Palanpuri, professor of Hadith and a Deobandi scholar argues:

> It appears that the products of the madrasas today do not achieve the standards expected of them. The cause of this is not the syllabus of the madrasa, but, rather, the lack of adequate experts in various disciplines, the carelessness of the students and their unwillingness to work hard.[5]

Traditionalist Ulama and the Challenge of Reform

The debates over madrasa reform reflect different understandings of appropriate Islamic education and indeed of Islam itself. As many 'traditionalist' ulama see it, since the elders (*buzurgs*) have evolved a perfect system of education, and since Islam itself is the ultimate truth, there is no need to learn from others. To attempt to do so is sometimes regarded as a sign of weak faith and as a straying from the path that the elders of the past have trod. Change in the madrasa system is, therefore, often considered as threatening the identity and devotional intensity of the faith. At the same time, and perhaps more importantly, it is considered threatening to undermine the power of the ulama as the leaders of the community and their claims of speaking authoritatively for Islam. Traditional ulama often see proposals for madrasa reform as interference in, if not an invasion of, what they regard as their own territory. Since their claims to authority as spokesmen of Islam are based on their mastery of certain disciplines and texts, quite naturally any change in the syllabus, such as the introduction of new subjects or new books or the exclusion of existing ones, directly undermines their own claims. Moreover, they fear that the introduction of modern disciplines in the madrasa curriculum might lead to a creeping secularisation of the institution as such, as well as tempting their students away from the path of religion and enticing them towards the snares of the world. Proposals for reform of the madrasas by incorporating modern subjects are sometimes seen as hidden ploys or even as grand conspiracies to dilute the religious character of the madrasas. Religion is here understood as a distinct sphere, neatly set apart from other spheres of life. This is readily apparent in the writings of many ulama. Take, for instance, the following statement of Ashraf 'Ali Thanwi, a leading early twentieth-century Deobandi '*alim*:

> It is, in fact, a source of great pride for the religious madrasas not to impart any secular (*duniyavi*) education at all. For if this is done, the religious character of these madrasas would inevitably be grievously harmed. Some people say that madrasas should teach their students additional subjects that would help them earn a livelihood, but this is not the aim of the madrasa at all. The madrasa is actually meant for those who have gone mad with their concern for the hereafter (*jinko fikr-i akhirat ne divana kar diya hai*).[6]

Other traditionalists may not go to such lengths in denying the need for inclusion of modern subjects in the curriculum, but, while accepting the need for reform, might argue that this should be strictly limited, and must not threaten or dilute the religious character of the madrasas. Madrasas, they argue, are geared to the training of religious specialists, and so it is important that worldly subjects must not assume the upper hand over religious instruction. Instead, it is enough, they insist, if the students are able to read and speak elementary English, perform basic mathematical problems and are familiar with the basic social sciences, albeit suitably 'Islamised', and so to that extent they welcome efforts for reform. It is enough, they stress, that the madrasa students gain a general familiarity with these subjects so that they can function in the modern world. It is also argued that if too much stress is given to modern subjects in the madrasas, the students' work load would be simply too great, which in turn would be 'of little use to either the faith or the world' (*na din ke kam ka na duniya ka*).

While these arguments may not be without merit, the opposition of some ulama to proposals for reform in the madrasas must also be seen as reflecting the challenges that they perceive from Muslims articulating a different vision of Islam and Islamic knowledge. If all knowledge, if conducted within the limits set by the Qur'an and the Prophetic Tradition, is Islamic, as many reformists insist, the monopoly over the authoritative interpretation of Islam enjoyed by the 'traditionalist' ulama is considerably undermined, if not eliminated altogether. If, as some reformers see it, a pious Muslim scientist, researching the human cell or the stars in order to discover the laws of God, is as much an *'alim* as one who has devoted his whole life to the study of the *Hadith*, the superior position that the 'traditionalist' ulama claim for themselves based on their expert knowledge of certain classical texts is effectively undermined.

Yet, madrasas are far from being completely immune to change and reform. Likewise, few ulama could claim to be completely satisfied with the madrasas as they exist today. Indeed, leading ulama are themselves conscious of the need for change in the madrasa system. As their graduates go out and take up a range of new careers, in India and abroad, and as pressures from within the community as well as from the state and the media for reform grow, madrasas, too, are changing. Change is, however, gradual, emerging out of sharply contested notions of appropriate Islamic education.

Reform: The Deobandi Case

The dilemmas that accompany change are well illustrated in the case of the Dar al-'Ulum at Deoband, often considered to be a major bastion of ulama conservatism in South Asia. The Deobandis stress conformity to traditional understandings of Hanafi *fiqh*, and they tend to see the solution to all contemporary problems as lying in a rigid adherence to past fiqh formulations. New ways of interpreting Islam are seen as akin to heresy and 'wrongful innovation'. As Mumshad 'Ali Qasimi, a critic of Deoband who is himself a product of the madrasa, says, the traditional ulama 'don't want to change. They are scared of the light because they have got used to darkness'.[7] However, today, there is mounting pressure from within the broader Deobandi fold for reform in the system of madrasa education.

Faced with increasingly vocal demands that Deoband reform its syllabus, in October 1994 the madrasa organised a convention attended by a large number of teachers of Deobandi madrasas from all over India. The convention was ostensibly held to discuss the question of syllabus reform of the madrasas at length, but the inaugural lecture delivered by the rector of the Deoband madrasa, Maulana Marghub ur-Rahman, suggested how far the organisers were really willing to go in accepting change. The Maulana insisted that there was no need to introduce modern education in the madrasas. There were thousands of schools in the country, he pointed out, and Muslim children who wanted to study modern subjects could enrol there instead. Introducing modern subjects in the madrasa would, he argued, 'destroy their [religious] character'. He argued that Islam had clearly divided knowledge into two distinct categories of 'religious' and 'worldly'. 'The paths and destinations of these two branches of knowledge', he claimed, 'were totally different', indeed mutually exclusive. 'If one seeks to travel on both paths together', combining religious and worldly knowledge, he asserted, he would 'get stuck in the middle'. Hence, he stressed, madrasas must remain 'purely religious', as the Deobandi elders had themselves insisted.[8]

Predictably, the convention concluded with a unanimous decision not to make any concessions to those who were clamouring for reform of the madrasa curriculum. The convention passed a resolution declaring that because Islam was a 'complete and perfect way of life' (*mukammil din*), it provided 'solutions to all problems'. Hence, to meet the challenges of modern life, Muslims needed to rely 'only on the Qur'an, Hadith and jurisprudence', and there was no need for 'Western knowledge and culture'.[9] The only change in the madrasa syllabus that the convention agreed to was merely cosmetic, and entailed adding a couple of books for some subjects and to reduce the number of texts for others. As one critic, himself a graduate of the Deoband madrasa, caustically remarked:

> It seems that the convention had not been organised to seriously discuss the madrasa curriculum, to make suitable changes in it in accordance with changing social conditions, to meet modern demands and to improve the functioning of the madrasas. Rather, it appears to have been held simply to announce that all is

> well with the madrasas, and that because they worked well in the past they will continue to do so, and to accuse those who demanding reform of having dubious intentions. If this indeed was the intention of this convention, there was no need to hold it. To prevent one's own weaknesses from being publicised and to proclaim the victories of the past is not a constructive approach.[10]

Despite the great reluctance of the administrators of Deoband to allow for any significant reform in the madrasa system, the winds of change are being felt today even in the hallowed portals of the Dar al-'Ulum. In fact, the above-mentioned convention was probably owed to, among other factors, the increasingly vocal demands of some Deobandis that the madrasa needed to change with the times. Not every Deobandi is a die-hard conservative, and not all of them are opposed to change in the madrasas. Qari Muhammad Tayyib, the rector of the Deoband madrasa prior to Maulana Marghub ur-Rahman, seemed to be somewhat more flexible and open to change than his successor. Addressing a government-sponsored conference on madrasa education, he argued that while no one could agree to change the teaching of the Qur'an in the madrasas, as far as those subjects or books that were considered 'servants of the Qur'an' (*khadim-i Qur'an*), they could be altered according to changing conditions. He argued that the ways of understanding the Qur'an may change over time. In the past, when Greek philosophy or Sufism were dominant, the Qur'an was understood through their eyes. In today's 'scientific age', however, the Qur'an needs to be studied from a scientific perspective, generating new ways of expressing the eternal truths of the sacred text. Therefore, he went on, books or subjects (specifically philosophy and logic) used to study the Qur'an must change with the times. In other words, he argued, there was room for reform in the madrasa syllabus, but he insisted that it was for the ulama alone to decide the direction and extent of the reforms.[11]

The growing pressure for change at the Dar al-'Ulum is owed, in part, to the influence of young Deobandi graduates, who, after completing their studies at the madrasa, go on to regular universities for higher studies or have accepted a range of occupations in India and abroad, but continue to maintain a link with their alma mater. Aware of the rapidly changing world around them, from which madrasa students are thought to be insulated, they help transmit new ideas that, in turn, have given birth to new initiatives at Deoband itself. An important role in this regard is played by the

Tanzim-i Abna-i Qadim, the Old Boys' Association of the Deoband madrasa, with its headquarters in Delhi. It has the following ambitious list of aims and objectives:

- To set up study centres and libraries to promote awareness about national and international affairs.
- To promote the study of the Qur'an and Hadith, the movement of Shah Waliullah [an eighteenth-century Indian Muslim scholar revered by the Deobandis] as well as of non-Islamic movements and to publish literature on these.
- To publish articles in newspapers and journals on religious issues and on social reform.
- To promote religious as well as modern education.
- To establish shari'a committees in Muslim localities consisting of ulama and imams of mosques to solve disputes in accordance with the shari'a.
- To promote social reform in accordance with the *shari'a*, e.g., discouraging wasteful expenses on celebrations, dowries, un-Islamic practices and unwarranted divorces.
- To encourage Muslims to get involved in social work to help the poor.
- To work along with people of other religions and castes for common social aims and for the general relief and development of everyone, irrespective of religion and caste.
- To promote interaction and good relations between people of different religions.
- To remove misunderstandings about Islam and Muslims among non-Muslims.[12]

The Association publishes a monthly magazine in Urdu, the *Tarjuman-i Dar al-'Ulum*, which is widely read by graduates, students and teachers of the Deoband madrasa as well as of various other madrasas affiliated with Deoband. The magazine serves as an important vehicle for the transmission of new ideas, including issues related to madrasa reform. In contrast to many ulama at Deoband itself, it insists on the need for reform in the madrasa system if madrasas are to play a constructive role in society. It advocates a controlled modernisation, seeing this, not as a departure from, but rather as a return to Islam and the vision of the Deoband's founders. Its advocacy of a return to the authentic Islamic tradition serves to facilitate change and reform, rather than to oppose it. Thus, for instance, in an article published in the magazine, Zain ul-Sajid bin Qasmi, a Deobandi graduate and now a teacher of Islamic Studies at the Aligarh Muslim University, emphasises that madrasas can no longer ignore modern challenges. 'We need ulama who are familiar with both religious as well as modern knowledge to serve the community and reply to the attacks on Islam from the West in the West's own language'.[13] While this proposal obviously suggests a defensive posture vis-à-vis the challenge of the West, it also signals a recognition of the importance of modern knowledge and might even represent an Islamic appropriation of modernity itself.

In a similar vein, another contributor to the journal, the Deobandi graduate 'Abdur Rahim 'Abid, writes that many younger ulama today rightly feel that the madrasas need to broaden their curricula in order to include basic education in subjects such as mathematics, science, the social sciences, Hindi and English. It is not necessary, he stresses, that students at madrasas be given detailed instruction in these modern subjects, but they should be. familiarised with them on at least an elementary level. He recognises that this might be construed by some as a betrayal of the Deobandi tradition, but assures his readers that in actual fact it is not so. He informs them that the founder of the madrasa Maulana Qasim Nanotawi arranged for Sanskrit to be taught at Deoband in its initial years, and that another leading reformist *'alim*, Ashraf 'Ali Thanwi had, likewise, suggested the need to include Hindi as well as basic modern law in the madrasa curriculum.[14] In other words, he writes, the Deobandi elders felt that the madrasa syllabus should be made more dynamic in order to equip would-be ulama for the changing conditions of the world around them so that they can provide answers to modern questions and challenges. However, he notes with distress that when a Muslim doctor based in the US offered to donate several computers to the Dar al-'Ulum for the students, the madrasa authorities declined, saying that they would be of no use to them. He laments that the madrasa's authorities, by opposing modern knowledge, are actually working against the original vision of the Deoband's founders.[15]

These critiques of conservatives from inside the Deoband are routine in the pages of the Association's magazine, and reflect an increasing dissatisfaction among several younger Deobandis with what they see as the inflexible, authoritarian conservatism of some of the madrasa's authorities.

Waris Mazhari, editor of the *Tarjuman-i Dar al-'Ulum* is a graduate of the Deoband madrasa who later studied at the Nadwat ul-'Ulama in Lucknow and then at the Jami'a Millia Islamia in New Delhi. Besides editing the journal, he is involved in a number of projects promoting Islamic as well as modern education among Muslims, including madrasa's graduates. Like many other contributors to the journal, he is also critical of various aspects of the Deoband madrasa, particularly its curriculum, because 'in many respects it is irrelevant, and is not able to meet the challenges of modern life'.

Mazhari advocates a thorough revision of the texts used at Deoband, particularly those used for core subjects such as theology and jurisprudence. The theology books still being used at Deoband, he points out, are largely based on ancient Greek philosophy, having been written at a time when it was still considered a major challenge to Islam. The books also focussed on combating various other rival schools and sects, such as the Kharijites and the Isma'ilis, and so these texts deal at great length with their doctrines in order to refute them. However, he emphasises that the challenge from Greek philosophy and the rival sects no longer exists today, and so the traditional theology books are largely irrelevant. What madrasas need today, instead, he advises, are theology books that deal with the confirmed findings of modern science and that seek to engage with contemporary ideological challenges, such as materialism, existentialism, atheism, Marxism, post-modernism and so on. For this he suggests introducing new commentaries on the Qur'an. The medieval Qur'anic commentators, whose books are still used in the madrasas, certainly did a great service to the faith, he insists. However, he adds, they were, after all, just human beings and no matter how pious they may have been they were certainly not infallible. When they interpreted the Qur'an they always emphasised the fact that it was a human effort, admitting that no human being could fully reveal the will of God as expressed in the Qur'an. Hence, to regard their commentaries as the ultimate word on the Qur'an, as many conservative ulama seem to do, is wrong. Many medieval commentaries, he says, also suffer from the influence of concocted *hadith* reports and from polemical debates and controversies. Moreover, the commentators were naturally also influenced in their thinking by their own social circumstances, by the general prevailing social environment as well as by the then available knowledge, and all this is reflected in the various commentaries written over the ages. Hence, he stresses that today with social conditions having undergone such a radical transformation and with the vast expansion of human knowledge, new interpretations of and commentaries on the Qur'an are needed. 'Since Muslims believe that the Qur'an is of eternal validity and provides guidance for all times', he observes, 'newer interpretations and commentaries of the text are needed as times change, in order to show the relevance of the Qur'an in each new age'.

Similarly, Mazhari also advocates radical reform in the teaching methods of Islamic jurisprudence or *fiqh*, which occupies a central place in the present madrasa curriculum. He is opposed to the practice of blind *taqlid* of jurisprudential precedent and argues that *fiqh* must continue to evolve over time, for as conditions change and new issues emerge, new *fiqh* responses must be articulated. He calls for the need to exercise *ijtihad* to examine matters afresh and to take into account new developments. He further agrees that in matters of faith (*'aqa'id*) and worship (*'ibadat*) and other areas that are specifically covered in the Qur'an, there can be no *ijtihad*, for these are eternal. However, in major areas in the domain of social transactions (*mu'amalat*) one must, he says, be open to the possibilities of new interpretations. He regrets that this is strongly discouraged in the Indian madrasas, suggesting that this could be because it would undermine the authority of the conservative ulama, whose claims of being the spiritual guides of the community rest on their knowledge of the classical texts. He is hopeful, however, because the younger generation of Islamic scholars are increasingly more willing to articulate their disagreements. 'While we respect our predecessors and cherish their great contributions', he says, 'we must not go to the extent of putting them on a divine pedestal, for the "worship of elders" (*buzurg parasti*) is strongly condemned in Islam.'

Mazhari's vision for the reform of the madrasas is not limited simply to their curricula, however. He recommends that the madrasas that have the necessary funds should make arrangements for the vocational training of those students who do not want to go on to become professional ulama. He suggests that community leaders pay more attention to educating the girls – both Islamic and modern. In this regard, he is critical of many ulama who are not in favour of higher education for girls, arguing that their stance is not in accordance with the Qur'an. He cites an article he wrote for his journal that lauded the achievement of a Muslim girl who came in second in the Indian Police Service examinations in 2001, presenting her as a model for other Muslim girls to follow. He received a number of angry letters from ulama criticising the article, but, he adds, several Deoband graduates wrote him to congratulate him for the article.[16]

The influence of the new thinking as represented by individual ulama associated with the Old Boys' Association, on the one hand, and the growing wave of attacks on madrasas, on the other, is today forcing Deoband's authorities to consider the introduction of limited reforms in their syllabuses and administrative methods. The media hype concerning the Deobandi's connections to the Taliban is said to have forced the authorities of the madrasa to relent and allow some of their students to take English and computer classes so that they can respond to the journalists and put their fears to rest regarding madrasas' alleged involvement in terrorism. The madrasa has arrangements for 25 students who have passed the *fazil* course (the advanced course that takes the student beyond the graduate or *'alim* level) to study in each of the two new departments. The madrasa has also launched a media department to document media reports on Islam and Muslim issues, to have a liaison with journalists and to prepare reports and articles on issues related to the madrasas. Several leading Deobandi authorities are now encouraging Muslims to take both religious and modern education, exhorting them to establish both madrasas and modern schools where arrangements should be made for the proper Islamic education of their children. Contrary to the image of Deobandis as hardcore conservatives and vehemently opposed to change, many Deobandis today would readily agree with Muhammad Aslam Qasmi, *Hadith* teacher, when he insists that Muslims must enrol in both modern and Islamic education, 'in a balanced way'.[17]

The changes that are slowly making their presence felt in Deoband are not an isolated exception. In fact, the voices of change in the madrasas have been gaining strength in recent years, but are not particularly new. The urgent need for madrasa reforms has been consistently articulated since colonial times by Muslim reformers, including many ulama themselves, although the actual pace of reform in the madrasa has been slow, while the limits and actual content of the reform programmes are still hotly debated.[18] In a recent survey, Siddiqui discovered that the majority of the over 450 madrasas that he studied in Delhi were in favour of curricular reform and the teaching of modern subjects, at least in the elementary classes.[19] Likewise, Qamruddin, in his survey of 576 madrasas throughout India, estimated that over 96 per cent of the madrasas were in favour of the introduction of modern subjects in order to ensure a better future for their students.[20] Yet, despite this widespread desire for reform, as Muhammad

Qasim Zaman rightly notes, 'The significance of the initiatives towards reforming the madrasa itself remains to be appreciated'.[21]

In South Asia today, advocates for reform in the madrasa system include both trained ulama, madrasa graduates, as well those educated in modern schools, including self-defined Islamists and Muslim modernists. Some of them have studied in madrasas and have then gone on to receive their higher educations in regular universities. Others may have been traditionally-trained ulama, whose sons have studied in universities and have then joined them to help improve the functioning of their madrasas, a phenomenon that has become increasingly common in contemporary India, particularly in the cases of some madrasas that are affiliated to official madrasa education boards in various Indian states. It is important, however, not to exaggerate the differences between the 'traditionalists', 'Islamists' and 'modernists'. While these categories may be useful for heuristic purposes, in actual fact, they do not exist as separate, neatly identifiable types. Instead, they represent a wide range of opinions with one blending almost imperceptibly into the other. It is often the case that an individual, who, for instance, could be defined as a 'traditionalist', might express 'modernist' or 'Islamist' sympathies in some significant situations.

Islamists, Muslim Modernists and Madrasa Reform

The voices for madrasa reform reflect a wide range of community agendas. Advocates of reform represent considerably different political positions, from those who consider themselves as completely apolitical, to those who feel that reform is needed in order to integrate madrasa students into the wider society, to those who insist on reform in the belief that it is only by combining Islamic with modern, particularly scientific, education, that Muslims can win political power and establish an Islamic state, in the absence of which Muslims are believed to be incapable of leading truly Islamic lives. Advocates of madrasa modernisation share a commitment to Islamic tradition with their opponents and present their schemes for the modernised madrasa as a return to the authentic tradition as represented by the Prophet and his companions, rather than as a radical departure from it. The very notion of the authentic Islamic tradition, being a social construct and an ongoing evolving project, is itself fiercely contested. Thus, different versions of what constitutes the authentic Islamic tradition are advocated and debated in the course of discussions about madrasa reforms.

Advocates for the introduction of modern subjects in the madrasa curriculum are also aware of the limits of reform, and there is considerable debate about how far reform should proceed. This tension centres on the perceived role and function of the madrasa. Those who see the madrasas' function as the training of students to become religious professionals argue that modern subjects should be allowed only insofar as they might help their students understand and interpret Islam in light of modern knowledge. Others, recognising that not all madrasa graduates will end up becoming professional ulama, have suggested the creation of two streams of madrasa education. The first stream includes students who want just a modicum of religious education and prefer going to a regular school. They would be taught basic religious subjects along with modern disciplines. The second stream would cater to students who want to become a professional ulama, and their education would focus on religious subjects, teaching modern disciplines only to the extent necessary for them to interpret Islam in light of contemporary contexts. On the other hand, a vocal minority has insisted that an entirely new system of education must take the place of the traditional madrasas, where a unified syllabus, based on a harmonious blend of religious and modern subjects would be taught in equal proportions, and whose graduates could then go on to pursue a range of occupations, both religious and secular. Some critics go so far as to suggest that the larger madrasas, after being suitably reformed, should be converted into universities funded by the state, with smaller madrasas remaining affiliated to them. This, however, is not a widely shared view.[22] More acceptable is the suggestion that madrasa education be reformed to allow madrasa graduates to apply to regular universities after having finished their basic religious education.

While advocates of reform seem to agree on the importance of the madrasa as an institution geared to the preservation and promotion of Islamic knowledge and Muslim identity, there is a considerable variety of approaches to the nature and extent of the reforms as well as the rationales employed to advocate their cases. However, there seems to be a consensus that the core of the reform project should consist of modifying the syllabus and teaching methods, in particular emphasising the teaching of modern subjects, such as mathematics, the social and the natural sciences and languages such as English and Hindi. New books for teaching religious subjects and the excision of certain subjects and texts considered outdated or irrelevant in today's context are also generally advocated. Although some proponents of reform go so far as to call for new ways of imagining Islamic theology and law, these are clearly in the minority.

The reformists' rationale for introducing modern disciplines into the madrasas is principally framed in four ways. Firstly, modernisation is seen as a recovery of the authentic, holistic Islamic understanding of knowledge as all embracing, covering both worship as well as social relations and worldly pursuits, knowledge of God and of His creation. Secondly, it is seen as indispensable so that the ulama may recover the quick decline of their authority as spokespersons for Islam. Thirdly, it is expressed as a necessary means for Muslims to prosper in this world as well as the next. Finally, it is considered as essential in order for the ulama to engage in *tabligh*, or Islamic missionary work. All these are intertwined with a new, more activist understanding of the role of the ulama. The ulama are no longer restricted to just teaching in the madrasas. Rather, armed with both modern and traditional knowledge, they can again become leaders in the community.

Madrasa Reform and the Worldly Prospects of the Ulama

Advocates for reform see the present syllabus used in most South Asian madrasas – generally some variant of the *dars-i nizami* – a syllabus prepared in eighteenth century north India, as stagnant and in many respects no longer in tune with the demands and needs of the times. This notion is thus based on the understanding of practical 'usefulness', with much of what madrasas today teach no longer being considered 'useful' or 'relevant'. While it is recognised that the dars-i nizami syllabus did indeed produce its share of brilliant scholars, it is also stressed that it was a product of a particular society and way of understanding the world, suited to the particular social and administrative needs of its times. However, now that social conditions have changed drastically and human knowledge has vastly expanded, the madrasa curriculum must also change, so that madrasas can provide a 'useful' and 'relevant' education.[23] This is regarded as particularly important for the future economic prospects of madrasa students.

The notion of 'useful' knowledge is itself a novel one, and one that can be traced to colonial discourse about what constituted appropriate learning. As we have seen, the classical ulama insisted, as many traditionalist ulama indeed still do, on the central importance of 'pure intention' (*sahih niyyat*) in the acquisition of knowledge. The quest for knowledge was, ideally, seen as being motivated simply to acquire God's favour, and students were sternly warned against any base or worldly motives. Knowledge, it was stressed, was a divine gift, and should only be used to do God's will, not as a means for worldly advancement. Yet, today, numerous Muslim scholars including even some traditionalist ulama, are arguing that madrasas should more seriously take the worldly prospects of their students into account when framing their curricula.

The 'useful' knowledge that should be included in the madrasa curriculum is described differently by different reform advocates. It generally includes the basics of the modern natural and physical sciences, as well as Hindi and English. The need to include these subjects is often framed by the classical notion of 'pure intention', and thus does not appear to be motivated by worldly concerns. It is sometimes expressed as a way to help salvage the sagging prestige of the ulama and reinforce their moral authority. Thus, a Deobandi graduate writes, for instance, that the ulama's lack of basic Hindi or English skills, often lead to feelings of 'humiliation' when they 'step outside of the four walls of their madrasas', and 'have to depend on others for even such elementary things as filling out a train reservation form'. This leads to a loss of prestige on the part of the ulama, which augurs ill for Islam.[24] Thus, the emphasis is on the notion that unless modern subjects are added to the curriculum, which will enable madrasa students to remain abreast of contemporary developments, there is little to stop the growing irrelevance of the ulama in the eyes of the general Muslim public.[25]

For many advocates of madrasa reform, including, though not solely, the Islamists, modernisation is proposed as a means of doing away with or at least reducing the rigid dualism that sets modern educated Muslims apart from the traditional ulama. If the madrasas were to incorporate modern subjects into their curricula they might also begin attracting students from better-off families, thus undermining the existing educational dualism, as well as improving the standards of the madrasas and, as one *'alim* suggests, the moral standards of the students.[26] Incorporating modern subjects into the madrasa curriculum is also seen as a particularly urgent issue given the increasingly visible and strident Hinduisation of the secular education system. Some suggest that in order to protect Muslim children studying in modern schools from Hinduisation and 'intellectual apostasy', madrasas need to incorporate modern subjects so that parents begin sending their children to the madrasa to prevent them from becoming delinquent. This appeal for madrasa reform is thus inextricably linked to broader concerns dealing with the maintenance of community boundaries and identities. It is also related to efforts by some ulama to reach out to modern educated Muslims, who are seen as having virtually abandoned their faith, in an effort to lure them back to Islam. In other words, it is seen as a way of extending and reinforcing ulama authority over modern-educated Muslims lost to their faith. As some Islamists envision it, this attempt to build bridges between the ulama and modern-educated Muslims may ultimately result in fusion of their distinct identities, leading to the formation of a new class of ulama, firmly rooted in the Islamic tradition but, at the same time, fully capable of functioning in the modern world. As a Deobandi *'alim* pointed out, it seeks to 'put an end to the war between the minister and the *maulvi*'.[27] However, the mere introduction of certain 'modern' subjects in the madrasa curriculum may not be enough to 'modernise' their worldview, especially given the fact that few ulama advocates of reform mention the need to revise their own understanding of traditional Islamic jurisprudence and theology.

Introducing modern subjects into the madrasas is also seen as providing madrasa students with substantial real-world benefits. Given the fact that madrasa teachers are often poorly paid and that the career prospects of madrasa graduates are limited and not particularly lucrative, this is a particularly pressing concern for many advocates of reform. Reforming the madrasa curriculum is regarded as essential in dealing with a central problem for many madrasa students, that of employment in an economy for which they have little or no training. The problem of suitable employment for madrasa graduates has now become a particularly serious one. With Indian independence in 1947, the absorption of Muslim-ruled princely states and the eclipse of the Muslim feudal nobility, numerous madrasas and ulama have lost valuable sources of patronage. The problem has only been exacerbated in the face of general Muslim economic backwardness and the rapid increase in the numbers of students matriculating from the growing numbers of madrasas each year.

Many ulama have responded to the issue by dismissing it altogether. They believe that the madrasa exists to train religious specialists, not petty clerks. Madrasa students, they insist, should not be concerned with where and how they will earn their livelihood, for God shall provide for them.[28] It has also often been argued that religious knowledge should be sought for its own sake, and not as a means to worldly advancement.[29]

Despite the widespread reluctance to discuss the issue, some writers, including many ulama themselves, today recognise that employment is indeed a fundamental concern for madrasa students, most of whom come from poor families, and are sent to the madrasas by their parents in the hope that upon graduation they will be able to earn a livelihood as imams in mosques or as teachers in *maktabs* and other madrasas. They see the introduction of modern subjects as an important way of addressing the problem of acute unemployment among madrasa graduates, because, they argue, the existing avenues of employment for them, mainly as teachers in madrasas or imams and *mu'azzins* in mosques, is limited. If madrasas were to include a basic modern curriculum, it is suggested, their students may be able to later enrol in colleges and aspire to new and better careers. Madrasa graduates, if is emphasised, will thereby be able to financially support themselves, thus lessening their burden on the community.[30] Several reform advocates have suggested that madrasas should introduce technical and vocational training for those students who do not wish to seek religious careers so that they can earn a respectable livelihood upon graduating from the madrasa.[31]

The question of the empowerment of the Muslim community as a whole, under the leadership of the ulama is related to the concern for shoring up the authority of the ulama and improving the economic conditions of madrasa students. Islamists as well as many traditional ulama sometimes present the modernisation of the madrasas as linked to the quest for political empowerment. This argument is sometimes expressed in terms of an overarching commitment to a worldview in which Islam is irreconcilably set against other religions in a desperate struggle for power, with the assertion that, as the only true religion in God's eyes, only Islam deserves to rule. This obviously reflects the deep and painful awareness that Muslims have been marginalised in the global order as they yearn for an age long past when they were masters of much of the world. This is sometimes framed in global terms in the form of a struggle between Islam and the West for world domination. Thus, Sayyid Muhammad Rabe Hasni Nadwi, rector of the Nadwat ul-'Ulama madrasa in Lucknow, north India, argues that Muslims need to acquire more modern knowledge, of both the natural and social sciences, albeit suitably Islamised, in order to 'defeat the West using the enemies' own instruments'.[32] Similar statements are often voiced by many other ulama and, of course, by Islamists.

Caution is advisable in taking these statements at face value, however. While they undoubtedly represent a deep strain of hostility towards other faiths and their adherents, they must be seen as reflecting a position of felt marginality and oppression and as symbolic statements of protest. Rather than actually setting Muslims against others militarily and politically, modernisation, suitably legitimised as a means for Muslim empowerment, may actually result in greater integration into the wider society. However, it can also be, as Arshad Alam argues, that in some cases the introduction of 'modern' subjects need not necessarily lead to a transformation in their own worldviews, with science and technology being employed for the cause of promoting traditional understandings of religion.[33]

Madrasa Reform and Muslim Missionary Activism

Introducing modern disciplines in the madrasa syllabus is also seen in the writings of many advocates of reform as central to the divinely ordained task of *tabligh* or the preaching of Islam. The ulama are regarded as having a special role in this regard, although *tabligh* is seen as a binding duty for all Muslims. It is stressed that Islam is for the entire world and not just Muslims, and the ulama must assume responsibility towards their fellow countrymen, the non-Muslim Indians, who are said to be 'in dire need of their guidance'.[34] Several writers argue that in order to become effective missionaries, the ulama must willingly adopt new forms of knowledge. If Muslims, the argument goes, were to lead the world in the development of knowledge, others would simply accept their leadership, and might even be inspired to convert to Islam. By mastering modern knowledge, the argument goes, the ulama would also be able to impress upon non-Muslims that Islam has the ideal solution to all worldly problems, and this might inspire them to accept the faith.

The writings of advocates of reform highlight noted ulama from the past who actively studied the languages, sciences and cultures of other peoples in order to more effectively carry on the task of *tabligh*. The figure of the eleventh-century Imam Ghazali, the most accomplished Islamic scholar of his time, often comes up in discussions. Ghazali is said to have studied Greek philosophy in order to refute those Muslims who had fallen prey to its snares and had dismissed religion as a human creation. By mastering Greek philosophy, he was able to refute its claims and argue for the superiority of Islam. Likewise, it is urged that present-day ulama must closely study, and indeed master, 'non-Islamic' philosophies – not for their own sake, however, but to expose them and assert the truth of Islam. A new science of Islamic theology (*'ilm-i kalam*) that seeks to present Islam in contemporary terms in order to appeal to the modern mind, is called for, one that seeks to present Islam in contemporary terms in order to appeal to the modern mind. For this, it is often stressed, the ulama must be familiar with various contemporary ideologies and knowledge systems that are opposed to Islam.[35] Numerous writers also suggest that in order to prepare effective Islamic missionaries and to rebut the claims of other faiths, there is a need for madrasas to teach comparative religion and English. Some have also argued for students learning computer skills and the use of the Internet in order to engage more effectively in *tabligh* work among people of other faiths.[36]

Critique of the Existing Madrasa Curriculum

Calls for madrasa reform, as we have pointed out, include both the introduction of modern subjects in the madrasa curriculum as well as the removal of subjects or books considered to be irrelevant or no longer useful. Reformists argue that since the world is in a state of continuous change, so, too, must the curriculum of the *madrasas* continue to evolve if madrasas are to maintain their relevance. In fact, they point out, the madrasa system has always responded to changes in the wider society. Change, however, they argue, must be selective and carefully controlled, and it must not result in the transformation of the madrasas into something entirely different or in a threat to what is seen as their specifically religious character. As they continue to absorb new developments and to respond accordingly, the madrasas must also continue to work to preserve, promote and transmit the Islamic tradition, for that is considered their primary function.

This controlled project of reform is based on a distinction between two forms of knowledge on which the madrasa syllabus is based: the transmitted (*naqli* or *manqul*) and the rational (*'aqli* or *ma'qul*) sciences. While the former are seen as immutable and valid for all time, being of divine origin, the latter are regarded as human products, which, therefore, can be reformed, removed or replaced. While the former are an end in themselves, the latter are regarded as simply a means for acquiring knowledge of the former. Accordingly, reformists argue, the rational sciences included in the existing madrasa curriculum must be replaced so that students can gain a better understanding of the primary sources of Islam, because in a changed world, these sciences, products of an age long past, are no longer adequate or properly intelligible.[37]

Besides the rational sciences of philosophy and logic, certain other subjects included in the present madrasa system are also regarded by numerous advocates of reform as unnecessary and in urgent need of reform or removal. One of these is the teaching of *'ilm al-ikhtilaf*, the discipline that focuses on the differences between the various schools of law and that all too easily lends itself to delegitimising other groups as heterodox or even un-Islamic. *'Ilm al-ikhtilaf* forms a central component of the syllabus in several madrasas today, because each *maslak* or school of thought and its associated madrasas regards the refutation of other Muslim groups as one of its primary functions. This serves to stress its own claims to Islamic authenticity. Those who see the teaching of *'ilm al-ikhtilaf* as unnecessary and even dangerous often complain that many madrasas play an inordinate role in promoting intra-Muslim conflicts by teaching their students to condemn all Muslim groups other than their own as virtually outside the pale of Islam. They suggest that books that tend to promote hatred against other Muslim groups should be excised from the syllabus.

Another contentious issue that is repeatedly discussed in the writings of the advocates of reform is the issue of *fiqh*, which constitutes the core of the madrasa syllabus. It is also the mainstay of the ulama's authority, because ulama are considered experts on the subject. A number of reformists who have pleaded for a revision of how *fiqh* is taught in the madrasas have recommended the inclusion of modern subjects in the madrasa curriculum in order to develop a new *fiqh* that is more attuned to contemporary India.

They emphasise that this is because the classical *fiqh* books deal with many issues that are no longer relevant and are also silent on contemporary matters that people are forced to deal with. Furthermore, many of the books on *fiqh*, as well as other subjects, currently still used in the madrasas are said to consist simply of commentaries upon commentaries or simply marginal footnotes, written in an archaic style and language. Many of these commentaries are said to further complicate rather than explain what the original books teach. Several of these books are said to promote 'heated verbal debates and quarrels and strife' and, hence, 'cannot open the minds of the students'.[38] It is thus suggested that these books be replaced by new, more accessible books on *fiqh* that deal with issues of contemporary concern and practical realities.[39]

This new Islamic jurisprudence that reform advocates seek to formulate necessitates *ijtihad*, or the skills of deducing rulings for new situations and problems from the Qur'an and *hadith*. Accordingly, the reformists suggest, the focus of the teaching of *fiqh* should be less about the details of jurisprudence (*furu'*) and more focussed on the principles of law (*usul*).[40] One writer even suggests that madrasas should familiarise their students with international law and comparative legal systems in order to 'meet modern challenges'.[41] Another leading *'alim* associated with the Jama'at-i Islami, a leading South Asian Islamist movement, recommends that madrasa students must be familiarised with the *fiqh* of other Muslim schools of jurisprudence in order to break the stranglehold of *taqlid* and inter-*maslak* prejudices. This *'alim* further insists on the need for an *ijtihad* based on a thorough study of the *usul-i fiqh* to deal with issues that the medieval compendia of *fiqh* either do not mention or do so in terms that are irrelevant today, including such subjects as religious pluralism, women's rights and social justice for oppressed peoples.[42]

Advocates of madrasa reform have also written extensively on the need for a change in the teaching of the core subject of *tafsir* or Qur'anic commentary. The original *dars-i nizami* devoted little attention to Qur'anic commentary, because it was envisaged as a syllabus to train government bureaucrats rather than religious specialists. Many Indian madrasas continue to pay scant attention to *tafsir*, using only a few texts by early medieval commentators that are now widely recognised as inadequate to teach the subject. Reform in the teaching of *tafsir* is generally articulated in two principal ways. Firstly, it is argued that the Qur'an is a simple, easily understandable book of practical guidance. Hence, it must be approached more directly and not with the help of outdated commentaries. Secondly, it is often argued that all commentaries naturally bear the imprint of their authors and their own socio-historical background. While the medieval *tafsir* literature is not dismissed as completely useless, it is argued that their authors were, after all, human beings and not infallible. Hence, it is stressed, no interpretation of God's word can be said to be absolute or to actually represent God's intentions in their entirety. Conceding that every interpretation of the text is partial and limited, some writers suggest that new commentaries, written by modern-day scholars, and taking into account modern developments in knowledge, should replace the outdated commentaries. This, however, does not necessarily mean that the medieval *tafsirs* should be totally ignored. This plea for reform is presented as a way of expressing the enduring relevance of the Qur'an in our day. It is also seen as proof of the Qur'an's divine nature, for if the Qur'an provides suitable guidance for constantly changing conditions, it must indeed be of divine provenance.[43]

Co-ordination Between Different Madrasas

Most madrasas function as independent bodies, run by their own management committees. In the case of the country's 7,000 Deobandi madrasas, each madrasa is autonomous in administrative matters, although the various madrasas share a similar ideology and commitment to what may be called a common Deobandi vision. Every madrasa is, in theory, free to formulate its own syllabus, select its own books, set its own standards, and conduct its own examinations. Because of this and its fierce inter-*maslak* rivalries, there is no central co-ordinating body for all of the madrasas. This presents major problems in matters involving the formulation of reform policies of the madrasa syllabus, improving educational standards, student exchanges between different madrasas, promoting unity among different Muslim groups and combating various challenges that the madrasas must collectively face. That the continued existence of sharp inter-*maslak* differences dooms all efforts to reform the madrasa system as a whole has long been recognised. Writing in the early twentieth century, Maulana Abul Kalam Azad, a leading Indian Muslim associated with the Congress Party and later India's first Education Minister, bitterly castigated the ulama of his day for their constant rivalries, going so far as to write, 'It may be possible for reptiles to live in a common habitat, but among the ulama one individual cannot agree to live in peaceful coexistence with another. Like dogs, they fight with sharp claws and teeth whenever a bone is thrown to them'.[44] In a more controlled manner, Tahir Mahmud, a leading Indian legal specialist, makes the same point:

> It is naïve to expect [that] the ulama of India, with their tremendous differences, would unanimously agree on a single item of reform, if they will even agree to discuss it ... In India, each group of ulama ... has its own interpretation of the Qur'an and Sunnah. They will take ages to express a unanimous opinion on any reform to be applied to all Muslims alike.[45]

A number of Muslim writers have called for the building of bridges between the many madrasas as part of a broader programme of madrasa reform. Thus, Muhammad Zafiruddin Miftahi, a mufti associated with the Dar al-'Ulum, Deoband, suggests that all Sunni madrasas, except those run by the Barelvis,[46] who are fierce foes of the Deobandis, should come together under one all-India madrasa board, with branches at the state, district and local levels. The proposed board would be responsible for preparing a common syllabus for the transmitted sciences, while each madrasa would be free to teach whatever modern subjects it wants. In order to gain general acceptance, the board would consist of ulama from various Sunni schools.[47] Another leading *'alim*, Muhammad Shams Tabrez, appeals to all Muslim *maslaks*, including even the Barelvis, to set up a single madrasa federation which would set up a common syllabus for all madrasas and which could work for their collective welfare. The board would set common standards and conduct common examinations for the madrasas under it.[48]

Given the fierce rivalries between madrasas of different *maslaks*, efforts to unite the madrasas under a common board have proved unsuccessful. Madrasas, like other such institutions, cherish their autonomy, and many would regard control by a higher institution as undue interference. Increasingly, however, leading madrasas of each *maslak* are moving towards the establishment of loose federations in order to streamline educational standards and examination procedures. In recent years, the growing fear and threat of interference by the state and attacks on the madrasas by extremist Hindu groups has further boosted the process, leading madrasas of each *maslak* to consolidate their ranks so as to more effectively respond to moves to control or regulate them. Separate federations have been formed, among others, by the Dar al-'Ulum, Deoband, the Nadwat ul-'Ulama, Lucknow, the Ahl-i Hadith[49] Jami'at us-Salafiya, Varanasi, and the nation's leading Barelvi madrasa, the Jami'at ul-Ashrafiya, Mubarakpur. Each federation is headed by an *amir*, generally the principal of the apex madrasa, and member madrasas all belong to the same *maslak*. Regular meetings are organised to flesh out plans and projects and to discuss common problems and concerns.

Reforms in Teaching Methods

Besides reforms in the curriculum of the madrasas, reformists have also written extensively on the need for changes in teaching methods. Many are critical of the 'book-centred' over 'student-centred' approach to education in the madrasas, which places too much emphasis on parroting entire sections of books without exercising reason or critical thought. As a result, few students actually comprehend what they are being taught. Even after years of poring over ancient Arabic tomes, writes a Deobandi *'alim*, few madrasa graduates are able to speak the language, having simply memorised a few sentences or chapters.[50] This problem is said to be exacerbated by the inordinate amount of emphasis that most madrasas put on particular books, which generally means memorisation, as opposed to actually learning a particular subject or discipline.[51] It has been observed that many madrasa managers and teachers strictly forbid students from reading books written by Muslim scholars from other *maslaks* and, indeed, any books not included on the prescribed syllabus 'which they believe might create doubts in their minds about the aims of the madrasas'.[52]

While the merits of some aspects of the traditional pedagogic styles and approaches are recognised, it is recommended that madrasas open up to learning new teaching methods from others, including from 'modern', secular institutions. These proposals are wide-ranging, and include the introduction of new methods of teaching language as used at various universities, which encourages students to debate and discuss issues, and trains them to write for newspapers, and organises cultural programmes in order to broaden the students' horizons. Some writers have suggested combining text-based learning with pragmatic learning, such as social work and inter-faith dialogue programmes. These efforts, it is argued, make madrasa students more aware of the world around them, which, in turn, can help them to be more effective in their future work as religious leaders. This would go a long way toward salvaging the sagging prestige of the ulama, by making them more relevant to people's daily concerns. At the same time, it would also help madrasa students develop a more contextually grounded and relevant understanding of their faith.[53]

In recent years, some madrasas have made considerable headway in reforming pedagogical methods. For instance, the Jami'at ul-Falah in Azamgarh, a madrasa run by the Jama'at-i Islami, now has a number of teachers with a bachelor's degree in education, almost all of whom are madrasa graduates. The English teacher at the Islamic Centre in Lucknow has a degree from the prestigious Central Institute for English and Foreign languages in Hyderabad. Exposed to new teaching methods in these institutions, these teachers may be encouraged to introduce reforms of the traditional teaching methods, although this has to date, been a slow process. An innovative experiment that may prove to be a major stimulus in this regard is the madrasa teachers' training centre that the Jami'at ul-Hidaya, one of the most progressive madrasas in the country, wants to establish in the near future. Thus far, however, no such regular institution exists, although some organisations such as the Uttar Pradesh Falah-i 'Am Trust in Lucknow, the Ta'amir-i Millat in Hyderabad, the Samastha Kerala Sunni Vidyavasa Board in Calicut, and the Centre for Promotion of Science in Aligarh, occasionally organise short-term training sessions for madrasa teachers where they are familiarised with new teaching methods.[54] Moreover, the Jami'a Millia Islamia in New Delhi, and the Aligarh Muslim University have both organised similar courses in recent years.[55]

The Pace of Reform

Given the current worldview of the traditional ulama, and the vested interests involved in maintaining the madrasa system as it is, it is hardly surprising that the actual pace of reform of madrasa education in India has been slow and halting. In the absence of mechanisms to make the madrasas accountable to the community, changes in the madrasa system have been mostly piecemeal and ad hoc, rather than wide-ranging and well planned.

Since each madrasa is an autonomous institution, with its curriculum set by its own management, reform in the system has thus far depended almost entirely on individual initiatives. In most cases, this has been done by the management on its own, often based on the personal whims of its principal or rector. Only a few madrasas have actively sought to involve academics from universities and trained education experts in reforming their curriculum. Typically, the involvement of outsiders in curriculum reform is seen as opening the door to 'irreligious' interference that will ultimately threaten the religious identity of the madrasa. Critics, however, argue that this opposition actually has more to do with the threats that university-trained specialists represent to madrasa managers regarding their authority even if Muslims still have a say in the running of their institutions.

The slow pace of change in the madrasa system might seem frustrating to the advocates of reform. However, it needs to be understood with some understanding, because critics of the madrasa system often ignore the important positive contributions of many madrasas in the field of Muslim education today and the critical financial and various constraints that they face. For the poor in India often the only available and affordable form of education is provided by the government school system. The standard of education provided by government schools, as the government itself concedes, is woefully inadequate. Teachers are frequently absent, and if they do show up, they spend little time actually teaching. Although government schools in theory provide a free education, poor families often find it difficult to meet the costs for clothing, books and food for their children. In many madrasas, on the other hand, these are provided free of cost.

In seeking to evaluate the actual pace of reform in the madrasa system, it is also important to bear in mind the considerable financial constraints under which most madrasas operate. Many of them might wish to provide a better education for their students and even to teach modern subjects, but are unable to do so for want of the necessary funds. Recruiting good teachers for modern subjects is often difficult, if not impossible, because many madrasas cannot afford the high salaries that these teachers demand. A related, broader issue involves the social background of the vast majority of the administrators, teachers and students in the madrasas. Most madrasa administrators and teachers come from poor or lower middle-class families, with little or no exposure to modern ideas or modern teaching methods. Being themselves products of traditional madrasas, they have been taught to believe that many aspects of modernity are a revolt against Islam. Not surprisingly, reform is thus often seen as an invitation to treason and apostasy. Like most other religious specialists, the essential task of the ulama is to preserve a received tradition and not to innovate or experiment. Hence, to expect the ulama to wholeheartedly embrace reform is unrealistic and impractical.

In the case of most madrasa students their social origins often also inhibit any enthusiasm for reform. Most of them come from poor families and are wholly dependent on the madrasa for their educations and living expenses. To demand reform in the madrasa system is a risky proposition that few students are willing to take up, because this may lead to expulsion. Modern-educated middle-class Muslims have not been very interested in madrasa reform issues, often viewing the madrasas as obscurantist. Few well-off families end up sending their children to a madrasa to train them to become a professional *'alim*. Because the general image of the madrasa is determined by a largely poor and deprived student population, madrasas often remain insulated from the kinds of changes and reforms that a more diverse student population may stimulate.

What also hampers reform efforts is the widespread and growing perception among the ulama and the Muslim community in India in general of the grave threat that militant anti-Muslim Hindu forces pose to Islam and Indian Muslims. This fear has a way of dampening any reform enthusiasm and only further serves to strengthen the forces of Muslim conservatism and the opponents of change. In this kind of charged climate, suggestions for madrasa reform are often perceived as sinister ploys by the 'enemies' of Islam to dilute the religious character of the madrasas, the 'forts of the faith'.

Although, as we have seen, reformists, including many ulama themselves, have advocated wide-ranging reforms in the traditional madrasa system, in actual fact, reform has been largely limited to the introduction of some new texts and subjects and the excision of others that are no longer seen as useful. In other words, reform has, so far, been peripheral, rather than structural or basic. Many madrasas have drastically reduced the number of books devoted to antiquated Greek philosophy and logic in their syllabus, and have replaced them with more books on *hadith*. In recent years, several madrasas have introduced the teaching of selected modern subjects, including basic English, and elementary social and natural sciences, along with Hindi and, in some cases, a regional language. However, in general, the standard of teaching of these subjects leaves much to be desired. These subjects are often not taken seriously by the teachers or the students, and are considered relatively unimportant compared to Islamic subjects. In many madrasas, these subjects are taught by teachers who themselves are traditionally trained ulama, who have had little or no exposure to modern knowledge or teaching methods.

Government Efforts at Madrasa Reform

In recent years, demands have been made for government regulation of the madrasas in the name of reform. These calls were certainly not unheard of in the past, but the rationale for government intervention through madrasa 'modernisation' was articulated in terms of helping the Muslims join the 'national mainstream', with madrasas being generally seen as 'backward', unconcerned with the world around them and generally resistant to change. Today, however, the rationale has shifted dramatically, with madrasas now seen as somehow too 'worldly' for 'proper' religious institutions, and allegedly churning out militant activists charged with a burning sense of mission to gain political power. Rather than representing a radical shift in the aims and methods of the madrasas as such, this new rationale is a reflection of the growing strength of Hindu chauvinism in India, which is based on an abiding hatred of the Muslim 'other'.

In several Indian states, governments have increasingly sought to control the madrasas, arguing that this is necessary in order to control 'terrorism'. However, they have failed to identify a single madrasa that is actually engaged in promoting 'terrorism'. In some states, those seeking to establish madrasas must secure permission from the state after ensuring them that they are not engaged in the promotion of 'undesirable' activities, a rule, however, that does not apply to similar Hindu institutions. Madrasas in some states are also required to furnish information about their student body to the state authorities. In large parts of India, madrasas are regularly visited by intelligence authorities, who on numerous occasions have been accused of unwarranted harassment. There have also been several cases of innocent madrasa teachers and students being shot dead or arrested by the police on trumped-up charges of 'terrorism'.

Calls for the state to intervene in India's madrasa system reflect the state's perception of madrasa autonomy as a challenge. Most madrasas are not dependent on the state for funds. Their financial independence is seen by state officials as providing the madrasas with a vast influence, over which it has little or no control. Madrasa independence is generally perceived, by government officials with a sympathy for Hindu nationalism, as a particularly potent challenge to monolithic Indian nationalism based on Brahminical Hinduism. As defenders of Islamic orthodoxy and Muslim community identity, and as alleged advocates of pan-Islamism or militancy, madrasas are regarded by the Hindu chauvinists as particularly menacing. Hence, Hindutva leaders have insisted on the need for more intense state monitoring and control of the madrasas, and some have even gone so far as to demand that the state close them all down. On the other hand, secular political parties in power in some states have sought to extend assistance to madrasas, aware of the considerable influence that the ulama wield among Muslim voters. Moreover, they are also appreciative of the efforts that madrasas are making to promote literacy among Muslims. The state's relations with the madrasas are thus determined by a mixed set of motives.

Ostensibly, the state's case for madrasa modernisation rests on two premises: that such modernisation is necessary to promote modern and rational thinking and that it is only by modernising themselves that madrasa students can become part of the nation's educational mainstream.[56] Some claim that madrasa modernisation is necessary for the promotion of national integration.[57] The assumption, therefore, is that a traditional madrasa education hampers integration, and causes Muslim children to be cut-off from the mainstream. The mainstream and the nation are generally viewed in hegemonic terms, as represented by a distinctly upper caste Hindu ethos. Joining the mainstream may simply be just a euphemism for shedding a separate Muslim identity and submerging it within a larger Indian identity that is defined in largely Hindu terms.

This suggests that the state's profession of concern for Muslim educational development through the modernisation of madrasas needs to be carefully and critically analysed. Critics point out that if the promotion of Muslim education was indeed a primary government concern, it should have paid more attention to establishing more modern schools in Muslim localities, which it has clearly failed to do. In fact, the level of educational provision by the state in Muslim areas is far below the level of other, particularly Hindu, areas, which leaves the state open to charges of obvious discrimination against Muslims.[58] Then again, proposals to legitimise state intervention in madrasas on the grounds of helping to promote modern and rational thinking seem completely hollow in the face of what is today seen as a concerted effort on the part of the Indian state to thoroughly Hinduise the education system, including the introduction of subjects such as astrology and Hindu rituals and mythology in the syllabus of schools and colleges. Not surprisingly, many Muslims view the state's efforts to interfere in the madrasas as being motivated by ulterior motives. One prominent Indian Muslim politician has even suggested that the real purpose of the government's proposals for modernisation of madrasas is to 'monitor what goes on inside the madrasas through a government-funded monitor in the form of a teacher of English, mathematics and sciences'.[59] In response to a state-sponsored report that recommended that madrasas should teach 'Vedic Mathematics' as part of a proposed modernisation scheme,[60] numerous ulama have argued that this is clear evidence that the state has been trying to dilute the Islamic identity of the madrasas through the backdoor while claiming to be assisting them.[61]

Government efforts to reform the madrasa have thus far taken, broadly speaking, three forms: (i) state governments establishing boards for madrasa education (ii) providing financial assistance to selected madrasas to teach secular subjects, and (iii) arranging for recognition of certain madrasas by certain state-funded universities.

Seven Indian states (Assam, Bihar, Madhya Pradesh, Orissa, Rajasthan, Uttar Pradesh and West Bengal) have government-sponsored madrasa education boards, which a number of madrasas are affiliated to. Not all of the madrasas in these states are members of the state boards, however, and madrasas are free to choose to join or not. Several of the affiliated madrasas receive some sort of assistance from various state governments, such as, teachers' salaries. In turn, these madrasas have to abide by certain norms laid down by the state, including in its curriculum. Graduates of most madrasas affiliated to the boards can go on to apply to regular colleges.[62] In late 2006, the National Commission for Minority Educational Institutions recommended the establishment of a Central Madrasa Board to the Government of India to provide funding and introduce curricular reforms in the madrasas. However, this proposal was met with stiff opposition from many madrasas and so has not been acted upon.

In recent years, the Indian Government along with some state governments have launched various small schemes such as providing paid teachers to teach modern subjects ostensibly to assist certain madrasas. In 1986, the Indian Government issued its new education policy, which included proposals for government intervention in madrasa education through a 'madrasa modernisation programme'. The Government's revised plan issued in 1992 suggested the introduction of modern subjects such as science, mathematics, English and Hindi in the madrasas, the expenses for which would be borne in part by the state.

Despite its claims of being seriously committed to madrasa modernisation, the government appears to have actually done very little in practical terms.[63] The funding for the madrasa modernisation scheme is said to have been woefully limited. In actual practice, it has proved extremely difficult for madrasas who wish to participate in the scheme to obtain financial assistance from the state. According to the rules of the scheme, madrasas would be only financed after receiving a security clearance from the state governments. This entails long and complicated bureaucratic hurdles and often the added burden of paying bribes to petty government servants, which madrasas either cannot afford or else simply refuse to pay.[64] What further compounds the problem is the fact that some bureaucrats apparently prefer to see the scheme fail. Thus, according to a report on the madrasa modernisation project in the state of Bihar, some state civil servants 'with a communal bent of mind' effectively sabotaged the government's scheme to help the madrasas financially by not disbursing the money allocated by the government. Apparently, the Ministry of Human Resources Development had authorised a sum of 4.3 million rupees to Bihar in 1999-2000 under the madrasa modernisation scheme, which was to be implemented by the Bihar State Madrasa Education Board. However, this money was never given to the Board, and Board officials claimed they had no knowledge of how it was spent. B.P. Srivastava, Bihar's upper caste Hindu education secretary and chairman of the committee dealing with the scheme, confessed that he had failed to submit a 'utilisation certificate' to the Central government that explained what happened to the money. He offered the specious argument that the money was not provided to the Board because it was 'pre-occupied with other matters'. Because Srivastava did not disburse the money, the Union Government decided not to allocate the 35.7

million rupees to the Bihar government which had been earmarked for the madrasa modernisation scheme for the coming year.[65]

In various other states, however, the scheme seems to have had considerable effect, and several madrasas have agreed to co-operate. In 2001, some 3,500 out of a total of 6,000 madrasas in Madhya Pradesh, with some 175,000 students, were receiving modest financial assistance from the state government for teaching secular subjects through the Madhya Pradesh Madrasa Education Board.[66] By 1999, some 600 madrasas in Rajasthan of a total of some 5,000 had been recognised by the state government, and several of them had received some sort of government funding. The government had allocated a sum of 20 million rupees for madrasas in that fiscal year, but since the entire budget could not be utilised, it was reduced to 7.8 million rupees in 2001. However, despite the drastic budget cuts, state-recognised madrasas seem to have performed exceptionally well in Rajasthan. According to one report, these madrasas had achieved new records, with between 90 to 100% of their students passing their examinations, as opposed to a pass-rate of 65% in government schools located in predominantly Muslim regions. 60% of the students in these madrasas secured a first division, while the figure for government schools was an abysmal 20%. Half of the passing madrasa students were girls. Impressed by the progress of the madrasas, the state government, in co-operation with several madrasas, had established a plan to appoint 'education workers' (*shiksha karmis*) to teach secular subjects in selected madrasas.[67] Moreover, the government had launched a scheme to distribute free science and other textbooks to selected madrasas through the Rajasthan Waqf Board.[68] In a state where only 0.15 per cent of the students in colleges and universities are Muslim, well below the community's representation in the state's population, the madrasas assisted by the government are clearly playing a major role in the promotion of literacy.

Another way in which the state has sought to engage with the madrasas is by allowing selected universities to recognise the degrees of certain madrasas, enabling their graduates to enrol therein for higher education and helping them join the educational mainstream. Several larger madrasas have managed to secure recognition of their degrees by Muslim universities such as the Aligarh Muslim University, Osmania University, Hyderabad, Lucknow University, Jami'a Millia Islamia and the Jami'a Hamdard, New Delhi. Madrasa students who join these universities generally enrol for courses in subjects such as Arabic, Urdu, Persian, Islamic Studies and History, but, increasingly, some are going in for other disciplines, such as English. Some madrasas actively encourage some of their brighter students to enrol in universities, in the hope that, equipped with modern knowledge, they would return to their alma maters to teach and help improve their standards. Indeed, a growing number of madrasas now include among their teachers former madrasa students who have also acquired degrees in regular universities.

Ulama Responses to State Assistance

For their part, the ulama seem to be sharply divided on the matter of madrasas receiving state patronage. Some, probably a minority, see no harm in receiving funds from the state, claiming that the state has not, at least as yet, linked its offer of financial assistance to any preconditions, such as the radical alteration of the content of their curriculum or interfering in their administration. On the one hand, many other ulama and Muslim leaders argue that accepting funds from the state will eventually lead to state interference in madrasa affairs, leaving them open to a subtle process of Hinduisation. They claim that by linking assistance to the modernisation of the curriculum, the religious content of the syllabus may eventually get watered down and that, burdened with the need to learn both religious as well as modern subjects, the students will end up doing well in neither.[69] It is also generally argued that the standard of education in government assisted madrasas is considerably lower than in independent madrasas, since in the former teachers, being paid by the government and assured of a permanent job, are no longer answerable to the madrasa management and do not take their duties seriously, being concerned simply with getting a regular salary. Hence, it is stressed, madrasas should avoid taking any money from the government. Thus, a noted Deobandi *'alim*, Mufti Muhammad Sulaiman Mansurpuri, warns the ulama not to fall prey to the blandishments of the state, asserting:

> To accept government aid from the state would lead to the death of the madrasas. It would be a gross violation of the aims of their founders, and would destroy their spirit of service to the faith .... It would lead to the madrasas be-

> coming the graveyards of the sciences of religion ... Because of this, no self-respecting *'alim* and servant of the faith can accept, even for a single moment, assistance from the government. We may suffer great financial hardships thereby, but we should reject government aid and rely only on Allah.[70]

Overall, then, the madrasas seem not to have been particularly enthusiastic about government offers of assistance, although there are notable exceptions. This, of course, has much to do with the fact that the state's professions of concern for Muslim education are viewed with considerable suspicion. Rather than look to the state for assistance to promote reform, today many madrasas are seeking to help themselves, developing innovative forms of Islamic education.

Notes

1 This madrasa, established in the latter half of the nineteenth century in the town of Deoband in northern India, sought to sustain the tradition of Islamic learning, perceived to be threatened under colonial rule, while at the same time crusading against many popular Muslim beliefs and practices that its founders saw as 'un-Islamic'. For a detailed study, see Barbara D. Metcalf, *Islamic Revival in British India: Deoband (1860-1900)*, New Delhi: Oxford University Press, 2004.

2 Quoted in Javed Ashraf Qasmi, *Faizan-i Dar al-'Ulum Deoband*. Ghaseda: Madrasa Abi bin Ka'ab Tahaffuz al-Qur'an al-Karim, 2000, p. 92.

3 'Abid Reza Bedar, in *'Arabi Islami Madaris Ka Nisab-o-Nizam-i Ta'lim Aur 'Asri Taqaze* (vol. 1). Patna: Khuda Bakhsh Oriental Public Library, 1995, p. 8.

4 Anwar 'Ali, 'Madaris-i Diniya Aur Hukumati Control' (part II), *Qaumi Awaz*, 19 June, 2002.

5 Quoted in Shaukat 'Ali Qasmi, *Rabita-i Madaris-i'Arabiyya Dar al-'Ulum: Qayyam, Ijtima'at, Sargarmiyan*. Deoband: Dar al-'Ulum, 1998, p. 22.

6 Quoted in Muhammad Zaid Mazhari Nadwi, *al-'Ilm wa-l-'Ulama*. Hathaura: Idara-i Ifadat-i Ashrafiya, 1996, p. 110.

7 Mumshad 'Ali Qasmi, *Tarikh-i Dars-i Nizami*. Bilaspur, Muzaffarnagar: Majma al-Bahuth al-'Ilmiya, 1994, p. 71.

8 'Dar al-'Ulum Deoband Zer-i Ehtimam Ijtima-i Madaris-i Islamiya Ka Ineqad', *Tarjuman-i Dar al-'Ulum*, November, 1994, p. 11.

9 Ibid., p. 13.

10 Ibid., p. 12.

11 Quoted in Javed Ashraf Qasmi, *Faizan-i Dar al-'Ulum Deoband*. Ghaseda: Madrasa Abi bin Ka'ab Tahaffuz al-Qur'an al-Karim, 2000, p. 92.

12 *'Amali Programme Tanzim Abna ul-Qadim Dar al-'Ulum Deoband*. Delhi: Tanzim Abna ul-Qadim Dar al-'Ulum Deoband, n.d., pp. 1-7.

13 Zain ul-Sajid bin Qasmi, 'Dars-i Nizami: Tarikhi Pas-i Manzar Aur Jadid Taqaze', *Tarjuman-i Dar al-'Ulum*, November 1994.

14 Thanwi is said to have argued for the inclusion of Sanskrit in the madrasa curriculum in order to 'spread Islam among the Hindus' and to 'rebut the Hindu scriptures'. Likewise, he is said to have recommended the learning of 'the languages and sciences of the infidels (*kuffar*) and the people of falsehood (*ahl-i batil*) in order to debate with them' (See, 'Islah-i Nisab Ke Liye Maulana Thanwi Ki Chand Tajawiz', *Tarjuman-i Dar al-'Ulum*, June, 1994, pp. 14-15.

15 'Abdur Rahim 'Abid, 'Madaris Ke Nisab Mai Tabdili Ka Masla: 'Ulama Kya Kahtey Hain?', *Tarjuman-i Dar al-'Ulum*, October 1994, p. 20.

16 www.sabrang.com/news/2004/madarsayogind.pdf.

17 ''Ilm-i Din Ke Sath Maddi 'Ulum Bhi Zaruri', *Qaumi Awaz*, 11 April 1995.

18 See, for instance, the several papers of ulama advocates of madrasa reform in *'Arabi Islami Madaris Ka Nisab-o-Nizam-i Ta'lim Aur 'Asri Taqaze*. Patna: Khuda Bakhsh Oriental Public Library, 1995.

19 Quoted in Ehtashamuddin Khan, 'Madrasas Want to Moderrnise, But Not Too Much', *The Fragrance of the East*, vol. V, no. 1, January-March 2003, p. 59.

20 Qamruddin, 'Modernising Madrasas', *The Times of India*, Bangalore, 8 July 2002.

21 Muhammad Qasim Zaman, 'Religious Education and the Rhetoric of Reform: The Madrasa in British India and Pakistan', *Comparative Studies in Society and History*, vol. 41, no. 2, April 1999, p. 295.

22 Sultan Ahmad Islahi, *Hindustan Mai Madaris-i-'Arabiya Ke Masa'il*. Aligarh: Idara-i 'Ilm-o-Adab, n.d., p. 152.

23 Khurshid Ahmad, *Nizam-i Ta'lim: Nazariya, Rivayat, Masa'il*. Islamabad: Institute of Policy Studies, 1996, p. 235.

24 Mumshad 'Ali Qasmi, *Tarikh-i Dars-i Nizami*, pp. 154-55.

25 Mujahid ul-Islam Qasmi (ed.) *Maqalat-i Sajjad*. Patna: Imarat-i Shari'ah, 1999, p. 72.

26 Muhammad Shihabuddin Nadwi, *Hamare Ta'limi Masa'il*. Bangalore: Furqania Academy, 1989, pp. 19-20.

27 Sayyed Manazir Ahsan Gilani, *Hindustan Mai Musalmano Ka Nizam-i Ta'lim-o-Tarbiyat* (vol. 1). Delhi: Nadwat ul-Musannifin, 1987, p. 303.

28 Muhammad Taqi 'Usmani, *Fazilat-i 'Ilm-o-'Ulama*. Delhi: Farid Book Depot, 1999, pp. 22-27.

29 Muhammad Wali Rahmani, *Dini Madaris Mai Sanati Ta'lim Ka Masla*. Munger: Jami'a Rahmani, 1981, p. 9.

30 Muhammad Nejatullah Siddiqui, *Dini Madaris: Masa'il Aur Taqaze*. New Delhi: Markazi Maktaba-i Islami, 2001, p. 11.

31 Rahmani, *Dini Madaris Mai Sanati Ta'lim Ka Masla.*, pp. 17-19.

32 Sayyed Muhammad Rabe Hasni Nadwi, *Musalman Aur Ta'lim*. Lucknow: Nadwat ul-'Ulama, 1997, p. 53.

33 Arshad Alam, 'Science in Madrasas', article online at: http://www.epw.org.in/showArticles.php?root=2005&leaf=04&filename=8583&filetype=html .

34 Habib ur-Rahman 'Azmi 'Umri, 'Dini Madaris Ki Zimmedariyan Aur Biradiran-i Watan', in *Dini Madaris Aur Unkey Masa'il*, Baleriaganj: Jami'at ul-Falah, 1990, p. 134.

35 Shihabuddin Nadwi, *Hamare Ta'limi Masa'il*, p. 15. The call for a new *'ilm-i kalam* goes back to the nineteenth century modernist, Sayyid Ahmad Khan.

36 Mohsin Usmani Nadwi, 'Madaris Ka Nizam-i-Ta'lim Aur Naya Challenge', *Islam Aur 'Asr-i Jadid*, vol. 32, no. 4, October 2000, pp. 107-08.

37 Muhammad Muhsin, 'Dini Madaris Ka Nisab', in *'Arabi Islami Madaris Ke Nisab-o-Nizam-i-Ta'lim*. Patna: Khuda Bakhsh Oriental Public Library, 1995, p. 102.

38 Mumshad 'Ali Qasmi, *Tarikh-i Dars-i Nizami*, p. 70.

39 Maqbul Ahmad Misbahi, 'Hindustan Aur 'Alam-i 'Arab ke Nisab-i Ta'lim Ka Taqabli Ja'iza, *Islam Aur 'Asr-i Jadid*, vol. 32, no. 4, October 2000, p. 83.

40 Abul 'Irfan Nadwi, 'Nisab-i Talim Aur Tariqa-i Ta'lim: Maujuda Ahad Ke Taqaze', *Islam Aur 'Asr-i Jadid*, vol. 12, no. 4, October 1980, p. 36.

41 Muhammad Rizwan ul-Qasmi, *Maqalat-i Sajjad*. Patna: Imarat-i Shari'a, 1999, p. 29.
42 Fazlur Rahman Faridi, 'Dini Madaris Ka Nisab-i Ta'lim Aur 'Asri Challenge', in *Kul Hind Dini Madaris Convention Souvenir*. New Delhi: All-India Milli Council, n.d., p. 86.
43 For details, see Yoginder Sikand, *Bastions of the Believers: Madrasas and Islamic Education in India*. New Delhi: Penguin, 2005, pp. 168-70.
44 Quoted in Moinuddin Ahmed, *The Urgency of Ijtihad*. New Delhi: Kitab Bhavan, 1992, p. 92.
45 Quoted in Ahmed, *Urgency of Ijtihad*, p. 93.
46 The Barelvis are associated with the tradition of the Sufi saints, whose cults were ardently defended against Deobandi and 'Wahhabi' attacks by Imam Ahmad Raza Khan, a traditionalist late nineteenth-century scholar from the Indian town of Bareilly.
47 Mufti Zahiruddin Miftahi, 'Madaris-i Diniya Aur Unke Masa'il', in *Dini Madaris Aur Unkey Masa'il*. Bilariyaganj: Jami'at ul-Falah, 1990, pp. 55-57. The Mufti writes that the Barelvis (whom he derisively refers to as 'Raza Khanis') dismiss all other Muslim groups as non-Muslim, and so cannot be expected to join the madrasa board.
48 Muhammad Shams Tabrez, ''Ilm-o-Taqwa Ki Buniyad Par Ta'lim-o-Tarbiyat', *Naqib*, Phulwari Sharif, 10-17 June 1996, p. 1.
49 The Ahl-i Hadith may be said to be somewhat like the South Asian counterparts of the Saudi 'Wahhabis'. They share some of the same understandings of what they consider to be 'true' monotheism, and harshly condemn Sufism as 'un-Islamic'.
50 Mumshad 'Ali Qasmi, *Tarikh-i Dars-i Nizami*, p. 82.
51 Mumshad 'Ali Qasmi, *Tarikh-i Dars-i Nizami*, p. 82.
52 Qamruddin, *Hindustan Ki Dini Darsgahe: Kul Hind Survey*. New Delhi: Hamdard Educational Society, 1996, p. 53.
53 Washim Ahmad, 'Psychology of Education: Madrasas of UP', *Economic and Political Weekly*, 25-31 March 2000 [http://www.epw.org.in/35-13/comm5.htm].
54 The Centre for Promotion of Science functions under the Aligarh Muslim University, Aligarh. One of its principal aims is to promote the teaching of science in madrasas, for which it organises workshops for designing appropriate teaching material as well as regular condensed courses on science for madrasa graduates. For details, see http://www.angelfire.com/sc3/cps.
55 Some madrasas have tried to introduce teachers' training courses but do not seem to have succeeded. The chief Barelvi madrasa in India, the Jami'a Ashrafiya in Mubarakpur, claims to have a two-year course, which at present has a mere 4 students undergoing the training.
56 'Prof. Joshi Has Designs on Madrasas', *The Milli Gazette*, 1-15 February 2000.
57 Nizam Elahi, *Modernisation of Madrasa Education Scheme in India*. New Delhi: State Council for Educational Research and Training, 2001, pp. 12-13.

58 For details, see Prime Minister's High Level Committee, *Social, Economic and Educational Status of the Muslim Community of India*. New Delhi: Government of India, 2006, pp. 49-86.

59 Syed Shahabuddin, quoted in Madhav Godbole, '*Madrasas*: Need for a Fresh Look', *Economic and Political Weekly*, 13 October 2001, p. 3890.

60 Nizam Elahi, op. cit., p. 21.

61 Comments by several ulama who were interviewed in the course of the fieldwork.

62 According to a 1998 report, the figures for the number of madrasas affiliated to selected state boards of madrasa education were as follows: Bihar (1600), Uttar Pradesh (375), Orissa (79) (Quoted in Mohammad Akhtar Siddiqui, 'Development and Trends in Madrasa Education', in A.W.B.Qadri, Riaz Shakir Khan and Mohammed Akhter Siddique, *Education and Muslims in India Since Independence*. New Delhi: Institute of Objective Studies, 1998, p. 78. In mid-2002, 507 madrasas in West Bengal were recognised by the state madrasa education board (*The Hindu*, 18 June, 2002).

63 Thus, the scheme seems to have almost completely 'flopped' in Maharashtra (with only six madrasas joining the project). Amin Khandwani, chairman of the Maharashtra Minorities Commission, alleged that one of the main reasons for this was that the state government had sorely neglected' the scheme (Shabnam Minwalla, 'Madrasas Need to Move With the Times', *The Times of India*, New Delhi, 3 December, 2001).

64 Interview with Zafrul Islam Khan, editor, *The Milli Gazette*, New Delhi, 2 January 2003.

65 Irshadul Haque, 'Bureaucrats Foil Madrasah Education Modernisation Programme', *The Milli Gazette*, 1-15 October, 2002, p.23.

66 'Educational Awareness Among Muslims: A Positive Step', *The Milli Gazette*, 15 April 2001, online at: http://www.milligazette.com/Archives/15042001/Art11.htm.

67 'Madrasa Modernisation in Rajasthan', *Islamic Voice*, June 2001.

68 'Winds of Change Sweep Rajasthan Madrasas', *Islamic Voice*, May 1997.

69 Khalid Saifullah Rahmani,, 'Nisab-i Ta'lim: Ek Ja'iza', in *Kul Hind Dini Madaris Convention Souvenir*. New Delhi: All-India Muslim Milli Council, 1994, p. 76.

70 Mufti Muhammad Sulaiman Mansurpuri, 'Sarkari Imdad Dini Madaris Ke Liye Sitam Qatil', *Tarjuman-i Dar al-'Ulum*, August 2003, pp. 19-22.

2 Change and Stagnation in Islamic Education

The Dar al-ᶜUlum of Deoband after the Split in 1982

Dietrich Reetz

Only very recently has the West taken any notice of Islamic schools in South Asia, where especially those following the purist Deobandi interpretation of Islam have attracted much media attention. They were accused of inspiring numerous radical Islamic movements in South Asia, including the Taliban in Afghanistan, sectarian movements fighting against dissenting Islamic groups in Pakistan, and separatist militants battling with the military and the police in Indian Kashmir.[1] While the vast majority of these schools focus on classical Islamic education and not on politics or militancy, it is the narrow theological and ideological outlook of their graduates that has repeatedly been the target of criticism.

The root of the problem is often seen in the resistance of these schools to change, as they cling to an age-old curriculum and time-worn patterns of instruction. The Western perspective of stagnation in these schools, however, appears to be biased and – worse still – frequently misinformed. While their methods of change may not conform to Western expectations, it is essential to realise that from their own perspective these institutions have undergone dramatic changes since the 1970s. The course and handling of these changes will be discussed here, using the example of one of its most prominent institutions, the Islamic seminary in Deoband, north India. The latter has become the leading seminary in the Deobandi school network, extending its influence throughout south Asia and to other parts of the Islamic world.

Since the early 1980s, two events have been instrumental in forcing the school to reconfigure its structure and agenda, and to adapt more resolutely to the changing times. The first was the symbolic centenary celebration in 1980, a public event that attracted more than 8,000 delegates, including Deobandi scholars, students, and activists from South Asia and other parts of the world.[2] The second was the split that took place in 1982, when one faction of the school's leadership and teaching staff, was driven out because of family loyalties, and this faction subsequently set up a rival institution, an incident that culminated in violent student actions and the temporary closure of the school. This paper will focus on several paradigm shifts that occurred in the wake of these two events. By paradigm we mean a set of principles and references that guide the self-organisation, operation, and self-perception of the school. As it adjusted to various internal and external challenges, the school's mode of operation gradually evolved from a personalised, closed, academic style to a more open, community-oriented, and overtly political and ideological approach.

These shifts will be discussed in relation to the principles of the school; its major educational subjects; the role of family politics; the mode of networking in Deobandi schools; the gradual modernisation of the institution and its teaching methods; and the strong articulation of non-religious concerns in ideology, politics, and society. Most of this data is being presented publicly for the first time. The various aspects discussed demonstrate the broad spectrum of change. Integrating these aspects requires an interdisciplinary approach widening the narrow confines of sociology and political science, and complementing them with a broader analysis more akin to an anthropological approach.

To understand the parameters of change as perceived by the Deoband school system one must go beyond the Western-induced framework of modernisation and look at the shifts that have taken place within these institutions. The Western modernisation paradigm measures Islamic movements against expectations of the promotion of economic development, social advancement and liberal democracy. These groups, however, rely on their own perspective based on their own movement's objectives. Within these parameters, they not only pursue universal goals such as missionary aims, but also reflect group-specific issues regarding expansion, control or leadership within the movement. Western analysts rarely see changes within these areas as legitimate or relevant, since they are not necessarily a reflection of modernisation in the West. But it seems wrong to conclude that such group-specific dynamics of change will only create obstacles for broader modernisation or preclude it altogether. In practice, such diverse objectives cannot be clearly separated as they become so tightly intertwined.

The principles of the school

The Deoband school has become known for its specific take on the interpretation of Islam. While it is mostly associated with a purist, Salafi-type of teaching, its philosophy presents a far more complex mix of historical, cultural and doctrinal aspects. Moreover, issues of competition and leadership within the emerging Islamic sector have also modified its message and forced it to evolve and adapt to changing circumstances.

The higher Islamic seminary, the Deoband Dar al-'Ulum, was founded in 1866 in northern India by Muhammad Qasim Nanaotawi (1832-1879) and Rashid Ahmad Gangohi (1829-1905). The intention was to address the supposed lack of religious education among the Muslims of British India. Religious scholars feared a loss of self-identity with the spread of Western values in society and English language instruction.[3] After the defeat of the anti-colonial uprising of 1857-58, in which many Muslim princes and scholars took part, Islamic institutions were suspected of disloyalty and sedition by the British rulers. Religious scholars decided instead to concentrate on the reconstruction of religious knowledge and religiosity. Politically, they preferred to prove their loyalty to the British during this period. A more radical section of seminary teachers emerged shortly after the turn of the century, however. The new head teacher Mahmud al-Hasan (1851-1921) and scholars like Husain Ahmad Madani (1879-1957) and Ubaidullah Sindhi (1872-1944) presented highly politicised ideas that challenged British rule, which they saw as a major impediment to true Islam in India and the Islamic world in general. Deoband scholars, in particular, identified with Ottoman rule, defending if after WWI and together with Mahatma Gandhi (1869-1948), they initiated the broad-based but unsuccessful Khilafat movement (1919-1925).[4]

The ideological foundations of the school were summarised in a set of seven principles that defined the school's concept (*maslak*).[5] These are: (1) conformity with Islamic law (*shari'a*), (2) Sufi-inspired self-purification and the search for spiritual perfection (*suluk-i batin*), (3) conformity to the principles that guided the Prophet and his companions (*sunna*), (4) reliance on the Hanafi law school, (5) certitude and stability in true beliefs with reference to the Hanafi theologian al-Maturidi, (6) removal of unlawful things (*munkirat*), and especially the refutation of polytheism, innovations, atheism and materialism, and (7) adherence to the principles personally embodied by the founders of the school, Muhammad Qasim and Rashid Gangohi. These are named after them and are referred to as 'a taste for Qasimism and Rashidism.'

Principles five and six form the basis of the reputed purism of the school. The interpretation of Islam by Deobandi scholars has veered over time in the direction of stringency. The school championed religious discourse in the reformist fashion of *islah* (reformation), which emerged in the Middle East in the late nineteenth century. The founders of Deoband as well as generations of students sought to spread true Islam. Deoband scholars were characterised by a marked orthodoxy, as well as by purism and asceticism. Relations between Deobandis and groups (*maslak*) representing other interpretations of Islam were burdened by controversy. The Deobandis attacked dissenting views, particularly those of the Barelwis, who represented the shrine-based culture of Sufi-Islam. The Barelwis were named after the town of Bareli, not far from Deoband, where their religious leader Ahmad Raza Khan (1856-1921) had once resided. Relations between Deobandis and Sufi-Islam were, however, not mutually exclusive. Most Deobandi divines were themselves active Sufi *shaykhs* who followed the Sufi path, or *tariqa*, which they perceived as being in accordance with the law and word of God, or *shari'a*. As staunch followers of the Hanafi school of law (*mazhab*) they were wrongly labelled Wahhabis, with whom they shared no more than a slight bent for the radical and purist interpretation of Islamic tenets. They anxiously distinguished themselves from other sects, notably the Shi'a and especially the Ahmadiyya, whom they considered heterodox. Over time the school became the head seminary of an elaborate network of schools and activities inspired by the ideas contained in Deobandi teaching and its interpretation of Islam. It introduced religious mass education in its own seminary through hostel-based study programmes and in numerous branches and *madaris* (schools) across and beyond the confines of south Asia.

Today's Deoband school stands out as an orthodox reference point for the rest of the Muslim world. It had spawned public activism in the form of an association of religious scholars known as the *Jam'iyat-ul-ulama-i Hind* (JUH), which had already emerged as a political party by the time of partition, and continued its political activities in Pakistan under the name of *Jam'iyat-ul-ulama-i Islam* (JUI). Its Indian counterpart, the JUH, concentrated on religious, educational and cultural activities.

While the formulated principles of the school have undergone little change, the different methods of implementation have reflected their evolution. Their practical application has repeatedly led to tension among scholars and students. During the nationalist anti-colonial movement this tension was largely played out in the polarisation between a more politically inclined faction and those who advocated scholarly pursuits as the primary objective of the school. The former group was represented by Hasan, Madani, and Sindhi, whereas the latter relied on the authority of Ashraf 'Ali Thanwi (1863-1943), the school's long-time patron, and on scholars such as Muhammad Anwar Shah Kashmiri (1875-1933) and Shabbir Ahmad 'Uthmani (1885-1949). This last group suffered defeat, which led to the expulsion of its scholars and several students from the school in 1927.[6]

A further evolution in the implementation of these principles after 1980 was marked by the growing prominence of development and social concerns. As will be discussed below, the introduction of computer skills in 1996 and the English language in 2002, albeit on a small scale, symbolised a new direction in the school's activities. The debate on the adaptation of the school curriculum to the changing requirements of society, in which some of the school's young graduates participated, was an additional reflection of this new trend.[7] The issue centred around whether secular subjects should be introduced or whether the institution should remain the preserve of theological teachings. These developments changed the parameters of the debate about the school's principles. Whereas in the late colonial period it had experienced the polarisation of political and academic orientations, it has now shifted to accommodate the juxtaposition of orthodoxy and development and community concerns.

The main courses in Deobandi teaching

Since teaching is the principal task of the Deoband school, processes of adjustment and change should also manifest themselves. The sense of continuity is particularly tenacious, however, as a survey of the major courses and degrees will reveal.

The most notable teaching element at Deobandi schools is the education of religious scholars (*'alim*, pl. *'ulama*). The curriculum covers a standard eight-year degree programme, whereby students become scholars of religion and law (ulama). In essence, it is comparable to a graduate degree, it is still based on the *dars-i nizami*, compiled and introduced by Mulla Nizamu'd-din (d. 1748). Students study the Qur'an, the Prophetic traditions, the principles of their, i.e., Hanafi, law school, along with a large number of often arcane commentaries written mainly by traditionalists (cf. Ahmad 1985). The degree consists of a number of licenses or *sanads* to teach the major works of Islamic theology. The licenses identify the line of teachers who have given instruction in the work throughout generations. Apart from *manqulat* or transmitted science, which is related to divine sources, worldly knowledge of a somewhat dated variety is represented by *ma'qulat* or rational science, and includes subjects such as philosophy and logic, as well as various branches of mathematics. Traditional medicine (*tibb*) is taught in a separate department. Modern subjects such as English, geography and history have long been conspicuously absent. A basic five-year Urdu medium curriculum prescribed by the government is taught at the primary level that precedes the *alim* course.

The grade of *'alim* (scholar) is conferred at the end of Class Seven, prior to the final year (*daura-i hadith*) that begins when students focus on the study of the Prophetic Traditions. Upon completion of Class Eight, students are considered graduates or *fazil*. They are then free to specialise (*takhassus*) in various directions and take courses of up to two years in different departments at the school. The number of students who take advantage of this opportunity varies from two to a maximum of twenty. The relevant departments include

- English language and literature;
- computer training;
- the Shaykh al-Hind Academy, which provides training in advanced theological research and religious journalism;

- the 'Defence of the Finality of the Prophethood of Muhammad' (*tahaffuz-i khatm-i nabuwwat*), which trains graduates to write texts and preach against the Ahmadiyya sect, but also to refute rival interpretations of Islam; this department operates in conjunction with the preaching department (*shu'ba-i tabligh*);
- Legal Consultation (*dar al-ifta*), which provides training in the writing of legal decisions (*fatawa*, sin. *fatwa*) in reply to inquiries from the Muslim general public.

Formal post-graduate courses (*takmilat*) are currently offered in Qur'anic exegesis (*tafsir*), in theology and the beliefs of the school (*ulum*), in jurisprudence (*fiqh*), and in Arabic literature (*adab*), after which students can obtain the highest degree available, *kamil*, which verifies that they are accomplished scholars or doctors of theology.[8]

Larger Islamic schools become more significant because of their special training of *muftis*. The Deoband school employs four to five *muftis* to answer legal inquiries about the legitimacy of certain actions and types of conduct under Islamic law. While Deoband concentrates on jurisprudence in the tradition of the Hanafi law school, to which most South Asian Muslims adhere, it also responds to inquiries regarding other law schools for which specialised scholars are available. In 1423 AH (2002) the Legal Department trained an additional 37 students.[9]

Courses to train students to become a memoriser of the Qur'an (*hafiz*) or a reciter (*qari*) are available. Basic Qur'an reading (*nazara*) and writing (*kitabat*) skills are taught separately. In 1423 AH (2002), 2,502 students attended the Arabic faculty, including the eight-class *'alim* course, while 717 students attended the non-Arabic faculty, including the primary classes and minor degree courses.[10]

The predominance of orthodox theology and religious training is evident from this teaching structure. However, changes are slowly emerging at the post-graduate level. A limited number of advanced students are exposed to non-theological topics. About a quarter of them focus on ideological and political issues at the Shaykh-ul-Hind Academy and the Finality of Prophethood Department, while the rest learn English and acquire computer skills.

From family networks to family power in the name of politics

Leadership in Deobandi institutions has traditionally been influenced by clan and family loyalties.[11] Deoband shares this trait with many other public bodies and educational networks in South Asia, irrespective of religious affiliation. The long-standing grip of caste and tribal structures on the social fabric is usually held responsible. Although Islam is potentially more egalitarian in social matters, in South Asia in particular, it failed to escape the influences of tradition. Religious schools – the Dar al-'Ulum and the *madrasas* – were also affected. Over time, key positions such as that of rector, head teacher or *hadith* teacher tended to become hereditary by default. Sons are deliberately groomed to assume the father's post at some point in time. Consequently family factions competing for control of the school and its resources emerge. Although it's a well-known fact, it is rarely discussed openly. The Muslim public in India and beyond was therefore deeply shocked when family feuds – i.e., between the Tayyib and Madani families – broke out in the prestigious Deoband school and eventually led to a split.

In hindsight, we can see that the centenary celebrations in 1980 and the concomitant preparations intensified the rivalry between these families for control of the seminary, especially as its long-time rector, Muhammad Tayyib, had by that time become increasingly frail and the issue of succession had emerged. Qari Muhammad Tayyib (1897-1983) assumed the post of *muhtamim* or rector of the Deoband school in 1929, a post he held until 1982. As the grandson of Deoband founder Qasim Nanaotawi, he embodied the classical tradition of learnedness and piety and had little interest in political manoeuvring.

The official version on the school website holds Tayyib and his advisors responsible for the debacle. It maintains that subsequent to the elaborate and highly successful centenary celebrations, Tayyib allegedly

> requested that the *Majlis-i Shura* provide assistance because his administration duties (*ihtimam*) were too much for a man of his advanced age. The *Majlis-i Shura*, as per request, elected the current *muhtamim* Marghub-ur-Rahman. Thereafter, he, [Tayyib] fell victim to the insincere policies of his close advisors. In December 1980, after returning from a trip to America, he appointed Maulana Muhammad Salim vice-rector (*na'ib muhtamim*) and Maulana Anzar Shah (Kashmiri) head teacher (*sadr-i mudarris*), all of these appointments were against school regula-

> tions. After the *Majlis-i Shura* protested he revoked his decisions. He then undertook the radical step of convening an illegal meeting (*ijtima'*) in which he announced the dissolution of the *Majlis-i Shura*. This incident disrupted the entire Dar al-'Ulum administration. The political turmoil within the administration left Muslims throughout the world with a sense of sorrow. In October 1981, the sad incident of the eviction of students from the Dar al-'Ulum with the help of police occurred, which led to its closure. The years 1981 and 1982 are well-known in the history of the Dar al-'Ulum because, in addition to the state of emergency, the Dar al-'Ulum closed its doors for five months (deprived of the sound of Allah and his prophet's words). The students retook possession of their Alma Mater on 23-24 March 1982 and the administration was resurrected under the supervision of the regular *Majlis-i Shura*.[12]

This account, which dominated the media and the official representation of the events at the time, seems to be at odds with the reflections of members of the defeated faction and the loyalist camp that remained at the school. Twenty-three years after these events these factions remain surprisingly unanimous in their criticism of the 'Madani faction',[13] which consisted of the offspring of Husain Ahmad Madani. Its main protagonists were Asad Madani (1928-2006), former president of JUH, and his son Mahmud Madani, general secretary of JUH. Respondents pointed out that Marghub was related to Madani and appointed solely to wrest control of the administration from the Tayyib family, which was related to Deoband's founder Qasim Nanaotawi and together comprised the larger 'Qasimi faction'. They stressed that during his time in office, Marghub demonstrated little scholarly inclination or capacity to enhance the administration. In 2004, he appeared frail and was on sick leave for long periods of time, during which deputy-rector Qari 'Uthman, Arshad Madani as head of the teaching department (*daftar-i ta'limat*), and another member of the Madani family steered the school through troubled waters.[14]

Respondents alleged that more scholarly and devoted teachers had left the old school as a result of the split. However, they basically agreed that they have been replaced by other teachers who are just as able. Asad Madani presented his nominees to the *Majlis-i Shura*. When Marghub was gradually judged as having failed his duties, Asad Madani was said to have laid claim to the chairmanship of the *Shura*. He remained politically active for the Congress Party. His son Mahmud tested the political waters for a regional party, the Rashtriya Lok Dal. While he lost the general party elections, he was elected on its ticket to the upper house of the Indian Parliament, the Rajya Sabha.[15]

The 'Madani faction' still draws sharp criticism for its approach in the matter. Some of my respondents regarded the current phase as a period of decline for the 'Madani faction's' control over the Deoband school. They claimed that the scholarly tradition had been replaced by a more policy-oriented superficial activism. Numerous issues remained unsolved, such as the maintenance of school buildings and student hostels. The library and the archives (*muhafiz khana*) showed signs of decline and disorder. Staff members frequently went on leave. Debates that might have redefined the role of the seminary and Islamic teaching in today's world were avoided or deliberately stifled.[16]

However, the current leadership portrays the period since the split as a success story marked by expansion and modernisation, as will be shown below.

Both of the quarrelling factions insist that the differences have less to do with principles than with personal matters. In 1982, the Qasimi group opened a new school called the Dar al-'Ulum (*waqf*) at another location. The name is derived from the endowment (*awqaf*) land to which they had laid claim in the process of partition. The old school was associated with the 'Madani faction' and portrayed the 'Qasimi faction' as the 'defeated' party that had caused the 'split', and accused them of causing the rift by founding a new school. Maulana Salim Qasim, Tayyib's son, became rector of the new school. Maulana Anzar Shah Kashmiri was nominated head of the teaching department. He represented a separate 'sub-faction' formed by the offspring of Anwar Shah Kashmiri, who are mentioned above in connection with an earlier conflict. He served as Shaykh al-Hadith and later head teacher of Deoband from 1915 to 1927. At the new school, the 'Kashmiri faction' seemed to be gaining ground, as demonstrated by a small but telling detail. A major gate to the premises, previously known as Bab-i Tayyib, has been renamed after Anwar Shah Kashmiri.[17]

In a typical illusory manner, the 'Qasimi faction' presented its school as the only true Deoband school, especially in its students recruitment flyers and brochures. In private, however, they were forced to concede that the old school was still regarded as the standard of reference. The 'Qasimi faction' considered themselves Deobandis in terms of school of thought (*maslak*) and beliefs (*'aqida*) and were waiting to be invited to join the network activities of the main school, an invitation they suggested would be favourably adjudged. In the meantime, they used the increased demand for religious education to consolidate and increase their own share of the market. This expansion was mirrored in the enrolment figures, which had already reached 1,500 and represented about half of the old school figure.[18] Since the new school was constructed on barren land, plans for expansion would be relatively simple. Meanwhile, the 'Kashmiri faction' established graduate training institutes for computer science and English (*ma'had al-anwar*) here. 'On principle', however, they do not provide these courses at their own Dar al-'Ulum so that students are not distracted from their religious studies.

The family networks that run the school relied on traditional forms of allegiance, while also appealing to Sufi traditions. They presented the family as constituting a line of transmission of blessing (*barakat*), which was passed down from father to son more reliably than to unrelated disciples. This argument was used when Tayyib was first appointed pro-rector in 1922 to refer to of the fact that he was a member of Deoband founder Muhammad Qasim Nanaotawi's family.[19] In the 1970s, the private privilege of family rule was replaced by a more competitive game of politics at the institution. Both the old and new school have now been placed firmly and unceremoniously in the hands of a family faction that no longer seems to advance arguments of spiritual blessing but instead exudes an attitude of sheer expediency based on political and economic survival.

From a School of Thought to a Network of Schools

Since its inception, the school has exerted its trans-local influence through its teacher, student and graduate networks, extending across a number of countries. They helped to set up a large network of school branches with a shared ideology and theological curriculum, which for the most part functioned autonomously. The joint tradition of legal thought embodied in the decisions of the school and its stalwarts, the missionary activities of school representatives, and the Tablighi Jama'at missionary movement led by Deobandi scholars were other historical bonding channels. This interaction, however, was largely personal and spontaneous, with little procedural co-ordination or formalisation. The way in which the school co-operates has undergone significant changes since 1980.

One remarkable development was how the Dar al-'Ulum set about formalising the influence it exerted as the head seminary of a particular school of thought. The centenary celebrations in 1980 were a welcome occasion to renew links with Deobandi schools in other parts of India, across South Asia, and beyond. Long invitation lists were compiled so that graduates from all over the world could be invited, although there had evidently been no regular contact with the majority of them prior to this. The Ayodhya controversy and the demolition of the Babri Masjid on 6 December 1992 seem to have marked a watershed in religious elite thinking in India. Several respondents confirmed that it brought home to Islamic leaders the fact that Muslims were now on their own in matters of religion, and could no longer count on the support or protection of a more or less well-meaning liberal and secular state. If Muslims wanted to preserve their religion and their place in society they had to be more assertive and show greater sympathy for the mainstream forces of society. Attacks by Hindu nationalist forces on the *madrasa* system and their teachings strengthened Islamic resolve to defend it, and this went hand-in-hand with the vigorous resistance to change. One solution to the dilemma was discovered in the formal organisation of the Deobandi *madaris*.

In the course of two meetings of like-minded Deobandi schools held on 29-30 June and 25-26 October in 1994,[20] the Association of Arabic Schools (Rabita Madaris Arabiya or RMA) was established, with its headquarters at the Dar al-'Ulum. As per March 2004, it had 1152 affiliated *madaris* across India. Once their rules and teaching practices had been appraised by the RMA, their certificates (*sanad*) would be ratified. The RMA regularly convened meetings with rectors and head teachers to discuss new challenges and curriculum issues.[21] By and large it served as a forum for Deobandi scholars to close ranks and resist demands for ever far-reaching changes. At the same time, changes concerning several matters were being discretely sanctioned, mainly with regard to increased computerisation and the use of English. It also contributed to the prevention of substandard religious teaching in the burgeoning market of religious education presented in the name of the eminent Deobandi school of thought. In a sense, this was like branding their product and protecting its rights in a market that was both lucrative and expansive. The Qasimi faction' school remained excluded. In an interview, Anzar Kashmiri emphasised that they were not seeking affiliation with the RMA because they regarded themselves as the true embodiment of the Deobandi school. He pointedly added, however, that they would not object to being invited, implying that they obviously viewed the rift as a painful anomaly.[22] When Asad Madani fell ill in 2005, increased efforts were made to mend the rift between the two schools,[23] and these efforts may be accelerated now, following his demise.

Preliminary data on Deobandi schools affiliated to the RMA indicate another notable development, i.e., the expansion and diversification of the geographic impact of the Deobandi school of thought. Not surprisingly, the great majority of schools were located in northern India, primarily in the state of Uttar Pradesh (402 schools). Somewhat more unexpected, however, is the considerable number of affiliated schools in West Bengal (253), showing that Deobandi thinking has made strong inroads into a region where Sufi-oriented and ritualist Islam had a tradition of being very influential. From the same perspective, the substantial number of Deobandi schools in Jammu and Kashmir (44), in southern India, particularly Maharashtra (38) and Andhra Pradesh (23), and in Assam in eastern India (121) are also worth mentioning.

A look at the composition of students at the Deoband head seminary in 1414-15 AH (1994) confirms a similar pattern of geographical distribution. Here the preponderance of the two states of Uttar Pradesh and Bihar is even greater, accounting for 85% of the students in a typical year. However, the south Indian states of Andhra Pradesh and Maharashtra are represented by 50 students each (in a total student population of almost 3,000), revealing that Deobandi thought is gaining momentum and spreading its roots in the south as well.[24]

Formalising the school's network activities continued with the foundation of a graduate association, Tanzim-i Abna-i Qadim, in 1991.[25] Its establishment had already been suggested at the centenary celebrations in 1980. The earlier efforts of Ubaidullah Sindhi in this direction in 1909 remained fruitless. The new association now seems to be working successfully and has established its headquarters in Delhi. Not only has it introduced two post-graduate training institutes, one for spoken Arabic and one for English, it also edits a regular monthly, *Tarjuman Dar al-ʿUlum*, established in 1993 with a world-wide graduate audience. The journal features debates that explore in a cautious but resolute manner, occasionally pushing the boundaries of the Deobandi school of thought concerning the history of the school, the need to review the religious curriculum, the inclusion of worldly subjects, and relations with the West. It is particularly noteworthy that in the interests of strengthening the Deobandi school of thought, the association maintains contact with both the old school and the 'Qasimi faction'. This undoubtedly has to do with the reconstruction and updating of Deobandi ideas in the modern era, especially as it is run by a new generation of graduates aware of the need to adapt to changing circumstances. However, the more senior, conservative scholars who oversee the work of the Association as patrons try to limit and control change while, on the other hand, they do not shy away from imposing their will by disciplining insubordinate functionaries.

Although the networking of international Deobandi institutions, scholars and students clearly multiplied during this period, formal links for foreign graduates of the school in Deoband are less easy to quantify.[26] While enrolment increased impressively over the years, their significance has simultaneously experienced a sharp decline.[27] Annual enrolment has long since dropped below the all-time high of the 1950s and 1960s, and currently numbers approximately 30 to 60 graduates per year. Their composition has also undergone a radical change. Whereas numerous students from outside South Asia were enrolled here in 1980, they are now almost non-existent.[28]

The Indian government introduced formal restrictions on the enrolment of foreigner students in the late 1970s. They were initially made more stringent as a result of Hindu nationalist pressure and later anti-terrorism policies. Only students with an educational visa can be enrolled. Students have rarely been granted this visa for Deoband, as the head of the school's education department acerbically pointed out to me. The reason why Muslims are not allowed to study their own religion, he stated, is known only to the powers that be.[29]

Nevertheless, international links have not been totally discarded. Although it should be emphasised that responsibility for spreading Deobandi thought lies with the *madaris* that were established by Deobandi graduates specifically for this purpose. The organisation of a world meeting of Deobandi schools, 9-11 April 2001 near Peshawar, Pakistan as a symbolic celebration of the 150th anniversary of the Deoband Alma Mater, demonstrated the willingness of Deobandi scholars to assert themselves more forcefully on the international scene.[30] While the Deobandi politicians from Pakistan such as Fazlur Rahman attacked the West for its policies on Islam, the Indian representatives chose to highlight the educational achievements of the school in spreading Deobandi thought. This development was severely disrupted by the aftermath of the September 11 attack in 2001.[31] The Deoband school claimed that it was at the receiving end of what it regards as malicious attacks by Hindu nationalists and the West, who are intent on proving its terrorist association with either the Taliban or militant so-called *jihadi* groups in India and Pakistan, particularly in Kashmir. At the same time, Deobandi scholars in India and Pakistan continue to argue that the Taliban's responsibility for these events has never been proved. They believe that the attack of 9/11 was at best willfully engineered by the Americans, at the worst organised by Israeli agencies.[32] The reality gap in their line of thought is compounded by the isolation of their outlook and the limited access to both secular knowledge and information in English.

A major development in the expansion of Deobandi networking concerns its interaction with the missionary movement of the Tablighi Jama'at, which was founded in India in 1926 by the Deobandi scholar Muhammad Ilyas (1885-1944).[33] The strengthening of links between Deobandi activists, groups and institutions in South Asia and the rest of the world has been greatly supported by the world-wide expansion of *Tablighi* activities since the 1970s. Its national centres (*marakaz*) in India and Pakistan maintain their own Deobandi schools, where the *alim* course is taught. Numerous international students frequent these schools. Students from Islamic schools in the provinces and states attend the final year – *daura-i hadith* – to obtain a graduation certificate from the renowned Deobandi schools at the Tablighi centres. The leadership of the Tablighi Jama'at in Delhi enjoys a special relationship with the Islamic seminary in Saharanpur, not far from Deoband. Many former leaders of the Tablighi Jama'at graduated from here. This school also split along family lines, however. The offspring of Ilyas and the co-founder of the movement, Muhammad Zakariyya (1898-1982), constitute an extended family clan that controls many of the leadership positions both in the Tablighi Jama'at and the new Saharanpur school. Maulana Zakariyya and his disciples extended their influence throughout the world. They founded several new Deobandi schools, above all in South Africa and the UK, each of which maintains close links with the Tablighi movement and integrate Tablighi literature into their curriculum.[34]

Networking between Deobandi schools in India and other parts of the world has thus undergone a major change since 1980. It expanded and became much more formalised. The decline in foreign student enrolment at Deoband during this period, however, was not an obstacle to international co-operation between other Deobandi schools and graduates. Co-ordination of Deobandi institutions at the global level remains personalised, although the Tablighi missionaries and scholar networks have begun to introduce more formal elements.

From traditional to 'modern' Islamic teaching

Moreover, the Dar al-'Ulum rebounded more formally from its moribund state after the split. Following a brief break during the crisis years of 1982 and 1983 it expanded rapidly, as reflected in its budget figures, as well as enrolment and number of teachers. The manifested increase in enrolment has become a proud feature of the school's modernity as touted by its leaders. The programme to improve the school's administration was primarily directed at streamlining the organisation. Much attention was paid to the impact of two innovations on the curriculum: the introduction of English classes at the post-graduate level and computer courses. However, these courses were only acceptable within the parameters of the school's theological objectives. The more traditional technical education, on the other hand, which has been on offer for a long time, is currently suffering from neglect.

This change in the approach of the school leadership and the shift towards quantitative growth is evident in the budget.[35] Although data available for the pre-1989 period is patchy, it nevertheless leads to several conclusions regarding the volume and dynamics of the budget. By international standards, it is modest. Full-time education programmes for more than 3,500 students are currently being run on an annual budget of $1 million. Compared to the financial situations of other South Asian educational institutions, however, its budget growth is impressive. In the 32 years from 1971 to 2003, the budget in Indian rupies has increased by a factor of almost 50. Throughout this period it had an average annual growth rate of 12% (calculated on a cost basis). The period of most rapid annual growth was between 1983 and 1989, after which it gradually declined in the 1990s and almost stagnated after 2000, reflecting the deteriorating political environment for Islamic institutions.

Meanwhile, the administrative reports allow an educated guess regarding the number of staff employed at the Deoband school, although the reporting is inconsistent and the data frequently incomplete. Since 1989, the overall number of staff seems to have fluctuated between 240 and 280. The number of teachers was comparatively stable at approximately 50 between 1965 and 1979 but increased notably to 74 in 1997 and 92 in 2002. However, this was not enough to offset the intense growth rates in student enrolment. As a result, the student/teacher ratio increased rapidly throughout the 1980s and 1990s, but it has since shown a slight decline.

The 'Madani faction' prefers to point to the increasing enrolment, which has almost doubled since 1980 and reached 3,556 in the year 2002-03. This is regarded as proof of the school's revival since the split. Moreover, the annual number of graduates has almost doubled to 774. The rise in enrolment has put new strains on the school's administration. This in turn may have spurred greater reform efforts, which have been primarily directed at removing administrative bottlenecks. A pamphlet containing a summary of the changes brought about since 1982 lists seven administrative reforms directed at streamlining internal procedures.[36] They concern the following:

- the admission of new students, where written tests have been replaced by oral exams, allowing for the more efficient processing of applicants;
- the elimination of one of two mid-year examinations, lessening the burden on the education department;
- the introduction of anonymous code numbers for examination papers, ensuring impartial assessment;
- the supervision of teachers with regard to covering course material and supply of competent teaching staff;
- the appointment of capable Qur'anic readers (*mujawwidin*) and reciters (*qurra*) with a national reputation;
- greater efficiency at the department of memorisation of the Qur'an (*hifz*);
- the fusion of the Persian and (Urdu) religious studies departments for primary level students with a uniform course length of five years.

The report also lists six areas of expansion in the teaching department. They include improved supervision of the Class One to Class Four students of the *'alim* course, the recruitment of gifted students and trainees for teaching positions through scholarships, the increase in the numbers of classes offered each course year, and the adjustment of the post-graduate *takmil* courses.

However, innovations were not merely limited to those of an administrative nature. A number of new departments were established: the Shaykh-ul-Hind Academy in 1982-83, the *Tahaffuz-i Khatm-i Nabuwwat* in 1986, the Computer Training Centre in 1996, and the Department of English Language and Literature in 2002.[37] The latter acquired a particular symbolic significance in the long history of the seminary, concluding a debate that lasted for more than a century. While the chief arguments for and against the learning of English had already been presented by the first decades of the twentieth century, the factual introduction of the English language as came up against a purported 'lack of funds'. Interviews with those involved in the momentous decision of the *Majlis-i Shura* to go ahead with English courses were evidence that the old inhibitions and arguments were still very much alive.

There was a fear that learning English would lead to an imitation of the West, a grave doctrinal argument with Qur'anic connotations, and one that ultimately undermines Muslim religious identity, paving the way for their Christianisation. The apprehension was particularly acute during the colonial period. Mahmud al-Hasan grappled with the consequences at the opening of the Jam'iya Milliya in Aligarh on 29 October 1920:

> Those amongst you who are well informed will know that I have never given a religious decree (*fatwa*) declaring the study of a foreign language or of the sciences and arts of other nations as *kufr* (unbelief). But I state categorically that the final impact of English education in our view is that people are influenced by (dyed in the colour of) Christianity, or mock and abuse their religion and their co-religionists with atheist taunts, or begin to worship the government of the day. It is right for a Muslim to stay aloof from such education.[38]

Badruddin Ajmal, a wealthy perfume merchant from Assam, a Dar al-'Ulum graduate and *Shura* member, had taken the introductory English course early on. Several respondents claimed that he had developed close relations with the Madani family solely to obtain access to the *Shura*. He first raised the issue of the English language in 1994 and was rebuked. He was asked to prove that its introduction would not dilute the Islamic quality of the graduates, that the demand for English was genuine, and that learning the language would add a new dimension to the task of spreading the true Islam. He set up a post-graduate training institutes for ulama with his own money, the *Markaz al-Ma'arif* in Delhi and Bombay, where English was already being taught. In two-year courses they produced a small but fine batch of ulama, who were well-versed in English and made their way up the hierarchy of Islamic institutions in India as a result of the urbane aura they now exuded. One of these students, a Dar al-'Ulum graduate and today the head of a post-graduate training institute, was called to the decisive meeting in 2001, where the issue remained unresolved despite a prolonged debate.[39] Ajmal subsequently delivered the key argument that in today's computerised world, a proficiency in English was crucial to responding to the many questions on Islam raised by Muslims who do not speak Urdu, in particular those from southern India and abroad, where they frequently live in isolation without access to knowledge about the true Islam. Hence, English could and should be seen as a means of *tabligh* and *da'wa*, i.e., of spreading God's message to non-believers and the uninformed.

Missionary goals are still a significant argument in legitimising the study and knowledge of English. When in this class I asked about their motives for studying English, the students were unanimous in replying that it served to spread Islam. In private, some acknowledged that many among them watch films in English on television and in the cinema, or that they contemplate secular career options – something categorically rejected by the purist Deobandi dogma.

Some Deobandi *madaris* still reject the idea of teaching English, not to mention other worldly subjects. Not unlike the elders of the new wing of the famous Saharanpur Madrasa Mazahir al-'Ulum, which split on similar lines to the Deoband school, they argue that learning English will distract students from their religious vocations, for which the community has made sacrifices to provide them with free educations.[40] In other words, they feel the need to 'trap' students from poor family backgrounds in the religious profession by refusing them access to English. They have also argued that the number of clerics per Muslim in India was still comparatively low compared to that of Christians in the West. Another line of argument equates engineering schools with madrasas, which simply specialised in religious education. The students could choose, the curriculum came with the respective specialisation. The latter argument sounds particularly odd since the traditional curriculum also contained the rational sciences, which were originally for secular use. The current narrow religious specialisation of the *madaris* was merely the historical result of Western and colonial influences, which in the nineteenth century had deprived religious schools of their standing as educational institutions in the secular realm.

While many ulama in India, Pakistan and Bangladesh defend the exclusively religious profile of the current *madaris*, some are hoping to regain their mainstream roles in education. It is interesting to note how a technical or economic vision of modernity is used by the ulama to advocate for change. They describe computer training, for instance, as a 'requirement of the modern era' (*'asr-i jadid ka ahm taqaza*).[41] This argument is related to an old inner-Islamic debate in South Asia about the need to update Islamic knowledge in line with the contemporary era (*'asr-i hazar*). Similar to the West's concepts of modernisation, computer knowledge is seen here as the key to obtaining an 'Islamic' view of modernity. Computer knowledge is accepted – like English – as long as it serves the school's religious objectives. In this context, the Deoband school sees the value of computers in how much easier it makes the study and reproduction of religious texts in Urdu, the most popular service offered by the computer centre. It makes the production of pamphlets and tracts for the propagation of the school's tenets (*da'wa, tabligh*) much easier, and thus further enhances its public religious profile. The centre charges a fee for other departments at the school that seek assistance with Urdu texts. The centre earned a total of 33,749 rupees on this service in 1423 AH (2002-03).

The computer centre also offers Internet access, but the number of computers is negligible. Students are only permitted to use the Internet for educational purpose and are closely monitored. However, students interested in using the Internet are free to use the Internet cafés in town in their spare time, although not many of them take advantage of this opportunity. The computer centre is thus expected to slowly change the graduate profile. By 2003, 152 students had been trained here. Due to the anxiety of unlimited access to uncontrolled information, and the lack of facilities and space, the number of new students is currently restricted to 20 per year.[42]

The computer department's proposals in the administrative report show that its role will continue to gradually expand in line with the increased computerisation of the school administration and its functions. The computer department requests the construction of new rooms to house separate divisions for administration, computer teaching, and computer and Internet access.[43] The proposals pointed out that it has to process increasing numbers of e-mail inquiries from outside, no less than 1,813 in 2002-3. The more important ones are translated and sent to the respective departments for reply. 268 legal inquiries (*istifta*, i.e., requests of a *fatwa*) were received by e-mail during the year, all of which emphasised the significance of the Internet for specific Islamic purposes. These details were apparently considered conclusive proof of the legitimacy of this new means of communication for the school elders. Moreover, 51 applications from other countries were received by e-mail that year.[44]

A major function of the computer centre is the maintenance of the school website, which is a key instrument in disseminating information about the school to the outside world.[45] The centre's online publications in 2002-3 included a general introduction to the school on its Arabic-language web pages, over 300 pages in Urdu dealing with the curriculum and system of education, the school's admissions regulations, departments, services and scholars, as well as its legal recommendations (*fatawa*) and publications, the 250 pages of Rizvi's *History of the Dar al-'Ulum* in English, and 18 news items in English, Urdu and Arabic.

New challenges for the computer department with regard to the Web site as outlined in the administrative report include the translation of more material into Arabic, English and Hindi, and the expansion of computer facilities to expedite replies to legal inquiries (*fatawa*). The department stressed that it had received numerous e-mails congratulating the school on its new online services and further encouraging its expansion. This feedback has in particular come from the UK.

The Web site illustrates the contradictory impact such technical innovations can have, which is not unlike the role of printing in religious mobilisation. The technically-minded young ulama, who do not want to be left behind by secular institutions in the presentation of Islam on the Internet, are attracted by the sense of competition. On the one hand, this has raised the ideological profile of the school and strengthened sectarian orientations. On the other hand, it has increased transparency, making religious arguments – and the inner workings of the school administration – more widely accessible, a decided move in the direction of democratisation.

Technical education at the school has long since included vocational training. The Dar al-'Ulum introduced this department (*dar al-sanaye'*) in

1945.[46] Students were to be given hands-on training in crafts, a measure that would improve their chances of employment later on. The crafts taught, however, were selected entirely in accordance with the needs of the school and the scholarly disposition of the ulama.[47] Today the department has three divisions: (1) tailoring of school uniforms (*khayyati*) where four students were employed on a full-time basis and 75 part-time students in 1423 AH; (2) bookbinding (*tajlid*), where books are repaired and the registries of various departments bound by one permanent staff member assisted by four students; and (3) embroidery (*kashida kari*), where one staff member teaches students the art of embroidery, although the position was vacant at the time of the 1423 AH report.[48]

The various 'modern' changes that have been implemented by the school reveal the quantitative, technical and functional vision of modernisation pursued by the school elders in the strict interests of ideological goals. These goals are being reinterpreted in the process to make room for further improvements. This reflects a paradigm shift in the school's self-image, but also in its everyday operations.

From Religious Education to Political, Ideological and Development Concerns

The institutionalisation of non-religious concerns must be seen as a further trend in adapting to modernising influences, and refers in particular to political and ideological debate, and development issues, all of which focus on the status and perspectives of the Muslim community in India. The school maintains separate departments for these subjects, the more active and more prominent of which were established only after 1980. Other formats to propagate the political and ideological concerns of the school include its periodical, student clubs, and Deobandi NGOs founded by graduates. The NGOs introduced a 'Deobandi universe' of interrelated graduate institutions, thereby responding to the need to create jobs for graduates, but also to participate directly in development efforts. The social impact of the school can be detected in the urban life of Deoband, which has become a high-profile Islamic university town.

Ideological debate should be understood here as the promotion of a polarised and reductionist world view. In the case of the Deoband school, it emanates from theological and doctrinal concepts showing a preference – or bias – for a specific interpretation of Islam and its practice, and of the world that surrounds it. This ideological debate contributes to the drawing of battle lines between followers and opponents, where doctrinal concerns are directly linked to internal, political, and international issues. It can be read as a consequence of purist pretensions, where prevailing worship practices and conduct are not accepted as such but assumed to be in need of cleansing.

A separate body to channel and support debate in defence of the 'Finality of Prophethood' – the All-India Majlis-i Tahaffuz-i Khatm-i Nabuwwat was created in 1986.[49] Its headquarters is run as a separate department at the Dar al-'Ulum. This organisation's name is a euphemism for a sectarian perspective on Islam, which does battle with perceived enemies that supposedly question the finality of Muhammad's Prophethood or the status of Muhammad as the 'seal of the prophets.' The first to be challenged were the Ahmadiyya, in response to claims by their founder Mirza Ghulam Ahmad (1839-1908) and subsequent leaders to some degree of prophethood. Enemies were spotted everywhere. The publications of the Majlis targeted not only the allegedly heretical Ahmadiyya, but also Shi'a, Christians, Hindus, Barelwis, Jama'at-i Islami, and Ahl-i Hadith. The organisation has also spawned a world body of unmistakable radicalism.[50] Its local chapters, particularly those in Pakistan, regularly make news with their persecution of Ahmadis. The Pakistani branch is notorious for its links with other sectarian organisations, such as the Sipah-i Sahaba and jihadi groups.[51] The Deoband office focuses on the formulaic reproduction of pamphlets targeting the above-mentioned groups. Local chapters enjoy a wide degree of autonomy, albeit the existence of a global network and mutual support cannot be denied. The co-ordinating function of the Indian organisation appears to extend to Nepal. It conducts camps throughout India to train scholars in the rejection of Ahmadi ideas.[52] As there are few Ahmadiyya in India, the camps were mainly used to mobilise followers and help the scholars get an ideological focus.

One scholar stands out in the 1423 AH (2002) report in the context of sectarian preaching, i.e., Maulana Qari 'Uthman, who was in charge of most of the high-level attacks on Ahmadi ideas. He is the senior vice-principal of the school and practically runs it when the principal, Maulana Marghub, is either too ill or too frail to attend to his duties. From the extensive coverage of the department's activities in the administrative report we can infer that honing the sectarian profile of the school is still a high priority. The school is thus by design a major ideological institution beyond its educational pretensions.

The *Tabligh* office is closely connected to the Finality of Prophethood department, which is much older, having been founded in 1907.[53] It continued its mission with great zeal in 2002-3. Its three full-time preachers have a gruelling schedule. Maulana Muhammad Yamin, Maulana Muhammad Irfan and Maulana Rashid each participated in two to three hundred missionary programmes, where they delivered more than 400 speeches during the year.[54]

The aim of the Shaykh-ul-Hind Academy, established in 1403 AH (1983), was to support academic in-depth studies with more sophisticated arguments for the defence and dissemination of the beliefs of the school's founders. Staff members are responsible for writing many of the public speeches delivered during the missionary work (*tabligh*), as well as those delivered by the rector and other luminaries on political issues. This function falls under the category of post-graduate specialisation or *takhassus*. The two-year course was attended by seven students in 2002-3.[55] It enables selected graduate students to practice Islam-related journalism and research. One particular case attracted public attention while I was in Deoband. A student was expelled from the Academy for publishing an article in which he supported the demand for the introduction of secular subjects in the school curriculum. He was heavily criticised for having revealed his association with the Deoband school. This demonstrates that the debate has penetrated the very heart of the school's ideological institutions, and it is only a matter of time before these kinds of debates will be conducted more openly.[56]

The school periodicals address matters dealing with ideology, politics and development, and are closely related to the above-mentioned departments.[57] The administrative reports make constant reference to their financial difficulties, stating that the subscriptions are inadequate. Besides, the school tends to give away complementary copies. As school organs, the periodicals are closely monitored. More recently, the school has begun to feature the latest issues of the monthlies *Dar al-'Ulum* and *Al-Da'i* on the Internet.[58] It also runs a printing press and its own bookshop, which stocks religious texts reflecting the school's philosophy. Many of its publications discuss the evolution of the Deoband school, including the works of its prominent ulama and its official history by Sayyid Mahboob Rizvi.[59]

PERIODICALS PUBLISHED BY THE DEOBAND SCHOOL

Periodical	First published	Circulation
Mahinama Dar al- ʿUlum (Monthly)	1360 ah (1941)	3,081 (1423 ah)
Mahinama al-Rashid (Monthly)	1332 ah (1913)	[Discontinued]
Mahinama al-Qasim (Monthly)	1328 ah (1910)	[Discontinued]
A'ina Dar al-ʿUlum (Bi-weekly)	1,000 (1423 ah)	
Mahinama al-Daʿi (Arabic)	1396 ah (1976)	1,000 (1398 ah)
Risala Daʿwa al-Haq (Arabic)	Discontinued (1396 ah)	237 (1394 ah)

There are more than 100 student clubs (*talaba ke anjumanen*) active in the school and they deserve particular attention. Structured according to the original geographical origins of the students, their aim is to facilitate learning. Some of them reflect the interest in promoting the study of Arabic literature and language (*an-nadi al-adbi*). Office bearers are elected, albeit under the direction of the teachers, who guide the groups as patrons (*sarparast*). Those in office design the wall newspapers (*diwari parche*), which adorn the walls and trees of the inner courtyards where students learn the basics of religious journalism. Most are written in the vernacular, while some are produced in regional languages, such as Bengali, Tamil, Nepali, or in Arabic. One wall newspaper announces school events, news and special announcements, such as the arrival of guests. The clubs have their own libraries and they hold regular meetings, primarily on Thursdays, which function as debating societies. Although free speech is practised here in the manner of a prayer leader addressing a congregation, topics cannot be freely chosen, but strictly reflect doctrinal and ideological concerns. In practice, the wall newspapers serve as a powerful means of maintaining control over students' minds and sharpening the doctrinal profile of the school.

The fact that student unions were banned and have not been revived since the split is being questioned today. Loyalists point to a similar situation in the Jamiʿa Milliya, arguing that a ban on student unions and their removal are a matter of historical tradition in India. More critical voices point out that the incident discussed above, in which a student was excluded from the Shaykh-ul-Hind Academy for his public criticism of the school has shown the disadvantage of not having a functioning student union. The demand for a student union will probably get new support at the school in the near future.

The growing number of graduates at the Deoband school and other Deobandi madrasas has now spawned a number of auxiliary Islamic institutions operating as non-governmental organisations (NGOs)

Peripheral institutions created by or influenced by Deobandi graduates

Institution	Year
All India Ta'limi wa Milli Foundation	2000
Dar al-Qazi	1994
Markazi JUH	1992
All India Milli Council (AIMC)	1992
Tanzim-i Abna-i Qadim	1991
Islamic Fiqh Academy	1989
Institute of Objective Studies	1986
Markaz al-Ma'arif	1982
Jam'iyat ul-Ulama-i Hind (JUH)	1919

It is through these institutions that the nexus with the wider society and the secular Muslim elite is being re-established. Both the Institute of Objective Studies and the JUH champion the political causes of India's Muslims and their minority rights. Education is the concern of the Milli Foundation, the Milli Council, the Markaz al-Ma'arif, and the Tanzim-i Abna-i Qadim. The Dar al-Qazi and the Fiqh Academy investigate legal issues raised by India's separate Muslim Personal Law and its reconciliation with common law and the *shari'a*. It is conspicuous that some of them, such as the Markaz al-Ma'arif and the Ta'limi wa Milli Foundation, also support the introduction of secular and non-denominational schools, where students can practice their religions unhindered. Some of these schools are attended by local Hindus, albeit in small numbers.[60]

Another option for Deobandi graduates is to continue their education at a university or at one of the post-graduate training institutes mentioned earlier. Deoband still faces the problem of having its degrees recognised by secular universities. At the Jami'a Millia and Hamdard Universities in Delhi, and Aligarh University, the *fazil* degree was recognised as the equivalent of the Intermediate graduation certificate on the condition that the respective students passed supplementary tests in English. Moreover, the *fazil* degree was recognised as the equivalent of a bachelor's degree in Arabic and Islamic Studies at Aligarh University, as was the case at Al-Azhar University in Cairo and the Islamic University in Medina. The Hamdard University also recognised the Deoband degree in traditional medicine (*tibb*) as the equivalent of a bachelor's degree in *Unani* ('Greek') medicine and surgery.[61]

The school and its graduates have left a lasting impression on the life and economy of the small town of Deoband, which shot to prominence as a result of the school. Several graduates and drop-outs set up their own businesses, opening bookshops, general stores, a medical clinic, a pharmacy, a hotel, and a trading outlet for the famous leather stockings worn in the madrasas and exported to other countries throughout the world.[62] In 2003, Deoband had a population of approximately 110,000. Muslims constitute about 60% of the population, with Hindus and Muslims living more or less separately in different parts of town.[63] As a result of its many Islamic schools, Deoband has become a centre of Islamic education and Islamic studies comparable to the academic towns of Oxford and Cambridge in the West. According to the latest local description of Deoband, it is home to 109 madrasas.[64]

Although diverse in character and format, these changes demonstrate that the school is increasingly pre-occupied with non-religious concerns, which both shape its activities and mobilise its students and graduates. An outstanding characteristic of the school is that it remains in close contact with society, despite its often polarised and selective views on religion and social life. The school seeks to expand its legitimacy in this dialogue and to address student concerns and their social environment.

Directions of Change

Since the split in 1982, the school has undoubtedly undergone major changes. From the multitude of school events, this paper has focused on four major directions of change:

- from a family network to politics of influence;
- from a school of thought to a well-built network of schools that is becoming more formal and cohesive;
- from a 'traditional' mode of operation to the Islamist notion of modernity that includes expansion and technical professionalism;[65]
- from religious instruction to the wider pursuit of ideological, political and development concerns.

These changes illustrate the winding course of the Dar al-'Ulum Deoband. It faces the challenges of modernity but endeavours to tackle them in the spirit of its own largely ideological mission. It is clear that it is far from being an homogenous school of thought, because it is powerless to prevent the penetration of society's mainstream concerns and perspectives into its body politics.

Its graduates play a decisive role in the creation of new Deobandi institutions, which focus to a large extent on development and education issues. Girls' education,[66] computer knowledge, and language qualifications in English and modern Arabic are among the growing demands of the students.

Its administrative operations are also undergoing adjustments. The administrative reports analysed for this paper indicate that the school is becoming increasingly more professional by the year. The growth in transparency of the school's operations has been remarkable. Nevertheless, this does not mean it is becoming ideologically more flexible, as it grows more defiant in the face of what it perceives as mounting political adversity.

Looking at the Dar al-'Ulum Deoband, it is difficult to speak of a crisis of orthodoxy in Islamic education, or of Islamic education in general.[67] The school continues to expand at a rapid rate. At the same time, its financial resources have become more strained. Sustaining the standard of support for students in terms of hostels, food, or medical aid seems more difficult. The school is currently tapping into new private resources to upgrade its infrastructure. Income from the private sector, such as Badruddin Ajmal's contribution to the running of several departments (computers, English,

Shaykh-ul-Hind Academy, Finality of Prophethood) could significantly alter how the school is run, if only on the technical side.[68]

It holds fast to its ideological mission, training students in the school's narrow theological dogma and its ideological interpretation of the world. It continues to rekindle sectarianism and polarisation among Muslim groups in India and further afield.[69] Its graduates, however, are still divided over their activist role in society. Most are guided by a contemplative mood and personal piety. The rigours of the school's training make them humble and disciplined servants of the school's cause.

Debates on the school curriculum and its teaching methods will only continue to increase, although the grip that the conservative elders have on the school's philosophy is still strong and often uncompromising. The school itself is directly confronted with the problems and demands of a broader society, particularly when it comes to such practical issues as the application of Islamic law in India and other countries. These concerns will continue to stimulate debate and exert pressure on the Deoband school to adapt to changes in society.

The political and religious impact of the school in India and the rest of the Muslim world has gathered momentum since 1982. Its diversity has likewise increased. Although it became a national institution in India, with students from every Indian state, it remains firmly rooted in the northern Indian states of Uttar Pradesh and Bihar, and is highly influential in West Bengal and neighbouring Bangladesh. Pakistan is still a powerful Deobandi centre in its own right, with little evidence of direct influence from the Deoband school in India.[70]

The Dar al-'Ulum will continue to be the focus of international attention as long as militant groups in countries such as Pakistan, Afghanistan and Bangladesh adhere to Deobandi doctrine. Its networking in India is becoming increasingly formal and works through the Association of Deobandi Madrasas (RMA), whereas Deobandi scholars and schools are linked at the international level via public conferences, youth work meetings, and missionary objectives, but also through Tablighi Jama'at channels.

In the academic field, efforts have multiplied to understand the character and dynamics of Islamic schools.[71] However, much of it is politically motivated.[72] Detailed studies that take the concept of the schools and their approach into account, without refraining from critical assessment, are required. Measured against its long history, the Deoband school is under enormous pressure and is experiencing change at a breakneck speed. Whether this will suffice to ensure its smooth adaptation to a new and radically changing world remains to be seen.

Notes

1 Cf. Jeffrey Goldberg, 'The Education of a Holy Warrior,' *New York Times Magazine*, 25 June 2000. For a less sensationalist but yet negative reporting on Deoband affiliated networks in Pakistan, see the International Crisis Group reports *Pakistan: Madrasas, Extremism and the Military* (29 July 2002) and *Pakistan: Karachi's Madrasas and Violent Extremism* (29 March 2007).

2 21-23 March 1980, see *Mukhtasir rudad – Ijlas Sadsala Dar al-'ulum Deoband mun'aqida 21, 22, 23 March 1980* [Brief minutes of the centenary congregation at Deoband University convened 21-23 March 1980]. Deoband: Daftar-i Ijlas Sadsala Dar al-'Ulum Deoband. 1980, p. 17. In fact, 1980 marked 113 years of the school's existence since 1866.

3 Barbara Daly Metcalf, *Islamic Revival in British India: Deoband, 1860-1900*. Princeton: Princeton University Press, 1982.

4 Gail Minault, *The Khilafat Movement: Religious Symbolism and Political Mobilisation in India*. New York: Columbia University Press, 1982.

5 Cf. Reetz, *Islam in the Public Sphere*. pp. 316-318.

6 Dietrich Reetz, *Islam in the Public Sphere: Religious Groups in India (1900-1947)*. Delhi and London: Oxford University Press, 2006, p. 180.

7 See various issues of the journal of the Old Boys Association of the Deoband school, *Tarjuman-i Dar al-'Ulum* (Organ of the Islamic university), produced in Delhi.

8 *Sana 1422-23 AH dar al-'ulum Deoband men jadid ṭalaba ke liye zaruri qawa'id-i dakhila* [Entry requirements for the new students at Deoband University during the academic year 1422-23 AH]. Deoband: Daftar-i Ta'limat, 1422 AH (2001), pp. 15-16.

9 Administrative Report for 1423 AH (2002-3). Most of the school data refers to the Hijri calendar and the academic year, which begins annually on the first of Ramadan. For accuracy the Hijri references are preferred and converted according to the beginning of the academic year.

10 Administrative Report for 1423 AH (2002-3).

11 Reetz, *Islam in the public sphere*. pp. 182ff.

12 http://darululoom-deoband.com/urdu/introulema/3/g.htm, accessed 1 March 2006.

13 Author's interviews during field research in Delhi and Deoband in February-March 2004.

14 Idem.

15 *The Hindu*, 29 March 2006, http://www.hindu.com/2006/03/29/stories/2006032920401600.htm, accessed 1 July 2007.

16 My interviews with Deoband graduates in February 2004 – DR.

17 Photographs from the author's own collection, taken in December 2001 and February 2004.

18 Interviews by the author with Dar al-'Ulum *waqf* representatives from Feb-Mar 2004.

19 Cf. Reetz, *Islam in the Public Sphere*, pp. 183f.

20 http://darululoom-deoband.com/urdu/departments/show.php?dept=rabita.gif, accessed 1 March 2006.

21 See, for instance, All-India meetings of Islamic Arabic schools on 12 November 1998 and 30 April 2002. *Khutba-i Sadarat - Kul Hind Ijtima'-i Madaris-i Islamiyyah 'Arabiyyah 21 Rajab 1419 AH = 12 November 1998* [Presidential address – All-India Convention of Islamic Arabic Schools, 12 November 1998]. Deoband: Markazi Daftar-i Madaris-i 'Arabiyyah, n.d.; *ditto* for *Kul Hind Ijlas-i Majlis 'Umumi-i Rabita Madaris-i Islamiyyah 'Arabiyyah 16 Safar 1423 AH = 30 April 2002* [General session of the All-India Convention of the Association of Islamic Arabic Schools, 30 April 2002].

22 Interview on 28 February 2004.

23 On efforts to heal the rift, see: 'Whiff of breeze from Deoband,' *The Milli Gazette* (Delhi), vol. 6, no. 6, 16-31 March 2005.

24 Numbers of students by geographical origin are taken from *Naqsha-i ta'dad-i talaba-i dar al-'ulum Deoband – Daftar-i Ta'limat* [Table of student numbers at the Islamic University of Deoband, Department of Education] for 1414-15 AH (1994).

25 *Dastur-i Asasi – Tanzim-i Abna-i Qadim Dar al-'Ulum Deoband* [Founding constitution – Old Boys' Association Islamic University Deoband]. Delhi: Tanzim-i Abna-i Qadim, 1991.

26 See, however, Dietrich Reetz, 'The Deoband Universe: What makes a transcultural and transnational educational movement of Islam?', in: Dietrich Reetz, and Bettina Dennerlein (eds.), *South-South Linkages in Islam: The Making of Continuity and Disparity in the 19th-21st centuries. Contemporary Studies of South Asia, Africa and the Middle East*, Durham: Duke University Press, 2007, pp. 139-159.

27 5,078 foreign students graduated from the school between 1866 and 2001. *Dar al-'ulum* (Deoband 2001, no. 11), 43.

28 The *Naqsha-i ta'dad-i talaba-i dar al-'ulum Deoband – Daftar-i Ta'limat* for 1979 lists 34 foreign students, including 9 from Bangladesh, 5 from Nepal, 6 from Malaysia, and 9 from Africa; that for 2002-3 lists 61 foreigners, including 32 from Nepal, 27 from Bangladesh, and 1 each from Burma and Malaysia.

29 Maulana Arshad Madani, head of the education department at the Deoband school, in the course of interviews in December 2001 and Feb-Mar 2004 – DR.

30 See the report by Maulana Ahmad Kathrada, 'An eye-witness account of the 150 year Deoband Conference', in *Al-Jamiat* (Johannesburg), vol. 4, no. 8, June 2001, at http://www.jamiat.org.za/al-jamiat/june/sreport.html, accessed 15 March 2006. In was actually the 135th anniversary.

31 Rahimullah Yusufzai, *The News*, 12 April 2001, at http://www.institute-for-afghan-studies.org/AFGHAN%20CONFLICT/TALIBAN/deobandi_conf_2001.htm, accessed 1 July 2007.

32 Interviews with various respondents at the Deoband school in December 2001 and February 2004; also Maulana Abdul Ghafoor Haideri, JUI General Secretary, during a visit to Berlin with a Parliamentary delegation on 11-12 May 2004 – DR.

33 Dietrich Reetz, 'Keeping busy on the path of Allah: The self-organisation (*intizam*) of the *Tablighi Jama'at*,' in: Daniela Bredi (ed.), *Islam in South Asia* (= *Oriente Moderno*, 84:1). Rome 2004, pp. 295-305.

34 See the directory of Zakariyya's disciples in: Muhammad Yusuf Mutala, *Maulana Muhammad Zakariyya aor un ke Khulafa-i Kiram*. [Maulana Zakariyya and his venerable disciples]. 3 parts in 2 vols. Bury: Dar al-'Ulum al-'Arabiyya al-Islamiyya, 1986.

35 The following paragraphs are based on an analysis of the Administrative Reports, held in Archive of the Dar al-'Ulum Deoband. Summary data compiled by the author in February 2004.

36 Dar al-'Ulum Deoband shu'ba nashr-o-insha'at, *Dar al-'Ulum Deoband – 'Ulum-i kitab-o-sunnat ke amin, sarmayia-i millat ke pasban. Khidmat, halat, mansube*. [The Islamic University of Deoband – Guardian of Knowledge of the Quran and Sunna, Flagbearer of the Treasure of the Community. Its Service, Current Conditions and Future Plans] Deoband: Dar al-'Ulum, 1422 AH (2001).

37 After the website of Deoband school http://www.darululoom-deoband.com; Administrative Report 1423 AH / 2003

38 Miyan Muhammad, *Asiran-i Malta* [Interned on Malta]. Delhi: Al-Jam'iyat Book Depot 1976, p. 58.

39 My interviews in March 2004 – DR.

40 My interviews with Maulana Shahid and Maulana Muhammad Salman at the *Madrasa Mazahir al-'Ulum Jadid* Saharanpur on 2 March 2004 – DR.

41 http://darululoom-deoband.com/urdu/departments/show.php?dept=computer.gif, downloaded 01 March 2006.

42 Administrative Report for 1423 AH (2002-3), p. 11.

43 Ibid., p. 12.

44 Ibid., p. 12.

45 www.darululoom-deoband.com.

46 Sayyid Mahboob Rizvi,. *History of the Dar al-'Ulum*. 2 vols. Deoband: Idarah-i Ihtimam, 1980, vol. II, pp. 244ff.

47 Cf. Reetz, *Islam in the Public Sphere*, pp. 288.

48 Administrative Report for 1423 AH (2002-03), p. 32-33.

49 http://darululoom-deoband.com/urdu/departments/show.php?dept=k-nubowat.gif, accessed 1 March 2006.

50 *Alami Majlis Tahaffuz-i Khatm-i Nabuwwat*, 35 Stockwell Green, London, SW9. (http://www.islamicfinder.org/getitWorld.php?id=26201&lang); see their Web site at http://www.khatme-nubuwwat.org/; see also the Web site of the US branch of the *Irshad-o-Da'wat*, a pro-Ahl-i Hadith organisation that co-sponsors its international activities: http://www.irshad.org/finality/significance.php.

51 Muhammad Amir Rana, *A to Z of Jehadi Organisations in Pakistan*. Lahore: Mashal, 2004.

52 These camps took place once a year in 1988, 1990-95, 1997-98. See Dar al-'Umum, *Dar al-'Ulum Deoband ... Khidmat, halat, mansube*, p. 25.

53 Reetz, *Islam in the public sphere*, pp. 153ff.
54 Administrative Report for 1423 AH (2002-3), p. 20.
55 Ibid., p. 25.
56 The student's name was Arshad Fayzee. Based on interviews by the author in Deoband, March 2004.
57 Dietrich Reetz, 'Dar al-Ulum Deoband and its Self-Representation on the Media.' *Islamic Studies* (Islamabad: Islamic Research Institute), vol. 44, no. 2, 2005, 209-227.
58 http://darululoom-deoband.com/urdu/magazine/index.php, accessed 16 March 2006.
59 For a list of its publications, see http://darululoom-deoband.com/urdu/publications/publications2a.htm, accessed 16 March 2006.
60 Author's interviews in March 2004.
61 Ibid. and Ahmad 1985: 28.
62 Interviews and inquiries conducted by myself and my research assistant, a Deoband graduate, from Feb-March 2004, during which we listed at least 16 businesses in Deoband.
63 Salim Ahmad, *Mustanad tarikh-i Deoband* [Authentic history of Deoband]. Deoband: Maktaba Rah-i Islam, n.d., pp. 222, 31.
64 Ibid., p. 222.
65 For a discussion of various dimensions of Islamism, see Dietrich Reetz, Aktuelle Analysen islamistischer Bewegungen und ihre Kritik. In: *Forschungsjournal Neue Soziale Bewegungen*, Stuttgart 17(2004)4, pp. 61-68.
66 Mareike Jule Winkelmann. *'From Behind the Curtain': A study of a girls' madrasa in India*. Amsterdam: Amsterdam University Press, 2005.
67 A strong sense of crisis pervades such studies as: A. H. Nayyar, 'Madrasah Education Frozen in Time', in: Pervez Hoodbhoy (ed.), *Fifty Years of Pakistan: Education and the State*. Karachi: Oxford University Press, 1998, pp. 215-250; Qamaruddin, *Hindustan ki dini darsgahen. Kul Hind sarwe* [Religious schools in India. All India survey]. Delhi: Hamdard Education Society, 1994; Kuldip Kaur, *Madrasa Education in India: A Study of its Past and Present*. Chandigarh: Centre for Research in Rural & Industrial Development, 1990.
68 Author's interviews in March 2004.
69 Muhammad Yusuf Ludhianwi, *Differences in the Ummah and the Straight Path*. Karachi: Zam Zam Publishers, 1999.
70 Nayyar, 'Madrasah Education'; Jamal Malik, *Colonialization of Islam: Dissolution of Traditional Institutions in Pakistan*. Delhi: Manohar, 1996.
71 Jan-Peter Hartung and Helmut Reifeld (eds.). *Islamic Education, Diversity, and National Identity: Dini Madaris in India post 9/11*. Delhi, London: Sage, 2006; Yoginder Sikand, *Bastions of the Believers: Madrasas and Islamic Education in India*. Delhi: Penguin, 2005.
72 Alexander Evans, 'Understanding Madrasahs', *Foreign Affairs*, vol. 85, no. 1, 2006, pp. 9-16.

3 'Inside and Outside' in a Girls' Madrasa in New Delhi

Mareike Winkelmann

Introduction

Historically speaking, late-nineteenth-century Muslim reformist ideas influenced the establishment of the earliest public schools for Muslim girls. Prior to that period, education for girls in Islamic matters was mainly a private affair, but it eventually became one of the main issues of public discourse, as it unfolded in the then just introduced Urdu print-culture, in the reformist (male) madrasas, and in voluntary associations or *anjumans*, which formed the link between the domestic and public realms. By the early twentieth century, education for girls in the confinement of the *zenana* or women's quarters of the home existed side by side with the first public girls' schools for Muslim girls.[1] These developments, along with the overall increasing literacy, Urdu print culture, and the democratisation of access to Islamic texts were precursors to the establishment of girls' madrasas. While there are several valuable studies examining boys' madrasas in India, published information on their female counterparts is scanty.[2] In the course of my research my interlocutors suggested that the first larger, public girls' madrasas in post-Partition India still bore witness to the earlier forms of 'home teaching', for example in the preservation of value-oriented or *adab* education.

As practices are best discerned through participant observation, interviews, and informal conversations with students, teachers, and founders of girls' madrasas over a longer period of time, a large portion of my study is based on ethnographic fieldwork in a girls' madrasa in New Delhi, which hosts roughly 180 students between twelve and seventeen years of age. The madrasa that I shall henceforth call Jami'at al-Niswan was established in 1996 under the patronage of the Nadwat al-Ulama in Lucknow and recruits students from Delhi and other cities as well as villages from all over India.[3] The links between the Jami'at al-Niswan and the Tablighi Jama'at formally began via the Nadwat al-Ulama madrasa in Lucknow, as the founders of the girls' madrasa adopted its curriculum with its strong emphasis on Arabic. Moreover, the male founders of this particular madrasa and the male members of its core families are active in the lay preacher's movement known as the Tablighi Jama'at.[4]

This paper focuses on three issues, namely (1) the transmission of Islamic knowledge in the girls' madrasa, (2) the 'informal' curriculum through which the broader aim of moulding the person as a whole is achieved, and finally (3) the role of the Tablighi Jama'at in the everyday running of the madrasa.

Islamic Education for Girls

Recent reports claim that there are approximately 35,000 madrasas in India[5], which often form networks along lines of affiliation with various schools of thought, such as the Deobandis, the Jama'at-i Islami-i Hind, the Ahl-i Hadith, the Barelvis, and the Nadwat al-Ulama – all of which represent important and large Muslim organisations that emerged roughly between the late nineteenth and the mid-twentieth centuries.

To date, there is no central administrative institution or madrasa board, which creates an initial impression of relative opacity regarding the madrasas' organisational structure. Second, the opacity toward the outside goes hand in hand with the estrangement between Islamic and non-Islamic education in India, as the madrasas have largely remained outside the scope of state intervention for over fifty years. However, especially following the events of 11 September 2001, the madrasas have received increasing amounts of attention in the Indian media, and the need to establish a central Madrasa Board has been voiced frequently.[6] But the proposal has been perceived as controversial, because many Muslims feel that such a central

Madrasa Board would jeopardise the independent status of the madrasas and allow for too much state control.

Even though Islamic education in madrasas has a long-standing history in India,[7] public madrasas for girls only began to mushroom roughly in the last two decades. Until the Partition of India in 1947, Muslim girls were predominantly taught at home in Islamic matters.[8] Well-to-do families patronised Islamic lessons for girls from the *mahalla* or neighbourhood in their homes. This informal way of teaching did not conflict with the requirements of *purdah*, as the girls were taught by female teachers in the women's quarters of the home, known as the *zenana*. Accounts of what has been termed 'home teaching' for girls in Delhi have been preserved in oral histories of women who still remember the era prior to Partition. Moreover, the late nineteenth-century 'advisory literature' for women by authors such as Ashraf Ali Thanawi, Nazir Ahmad, and Altaf Husain Hali,[9] has preserved lively impressions and became a model later used in the establishment of the first girls' madrasas shortly after Partition.

As most of those who had once patronised Islamic home teaching for girls in north India had migrated to the newly formed state of Pakistan, a gap emerged in India that had to be filled with new forms of Islamic education for Muslim girls. The most common explanations given by people I asked as to why madrasas for girls were established in the early 1950s was the following: first, the earlier educational patrons had departed; and second, the Muslim minority in independent India had to find new ways of preserving their Islamic legacy and herein women played a pivotal role. As the saying goes, 'The mother's lap is the first madrasa'. In a study carried out by the Delhi-based Hamdard Education Society, it has been suggested that of the estimated 35,000 Indian madrasas only between 8 to 10% are madrasas for girls.[10] However, many Muslims remain unaware of or even surprised at the suggestion that girls' madrasas exist, even if they are located in their own neighbourhoods, which suggests that even the madrasa buildings are often, as it were, in *purdah*, hidden from public view.

A Glance Behind the Curtain

The Jami'at al-Niswan offers a five-year *fazila* degree course in Islamic Studies for girls between twelve and seventeen years of age.[11] The students hail from lower to lower middle-class backgrounds, from Delhi and from far-flung places across India, and are from both rural and urban backgrounds. The teachers have been recruited from the first two batches of graduates since 2001 and from two affiliated girls' madrasas in Malegaon and Lucknow. The founder's family originates from the Barabanki district close to Lucknow and claims Ansari background.[12] Moreover, the founder, his son-in-law who is the manager of the madrasa, as well as the fathers of two other teachers are closely affiliated with the Tablighi Jama'at, whose global headquarters in Nizamuddin lies in the direct vicinity of the madrasa. The above-mentioned ulama also studied in the Tablighi boys' madrasa known as the Kashf al-'Ulum, where two of them continue to teach to date. There are further ties between the madrasa and the Tablighi headquarters, such as the Thursday programme, as both the Jami'at al-Niswan and the Tablighi Jama'at organise women's *bayan* or lectures on Thursday afternoons.

The tiny school building hosts the almost impossible number of one hundred eighty students at present, but a larger compound has been acquired in Okhla, a Muslim neighbourhood in New Delhi. Once the construction of the school building has been completed, the madrasa will eventually host some one thousand students. Up to now, there are three to four hundred applicants annually, out of which only an average of forty-five students make it into the Jami'at al-Niswan. Recently, a total application stop has been implemented, as the school building is overcrowded. The requirements regarding *purdah*, which is a term that denotes both the veiling of the female body as well as the physical segregation of women from male spaces, are laid out in the madrasa's enrolment brochure:[13]

> '2. Rules and Regulations
> ... If the student has to go out, permission of the head teacher and the hostel warden must be requested.
> Students must always wear their school uniforms during school hours.
> Students must remember that the Jami'a is a centre of morality (*akhlaq*).
> The aim of the Jami'a is the reform (*islah*) of morality and actions (*'amal*).
> Students' behaviour should be in accordance with Islamic law (*shari'at*).
> Student dress should be in accordance with Islam.
> *Purdah* is to be observed at all times.

3. Holidays

... Students who go to *melas*, cinemas, or other places of entertainment will be expelled from the Jami'a.

Students are strictly prohibited to wear jewellery.

Students must observe the obligatory Islamic rituals (*'ibadat*).

Students must attend the daily gathering (*majlis*) of the virtues of pious deeds (*faza'il*).[14]

Students must fully respect the teachers, founders, and Islamic scholars (*ulama*) behind the Jami'a.

Students must stay avoid controversy and chaos (*fitna*) at all times. ...

4. Student's Pledge

I promise to observe these rules and regulations and that I shall study with great dedication and avoid things that are a waste of time and that I shall never display any immoral behaviour. I promise to dedicate 24 hours of every day to my studies in accordance with the timetable of the Jami'a and that I shall obey the command of those in charge of the Jami'a and accept any punishment if I break any of the rules and regulations. ...

6. Contact with Parents

Parents are permitted and encouraged to call the Jami'a during certain times, to enquire about their daughters' progress. Students are allowed to talk on the phone for three minutes., Students can go home to visit their parents every first Thursday of every month. When they are picked up from the Jami'a, the students must be accompanied by a *mahram* man whose photo is on file at the Jami'a.[15] A woman is not permitted to fulfil this function. A student cannot meet a *ghair mahram* man, even if he is a close relative of hers. One can meet students on Thursdays after 12 noon and Fridays from 9am to noon. Parents are expected to check regularly with the Jami'a about their daughters' progress and possible problems'.

Regarding the seclusion of women, Cora Vreede-de Stuers has raised the question of whether *purdah* excludes women from male domains or excludes men from female domains, similar to the argument made in Lila Abu Lughod's *Veiled Sentiments*.[16] There is a small front room at the Jami'at al-Niswan for the founder, the manager and their guests to meet, but what goes on behind the literal *purdah* or curtain is largely inaccessible for the men.[17] Even though it is the girls and women who 'observe *purdah*', one could also argue that men are excluded from the women's domain. However, the mobility of women outside these exclusively female domains is clearly more restricted than that of men, who are only excluded from a relatively small area in girls' madrasas.

The girls are allowed to leave the madrasa only for clearly specified occasions. For example, the students are allowed to go home on weekends on a regular basis. These visits home be it over the weekend, for the school holidays during the month of Ramadan or during the summer, one of the girls' 'guardians' (i.e., a male relative who is 'forbidden for the girl in marriage' or *mahram*) must pick up the girl from the madrasa, escort her home and bring her back to the madrasa on time. If he fails to do so, the family will be fined or the student may even be expelled. Male guardianship is thus central to the girls' mobility outside the madrasa. Many other students and teachers do not reside in Delhi and thus the issues of male guardianship and mobility are more complicated for them. For example, apart from those girls who come from remote areas in and around the capital, the Jami'at al-Niswan also hosts students from places as divergent as Lucknow, Bahraich, Bijnor, Saharanpur, Malegaon, and even Mumbai, to name but a few. These girls generally only visit their homes during the longer vacations during the month of Ramadan and over the summer, when the madrasa is closed. Otherwise, many students stay behind at the madrasa for most of the school year and hence their lives are marked by a sense of austerity, as the physical space is minimal with almost no diversions.

An Opportunity to Speak Up

Every Thursday between 11:30 a.m. and 2 p.m., teachers and students organise a weekly programme, which a few local women can also attend, including the female relatives of students and teachers from the neighbourhood. The programme is held in the largest part of the building on the ground floor, where approximately 200 girls and women can be accommodated in orderly rows of seats supervised by senior students. Every week the teachers in charge of organising the programme sit facing everyone else in a slightly elevated section of the hall. With the hand-written programme for the day in hand, they take turns announcing the students' contributions via a microphone, a gesture that appears somewhat exaggerated, considering that the space is not that big, and the technical equipment leaves a lot to be desired. The amplifier and sound system are located in the adjacent front room, where the manager sits with his guests and listens to what is going on behind the door that separates them from the girls.

When the teachers give the word, the students come to the fore and recite a portion of text from the Qur'an, present an interpretation of a Qur'anic text in Urdu (*tafsir*), recount *hadiths*, tell an Islamic story, or sing a religious poem called *tarana* or *na'at*. Simultaneously, one of the other teachers present may call students to the fore and reprimand them for performing poorly during the past week. While most of the programme is in Arabic, which most of the women attending from the neighbourhood are unable to understand, great care is taken that *tafsir*, or the exegesis of a Qur'anic text, is in Urdu. Moreover, following the formal exegesis of a Qur'anic text, the students explain the text again in their own words. Those sections of the programme are characterised by a contrastingly familiar tone and the students' explanations tend to merge with numerous moral appeals to the audience, in the style of the *adab* literature.

Adab or Moral Education

Although lessons in *adab* or 'moral education' only take up a relatively small portion of the schedule, namely eight hours a week, observations confirm that *adab* permeates the everyday affairs and overall atmosphere of the Jami'at al-Niswan. Moreover, introducing and grooming the students to the rules laid out by the community's understanding of *adab* appears to be pivotal when it comes to the madrasa's explicit aim of bringing about 'the *islah* (reform) of the *akhlaq* (morality) and *'amal* (actions), as the madrasa's brochure puts it. Finally, the admission papers also state that 'the students must fully respect the teachers, founders, and ulama behind the Jami'a'. The question is how these aims can be established and put into practice.

Apart from the formally scheduled classes in *adab*, during which texts such as Maulana Ashraf Ali Thanawi's well-known and much discussed *Bihishti Zewar*,[18] and the Arabic *Qira'at ur-Rashida*[19] are carefully studied beginning in the first year of their schooling, the *adab* is also transmitted, practised, and reproduced through a non-formal teaching regime, i.e., through rules, discipline, bodily control, and behavioural expectations, especially vis-à-vis those considered authorities in the madrasa. Hence, the overall aim of bringing about a sense of *adab* in the students is not limited to the formal didactic activities that take place in the classroom. As the teachers are barely older than their students, the students in turn feel free to interact with them in an informal way. Nevertheless, the students address the teachers using the formal *ap* or *appa*, instead of a less formal form of address such as by their first names or *tum*, which are other options, considering that some of the teachers actually graduated from the Jami'at al-Niswan a year earlier, and thus the girls interacted with them as fellow students only a year earlier. There is one exception to the use of *ap* or *appa*, namely in the case of the manager's wife, who at the same time is also the madrasa founder's daughter. Being in her late twenties, this young woman is the most senior teacher in the madrasa, and hence everyone respectfully refers to her as *badi appa* or 'big elder sister'. In her case, the fictive kinship relation expressed in the omnipresent reference to *badi appa* suggests that respect is not gained through family relations or ascribed status alone, but also through kindness and knowledge, as she is also considered the most learned young woman. *Badi appa*'s father teaches Arabic in the Kashf al-'Ulum madrasa for boys in the Tablighi headquarters and she received her secondary education in the Jami'at us-Salehat girls' madrasa in Malegaon, where she also learned Persian, apart from a fluency in Arabic, which is considered a marker of knowledge and status at the Jami'at al-Niswan.

The very first lesson the students learn about *adab* is that they have to show respect for their teachers, for books and their authors, and finally for the madrasa itself. One of the books used for the *adab* classes, titled the *Qira'at ur-Rashida*, includes stories about the lives of the Prophet, his Companions, and the first Caliphs. The stories deal with social etiquette, and teach the reader how to eat and drink properly, how to attend and organise marriages, or how to run a household with a view toward pleasing God. The teachers in turn ensure that the students not only understand the texts literally but also encourage them to find in their own lives applications of the examples highlighted in the texts.

Furthermore, the all-pervading effect of *adab* becomes more evident when we look at the case of a girl who initially worked in the Jami'at al-Niswan as a cleaner. The girl was in her early teens and stood out, as her *shalwar kameez* tended to be very colourful, in contrast to the students' otherwise sober, white, school uniforms. Moreover, her head was generally uncovered and her hair was sloppily tied back. After some time, a gradual change began to set in, as she began to linger around in the staff room more and more. From that point onwards, the cleaner was taught to read and write Urdu and Arabic properly, and apart from her ongoing chores, she was often found in a corner of the small staff room, her head covered by a clean white *dupatta* (loose scarf), reciting texts from her Urdu and Arabic primers. She no longer left her head uncovered, even though she still seemed rather new to the habit of covering it, and hence the *dupatta* often slipped off her head, revealing that she had also started to use hair oil, which had made her hair more shiny, and she tied it back more mindfully.

The girl's favourite pastime seemed to be observing and listening to the teachers' conversations in the staff room, while dedicating herself more or less fully to her studies. The former cleaner seemed to take pride in her newly acquired and visibly more demure appearance, as she spoke in a muted voice, tended to lower her eyes when addressing someone, and walked about in a much more lady-like manner than before. Even though her age was roughly the same as that of the other students, she did not socialise with them, and there did not seem to be a place for her among their circle. Nevertheless, her status in the Jami'at al-Niswan had changed, as she gained respectability through her interest in Islamic education. Moreover, as she began to show interest in what they were doing and a willingness to adjust to their dress and behaviour codes, the teachers seemed obliged to pay her more mind, instead of just ordering her to fetch them tea, clean up the floor or put away their breakfast dishes.

A second example is that of twin girls, around six years of age, who started coming to the Jami'at al-Niswan every day for their first lessons in reading and memorising the Qur'an. The girls were rather shabbily dressed with their make-do *dupattas* loosely covering their heads and they looked quite unhealthy, as if they were not used to being outside the house. Over the months, things began to change. First, their daily walks to the madrasa led to the young girls looking increasingly healthy, with their hair neatly brushed and oiled, and with their *dupattas* were properly tied around their heads. Second, while in the beginning the girls used to carry their Qur'ans wrapped in plain pieces of cloth, it wasn't long before they began to proudly carry their Qur'ans in beautiful green silken covers with matching buttons. Third, soon the girls were no longer seen with the Qur'an lying on a cushion or a pile of books in front of them, as both possessed ornamentally carved wooden Qur'an stands, which they folded up at the lesson's end and carried them under their arms together with their copies of the Qur'an. Finally, while in the beginning the girls had appeared quite anxious and scared, after a while they felt at ease in their new environment, even though they seldom spoke to anyone, as they studied in a strikingly disciplined fashion for girls their age.

Even though the girls learn that, according to Islam, they have the right to acquire knowledge and that they also have the right, for example, to ignore certain household chores considered 'un-Islamic', such as the extensive preparations for lavish weddings, this new level of self-assertion of these learned young women also has the potential for creating tensions in the domestic field.

For example, one teacher was made aware of her being overweight when she married into a family of very slender people. Adding to this teacher's misery was the fact that all of the younger female in-laws were also either teaching or studying at the Jamiʿat al-Niswan, although the young women were clearly taking her side by saying that they wished to be more like her. However, the young teacher was put under tremendous pressure to lose weight, because she admitted that her husband liked slim women and threatened to divorce her if she gained any more weight. Thus, she went on a strict diet and started exercising regularly. Her physical ideal of becoming thinner had nothing to do with Islam, she insisted, arguing that 'we (*ham log*) believe human beings are good the way God created us'. Nevertheless, she noted that, according to Islam, her primary duty was to please her husband and losing weight had everything to do with that. The young woman had tried to reconcile two conflicting issues, namely the idea that she should not alter her body because of community pressure and the notion that her primary duty was to please her husband.

Penetration of External Influences into the Girls' Madrasa

While there seemed to be an outright rejection of what is perceived as negative Western influences, there is also an awareness that one cannot entirely avoid coming into contact with certain aspects of Western culture. For the women and girls of the madrasa, avoidance of the outside world is practically impossible in the context of present-day cosmopolitan India, and this was made all the more evident on several occasions during my research there.

There is an obvious difference between declared demonstrations of piety and what actually happens in real life. For instance, when the students and teachers were asked what they had done during a vacation following Ramadan, most responded by saying that they had rested and studied, which suggested a continuation of the sober lifestyle observed in the madrasa. But spontaneous references to advertisements shown on television were often made in the staff room, implying that some of the young women do watch television; a 'revelation' they became very self-conscious about once the initial laughs had died down. However, it seems that generally the male family members are more exposed than women to what are regarded as forbidden 'Western influences', including media and film, often under the pretext that 'one has to know one's enemy' in order to find the best strategies possible to win him over to one's own cause, which is an argument often heard among the Tablighis.

For the staff and students of the madrasa it is almost impossible to avoid being exposed to these 'evils' in a multicultural environment, where, for example, Hindi film music is played in the bazaars. Evidence of this exposure resonates in the songs called *taranas* or *na'at*, which the students write and sing for their own entertainment as well as for the weekly occasion of a programme at school. The *taranas* and Urdu *na'at* are sung very often to popular Hindi film tunes, which must have found their way inside the madrasa somehow.

Hardly anyone at the Jami'at al-Niswan has had any contact with other non-Islamic forms of education prior to enrolment in the madrasa, because most of the students and teachers received their primary educations either in a *maktab* or in Islamic centres offering primary school educations for girls. As an exception to this rule, in the case of *badi appa* it was interesting to observe that both of her daughters attend the prestigious Delhi Public School every afternoon during its free Hindi classes. *Badi appa* has expressed her wish to see her children enrol in an English medium school on more than one occasion, even though, she considered the prospect highly unlikely, because, after all, 'these schools are only for rich people, not for poor people like us'.

The Jamiᶜat al-Niswan and the Tablighi Jamaᶜat

In the course of carrying out my research, the Tablighi Jama'at appeared time again, both physically and in conversations. As mentioned above, the Tabligh's international headquarters is located in the vicinity of the Jami'at al-Niswan. Hence, on my daily walks to and from the madrasa, I observed some of the activities in that part of the area, such as the arrival of overseas delegations, the departure of local delegations of Tablighi activists, preparations for major meetings and the like. Moreover, many bookshops, cassette tape peddlers, and petty traders affiliated with the Tablighi Jama'at often proved to be important sources of information with regard to both the Tablighi Jama'at's activities as well as the Jami'at al-Niswan's background.

Many of the male relatives of the students and teachers at Jami'at al-Niswan are active in the Tablighi Jama'at or teach in the Kashf al-'Ulum madrasa for boys inside the Tablighi headquarters. When students and teachers spoke about their male relatives' Tablighi activities, such as their regular travels 'in the path of God' (*fi sabil Allah*), they did so with admiration and sometimes also with a tinge of envy, because the lives of their male relatives represented the mobility and freedom they themselves did not have and because they valued their Tablighi activities highly. Some of the students and teachers expressed regret that such activities, best subsumed in the rubric 'travelling in the path of God', were not open to them, because they observe a very strict form of *purdah*.[20]

It is equally important to note that the men's travels also account for the Jami'at al-Niswan's most important recruitment strategy. In fact, the founder and manager regularly travel throughout the country to raise funds for the madrasa. Many students from places outside Delhi heard about the Jami'at al-Niswan from these travellers associated with the madrasa. Besides recruiting new students – which in the case of the Jami'at al-Niswan is a lesser concern as they are well connected with two similar girls' madrasas in Lucknow and Malegaon – the men also establish and maintain contacts outside India, which, in some cases, plays a role in the girls' marriage prospects. During my fieldwork, I was exposed to cases in which girls from the core families associated with the Jami'at al-Niswan married boys whose parents had settled outside India, in Saudi Arabia and South Africa, for instance.

Both the Tablighi Jama'at and the Jami'at al-Niswan represent institutions that are quite different from those in their immediate surroundings. For instance, they differ in their (temporary and limited) inversion of gender roles,[21] or in their disregard for the lavishness associated with household rituals such as weddings. With regard to the inversion of gender roles, it is noteworthy that in the Jami'at al-Niswan it is men who prepare the food for the students and teachers, while the latter in turn have to take care of the normally male job of cleaning the school building as well as laundering, since men are not allowed to enter the school building. Some observers have suggested that these forms of (limited and temporary) inversion of gender roles is typical of the Tablighi Jama'at as well, because the men who 'travel in the path of God' are left to their own devices in terms of taking care of their daily needs for the duration of their journey. Moreover, this particular Muslim group, in line with earlier reformist ideas, considers lavish ceremonies to be a major problem and a widespread social evil. They disapprove of big weddings, which are usually grand social events allowing the display of social status, which is considered a positive value in society. Both the Tablighi Jama'at and the Jami'at al-Niswan condemn such practices as they represent unnecessary and even sinful luxury. All of this affects the identity of the young women in the Jami'at al-Niswan; the height of a dowry is not much of a concern in this community and there is correspondingly less reason to fear the role of a *bahu* or daughter-in-law. Marriage is considered an act of piety to be consummated in a simple ceremony. Nevertheless, the young girls love discussing the gifts they may or have already received. However, the Principal reprimands them for these small signs of resistance, just as the wearing of jewellery and fancy clothes are frowned upon.

There is a sense of equality of the sexes regarding the actual pursuit of knowledge, the similarity of the girls and boys' curricula in the madrasa, but also with regard to *purdah*, as the concept is interpreted to denote modesty in dress and behaviour for men and women alike. The Jami'at al-Niswan also attempts to promote equality among the students with regard to sartorial modesty and discouragement of jewellery., However I did observe that there were exceptions and that the girls developed subtle strategies to project their individuality within the given constraints. For example, some students adorn their hands and feet with floral *mehendi* or henna designs, or they decorate their simple white blouses and trousers with hand-painted floral patterns, or they choose fine material for their dresses, or they wear jewellery after they get married and then justify it as abiding by their husbands' wishes, which, of course, have to be accommodated.

Both the Jami'at al-Niswan and the Tablighi Jama'at seek to create a milieu characterised by deep piety. In the case of the Tablighi Jama'at, this becomes explicit in the *Faza'il-i 'Amal*, the principal text that they use in their preaching, in which the processes of sanctifying everyday life and its actions are laid out in minute detail. The book teaches that certain virtues displayed in one's daily behaviour are valuable for the accumulation of *sawab* or merit for the hereafter. One of the *Faza'il*'s main teachings, namely that one should abstain from futile endeavours, is also central to everyday life in Jami'at al-Niswan. The young women never seemed to be idle and were always occupied with something useful, be it their studies, additional reading, handiwork or other chores.

Future Trajectories of Madrasa Graduates

With regard to the madrasa's curriculum, the official curriculum does not reveal that in many if not most cases, the books mentioned are not studied completely. For example, I observed that in the case of the *Hidaya*, the standard text on Hanafi jurisprudence, the chapters the girls were obligated to study suggests that the ambitious curriculum has often been narrowed down to fit the constraints of a five-year course (as opposed to the original sixteen and later eight years of study for boys). More importantly, these changes seem to have been made with the aim of reinforcing the madrasa's educational goals. In other words, the founder and administrator of the Jami'at al-Niswan set the curriculum, thus their underlying educational ideals determine what will be the focus of studies for the girls. As a result, by the time they graduate they can only legitimately claim to be well informed in Hanafi law in subjects that pertain to women, such as marriage, divorce, inheritance, and child custody, or subjects that were deemed appropriate to learn in the first place. Overall, the curriculum appears ambitious for a five-year course. Compared to Malik's list of the standardised madrasa curriculum according to the *dars-i nizami*, it also shows that many works have been left out (mainly those regarding *fiqh*, *usul al-fiqh*, logic, philosophy, mathematical sciences, astronomy, and rhetoric). But many other, newer subjects have also been added.[22] Overall, there seems to be a heavy emphasis on teaching the *Hadith*, both according to the curriculum and in practice.

When I asked the senior students at the Jami'at al-Niswan what they wanted to do after graduation, their first response was usually that they wanted to get married, while several expressed a desire to teach either in this madrasa or elsewhere.[23] When they speak of 'elsewhere', this suggests the possibility of an intellectual migration. It happens occasionally that a female madrasa graduate relocates in order to take up a teaching position in a girls' madrasa other than the one she graduated from, located far from her paternal home or that of her in-laws. The above trajectory provides an opportunity for a professional career to some of the (unmarried) teachers at the Jami'at al-Niswan, whose migration depends on the *ijazat* or permission from their guardians, i.e., their parents or husbands. When I asked teachers whether their parents found it difficult that they lived and worked so far away from home, they replied that their families considered it a religious honour to have a daughter who teaches in a madrasa.

The above examples indicate that *adab* is central to the madrasa's mission of bringing about reform through education when it comes to the morality and actions of the girls, although the ideals as stated in the Jami'at al-Niswan's admission statement may or may not tally with the lives the girls lead outside the madrasa, be it in their paternal homes or their own homes once they get married. The girls' point out that the acquired status of being knowledgeable in Islamic matters is sometimes acknowledged and sometimes not. In the case of the teacher who was trying to lose weight, we saw how fragile her position in the household was, despite her knowledge and her being a significant breadwinner in the family. Similarly, with regard to the obligation for all Muslims to seek knowledge, women and men may not be as equal as some of my interviewees claimed. At the formal level, women are still excluded from a variety of positions of authority, such as *muftis* and *qadis*. When I asked one of the teachers in the Jami'at al-Niswan what she thought about this issue, she replied that the ulama did not believe a woman could attain such a position. She also did she believe that a *mufti* course for women would ever be realised.

A number of Indian universities, such as the Osmania University in Hyderabad, Aligarh Muslim University in Aligarh, and the Jami'a Millia Islamia and the Jami'a Hamdard in Delhi, recognise the *fazila* degrees issued in well-established girls' madrasas as being equal to a '10+2' graduation level from a non-Islamic secondary school, or sometimes a BA in subjects like Arabic, Urdu, Persian, Islamic Studies, or Unani medicine.[24] This, however, is not yet the case for the Jami'at al-Niswan. The above concerns regarding recognition, funding, and the potential to expand are what characterise everyday life in this particular madrasa and are like those of most of the Indian girls' madrasas. Although at present, madrasa education for Muslim girls appears to be in transition, the demand for more and larger girls' madrasas also indicates the possible development of future trajectories for madrasa graduates in the labour market. India's girls' madrasas open up a limited range of future trajectories in the professional sector for Indian Muslim girls who hail from families where they may be the first female family members to find a paid job. Equally important, however, is that madrasas for girls between 12 and 17 years of age provide an Islamic alternative form of education that may persuade many parents to send their daughters to school instead of keeping them at home.

Notes

1 This overview brief is based on Gail Minault, *Secluded Scholars: Women's education and Muslim Social Reform in Colonial India*. New Delhi: Oxford University Press 1998; Barbara Daly Metcalf, *Perfecting Women: Maulana Ashraf 'Ali Thanawi's Bihishti Zewar*. Berkeley and Los Angeles: University of California Press 1990.

2 For more writing on boys' madrasas see: Barbara Daly Metcalf, *Islamic Revival in British India: Deoband, 1860-1900*. Princeton: Princeton University Press 1982; Jamal Malik, *Islamische Gelehrtenkultur in Nordindien. Entwicklungsgeschichte & Tendenzen am Beispiel von Lucknow*. Leiden: Brill 1997; Muhammad Qasim Zaman, 'Commentaries, Print and Patronage: Hadith and the Madrasas in Modern South Asia', *Bulletin of the School of Oriental and African Studies* 62 (1999), 60-81; Muhammad Qasim Zaman, *The Ulama in Contemporary Islam: Custodians of Change*. Princeton: Princeton University Press, 2002.

3 The name Jami'at al-Niswan is fictive, but it resembles the real names of girls' madrasas I encountered during my fieldwork. Madrasas offering higher levels of education are often named *jami'a*, which is also the term for university. On the Nadwat al-Ulama see Malik, *Islamische Gelehrtenkultur*.

4 On which, see Muhammad Khalid Masud (ed.), *Travellers in Faith. Studies of the Tablighi Jama'at as a Transnational Islamic Movement for Faith Renewal*. Leiden: Brill 2000.

5 Qamaruddin, *Hindustan Ki Dini Darsgahen* [Religious schools in India]. New Delhi: Hamdard Education Society 1997.

6 *See for example the* Milli Gazette *archives at: http://www.milligazette.com/Archives/15072002/1507200259.htm.*

7 See Nicole Grandin and Marc Gaborieau (eds.), *Madrasa: la transmission du savoir dans le monde musulman*. Paris: Arguments 1997.

8 See Minault, *Secluded scholars*.

9 For a detailed analysis of these and other authors, see Margrit Pernau, 'Motherhood and Female Identity: Religious Advice Literature for Women in German Catholicism and Indian Islam', in: Margrit Pernau, Imtiaz Ahmad and Helmut Reifeld (eds.), *Family and Gender: Changing Values in Germany and India*. New Delhi: Sage Publications 2002, pp.140-161.

10 Qamaruddin, *Hindustan Ki Dini Darsgahen*.

11 The madrasa system of education recognises a secondary degree, namely the *'alim(a)* degree, as well as a tertiary degree, namely the *fazil(a)* degree. Today, in the case of some girls' madrasas, the highest degree, namely the *fazila*, is recognised by a few Muslim universities as equal to graduation from a secondary non-Islamic school and sometimes as being equal to a BA degree in certain subjects.

12 It is interesting to note that the term *Ansari* here refers to two distinct caste groups of very different status: (1) the low caste of weavers in northern India referred to as Ansaris; and (2) a group of high-status Muslims who claim to be descended from the Ansar or Muhammad's helpers in Medina.

13 The translation of the following sections is the author's.

14 Again, there is an allusion to the above-mentioned *Faza'il-i 'Amal*, the instruction 'manual' central to the reformist work of the Tablighi Jama'at.

15 *Mahram* denotes a man not eligible for marriage to a woman, who can serve as her guardian until she gets married. Similarly, *ghair mahram* denotes an eligible bachelor and in whose company she should wear a veil, or in whose company she is not even permitted.

16 See: Cora Vreede-de Stuers, *Parda: A Study of Muslim Women's Life in Northern India*. Assen: Koninklijke Van Gorcum & Comp. Ltd., 1968, p. 42. and Lila Abu Lughod, *Veiled Sentiments: Honor and Poetry in a Bedouin Society*. Cairo: American University Cairo Press, 1987.

17 Qualification of this statement is necessary because the school building is so small that the men sitting in the front room are bound to hear what is going on inside the classrooms.

18 See Metcalf, *Perfecting women*.

19 The *Qir'at ur-Rashida* was written by Maulana Saiyid Abul Hasan Ali Nadwi of the Nadwat al-Ulama. It teaches social etiquette based on the exemplary lives of the first Caliphs of Islam.

20 Among this particular group of Muslim women, *purdah* includes wearing a *burqa* at all times when they step outside the madrasa or the face veil or *niqab* when they step outside their homes, the, wearing thick socks up to their knees and also putting on long black gloves until above the elbow, which goes for the hot summer months as well. The girls don't complain, in fact, they seem to take pride in this strict form of *purdah*.

21 See Barbara Daly Metcalf, 'Tablighi Jama'at and women', in: Masud (ed.), *Travellers in Faith*, pp. 44-58.

22 On the *dars-i nizami*, see Malik, *Islamische Gelehrtenkultur*, pp. 536-541.

23 The answers reflected the following order of preference: (1) get married; (2) teach in a girls' madrasa; (3) do *tabligh*; and finally (4) lead *jama'at* (women's gatherings).

24 The differences in how much madrasa degrees are recognised hinge on the standards and requirements of the respective government institutions in various Indian states.

4 Between Pakistan and Qom

Shi'i Women's Madrasas and New Transnational Networks

Mariam Abou Zahab

The Iranian revolution has had a major impact, directly and indirectly, on the presence of Islam in the Pakistani public sphere. Indirectly, it has contributed to the flourishing of various Sunni Muslim institutions and movements, including some radical ones. Both local and foreign sponsors, especially from the Arabian peninsula, who have wished to counter the revolutionary messages coming from Iran, have resorted to supporting the radical strain in Sunni Islam. But more directly, the revolution has galvanised the Pakistani Shi'i communities, as it did Shi'i communities all over the world, setting in motion a strong movement of religious intensification and purification, and creating or strengthening transnational networks that connected Pakistani Shi'is with their co-religionaries in Iran and elsewhere. This paper deals with one particular aspect of the resurgence of Pakistani Shi'ism, the emergence of women's madrasas and the movement of some of the best graduates of these madrasas to Qom in Iran for advanced studies.[1]

Shi'ism, in its various forms, has had a long presence in the regions that make up present-day Pakistan. Currently, Shi'is are believed to constitute 15 to 20 per cent of the population.[2] Most of them are Twelver (*ithna'ashari*) Shi'is, but there is also a certain presence of Isma'ilis, especially in Karachi and in the northern territories. According to local tradition, Shi'ism here goes back to the first centuries of Islam, when members of the Ahl-i Bait, the Prophet's family, fled eastward from Sunni persecution and found a safe haven on the banks of the Indus. The genealogies of the Pakistani *sayyids* (descendants of the Prophet) trace their family origins all the way back to the seventh century and believe their ancestors settled here soon after Husain's martyrdom at Karbala and the persecution of his descendants. Most *sayyids* in Pakistan are Shi'is.

However, the majority of Pakistani Shi'is are the descendants of Hindus who were converted to Islam by Isma'ili missionaries (*da'i*), whose presence in the region can be attested from the tenth century onwards.[3] The state of Multan in fact even adopted Isma'ilism as the state religion for a brief period in the tenth century, under an independent dynasty allied with the Qarmatis, until its conquest and incorporation into the Sunni Ghaznavid empire under Sultan Mahmud of Ghazna in 1010.[4] Another wave of conversions, this time to Twelver (*ithna'ashari*) Shi'ism, took place in the Safavid period (1505-1722). Isma'ili shrines in the Panjab and the present Northwest Frontier Province were taken over by Twelver Shi'a. Conversions to Shi'ism did not come to an end after the Safavid period but have continued to our day. A number of well-known Shi'i ulama and preachers today are converts from Sunni Islam.

The Shi'i population is highly fragmented and heterogeneous, divided into numerous ethnic, linguistic and social communities, with rituals and practices showing great variety from region to region and even from one city to another. The mourning rituals (*'azadari*) are particularly rich and complex, with apparent adaptations of Hindu rituals, but quite different from the more austere rituals observed in Lebanon, Iraq and Iran.[5]

In terms of gender relations, Shi'ism has often been considered as more liberal than Sunni Islam on the Indian subcontinent, and as offering a more important role for women in social life. Shi'i women have access to religious public spaces whereas. apart from visits to the shrines, Sunni women are not permitted to participate in public religious activities. Moreover, Shi'i religious law favours women more than does the Hanafi *mazhab*, especially in matters of marriage, divorce and inheritance.

Juan Cole has shown that women in urban circles in the Shi'i principality of Awadh (1722-1856) enjoyed a high degree of independence vis-à-vis men, which, together with the practice of gender segregation, "contributed to the development of a specifically feminine Shi'ite religious discourse that was ... more syncretic and innovative than the scripturalism of literate males."[6] Cole adds that these women believed in astrology and were much influenced by Hindu rituals. All this contributed to the elaboration of a distinct female Shi'i culture that is still very much alive among the *sayyid* families that settled in Multan, Lahore and Karachi as refugees (*muhajir*) after the Partition of British India.

One remarkable aspect of this relatively independent position of women combined with strict gender separation in Shi'i communities is the existence of a class of female informal religious experts. Many daughters of especially the poorer *sayyid* families remained unmarried, because they were not allowed to marry commoners and their families could not afford the high dowries demanded by the more well-off *sayyid* families.[7] These women were then trained as religious teachers and preachers. They would teach the Qur'an to the daughters of the aristocracy and during the month of Muharram they would lead women's gatherings (*majlis*) and recite the mournful stories of the martyrdom of Husain and the suffering of the other imams. The female religious experts constituted a widespread network of learning, independent of the male ulama networks.

In contemporary Pakistan, such celibate *sayyidas* are not the only class of educated women among the Shi'a, however. The Pakistani Shi'a, and especially the Urdu-speaking Muhajirs among them, have long given more importance to girls' education than the Sunnis. Before the 1980s, this concerned mainly secular education. Due to their relatively high educational achievements, Shi'i women were over-represented in the media (on television and in the English-language press) as well as in the professions (lawyers, doctors, academics) and in literature and the arts.

The Iranian revolution and its apparently empowering effect on women's social roles had a pervasive effect on the self-perception and ideals of south Asian Shi'i women, who took Iranian women as their role models. It was especially in the field of religious education and in the increased visibility of women in the religious space that the Iranian influence made itself felt. A number of girls' madrasas were established, initially with financial support from Iran. (It was especially during Khatami's presidency that the export of revolution gave way to the support of educational institutions as an instrument of foreign policy.)

Consequently, the number of women seeking a religious education or taking courses in such a madrasa while continuing their secular studies has increased tremendously. Moreover, since the mid-1980s, a growing number of Pakistani women have been going to Iran for advanced studies in the seminaries of Qom.

The remainder of this chapter discusses three of these new women's madrasas in Pakistan and the seminary for foreign female students in Qom, the Jami'at al-Zahra, where some of the best graduates of these madrasas have gone to continue their studies. These madrasas are located in very different geographical and social settings, were established for different reasons, and serve different constituencies. One is an urban elite institution in Lahore, that is highly 'Persianised;' another is a school in a Shi'a village with a largely *sayyid* population; and the third, with which I begin, is located in an isolated rural district, where Shi'ism is deeply anchored in local tradition and culture.

The Jami'at Khadijat al-Kubra

One of Pakistan's largest madrasas for girls is the Jami'at Khadijat al-Kubra in Pakki Shah Mardan, a remote Shi'a village about 40 kilometres from Mianwali, in a socially conservative area where the female literacy rate is particularly low. The founder of this madrasa is Sayyid Iftikhar Hussain Naqvi, a Shi'i *'alim* who was born in 1951 in the Multan district. Upon his return from studying in Iraq in the 1970s, Naqvi became a close associate of Allama Arif Hussain al-Hussaini, the most prominent leader of the reformist group among Pakistani Shi'i clerics, and he became actively involved in politics.[8] His first venture into education was his founding of the Madrasa Imam Khomeini for boys in Marri Indus, near Mianwali, in 1982. The Jami'at Khadijat al-Kubra began its activities in 1993 in a small house next to the boys' madrasa. Land was later acquired in Pakki Shah Mardan, where the madrasa was inaugurated in September 1996. In the first year, 40 girls received admission; currently the number of students is close to 200, and the school has some 60 full-time and part-time teachers, of whom 20 are men.[9] At the time of my last visit, in December 2004, a new dormitory was under construction, indicating that expansion was continuing. The madrasa attracts students from far afield, but the complex includes two institutions catering to the needs of the local community: a training centre where local girls are taught practical skills such as sewing, embroidery but also computer skills, and a dispensary. The current director of the madrasa is

Iftikhar Naqvi's daughter, Wajiha Naqvi, one of the early Pakistani graduates from the Jami'at al-Zahra in Qom.

Some of the students belong to clerical (*ruhani*) families, and could be said to be stepping into a known though previously male domain. They are a minority, however. The other girls have chosen to study in a madrasa because of their personal interest in religion, or because they perceived these studies as a way to advance socially. Quite a few students are from the northern areas (Gilgit, Baltistan), although this region has many madrasas supported by Iran. I also met a number of British Pakistani girls, who had enrolled in the madrasa both in order to receive a religious education and to get better acquainted with their own culture.

The madrasa offers four types of courses, each designed for a different audience. The curriculum follows the prescribed curriculum for Pakistani Shi'i madrasas elaborated by the Wifaq al-Madaris al-Shi'a (Union of Shi'i madrasas), the body in charge of religious studies that organises exams and issues degrees.[10] The courses are taught in Urdu, and many of the prescribed books are translations from Persian textbooks, published in Lahore in co-operation with Iranian publishers.

The first course, *fahm-i din*, which lasts three months, is a basic course intended especially for girls studying in government schools or living abroad. It consists of a basic knowledge of Islam: *'aqa'id* (the articles of faith) and *akhlaq* (morality); the girls are taught how to read the Qur'an and the *Sirat Fatima* (the life of the Prophet's daughter Fatima – the ultimate role model for Shi'i women); they learn the correct form of the rituals and memorise numerous invocations (*salawat*) to be recited daily.

Wajiha Naqvi explained the objectives of this course, which are that the basic knowledge imparted should enable the girls to develop their personalities and give spirituality a proper place in their lives. It should offer girls a better understanding of Shi'ism and also correct the negative image of madrasas in Pakistani society. Students are formally required to pass a matriculation exam, which means having successfully completed ten years of general education, before they can apply for admission. In exceptional cases, girls who have only completed intermediate level (8th grade) or even primary level (5th grade) of education, can be admitted if they have the required intellectual capacities and motivation and the courses are then appropriately adapted to their levels of education.

Wajiha Naqvi argues that there are good reasons for offering this type of basic religious education in a school context instead of, as was common in the past, at home. The family, she claims, is not the best environment for providing even this basic level of discipline; a more structured learning environment is needed. With more systematic methods of discipline, even those girls who do not continue their educations after this basic course will contribute to spreading the faith as 'silent preachers': by daily performing the prayers and wearing the *hijab*, they become role models for children and draw them towards Islam.

During the ten years that this course has been offered, about 500 girls have followed it. The madrasa attempts to stay in touch with the former students and has thus gradually built up a network of pious, committed young women.

The second course, which lasts a full year trains girls to be *muballigha* (female preachers) and *zakira* (the ritual experts who lead the *majalis*, the gatherings where the suffering and martyrdom of the imams is commemorated). The teaching focuses on memorisation and the practical aspects of the *majlis*. Students memorise Qur'anic verses together with their Urdu translation, they learn about the life of the Prophet and of the imams, and they receive basic notions of Arabic (in order to pronounce the Qur'anic verses correctly), *tafsir* (exegesis) and *fiqh* (jurisprudence). They memorise the songs of mourning, laments and elegies (*marsiyas*, *nohas*, and *qasidas*) that are sung during the *majalis*. The courses focus on the performing technique whereby the students view videocassettes of famous (male) *zakirs* and *wa'iz* (preachers),[11] and they learn how to write sermons in Urdu and in Siraiki (the local language) for various types of audiences. They also acquire the technique of reciting the *faza'il* (meritorious qualities) of the imams and *masa'ib* (misfortunes) of the Ahl-i Bait. A good *zakira* must have a strong voice, and she must be able to arouse emotions among the participants and make them cry.

The madrasa aims to produce a new type of *zakira*, different from the traditional *zakiras*, who lacked a formal religious education and learned their skills from their mothers or older, more experienced *zakiras*. The traditional religious ideas mediated by the old-style *zakiras* often bordered on the heterodox. The training of better qualified (and more orthodox) *zakiras* continues an earlier movement of reform of the *majalis* (*islah al-majalis*) and the rationalisation of ritual that was launched in as early as the mid-1960s by

Maulana Mohammad Hussain Dhakku. Dhakku's initiative at that time provoked hostile reactions from the more traditional elements, who called him a 'Wahhabi' intent on destroying religion. The revolution in Iran, however, gave a strong boost to the reformist effort to purify belief. As a part of their training, students are required to do textual research in preparation of their having to recount one of the episodes of the imams' lives. Their teachers have them compare the written texts with the popular oral versions told by traditional *zakiras* and denounce the latter as erroneous and heterodox.

Wajiha Naqvi says that she considers the *majalis* an excellent occasion for *tabligh* (predication), but that these are unfortunately mostly organised and led by men. Women do attend the *majalis*, but they usually return home after listening to the *faza'il* and *masa'ib*, without acquiring any religious knowledge. Therefore, educated women have had to take charge and organise separate women's *majalis* as a vehicle for the transmission of religious knowledge that is both accessible to rural women and adapted to their specific needs.[12]

In rural areas, where women are not highly educated and often illiterate, the graduates of this one-year course can make a significant impact on society because of their access to the women. *Muballighas* travel from village to village especially during the months of Ramadan and Muharram, delivering pious homilies, teaching the Qur'an, and leading invocations.

This second course has so far been completed by 120 students, some of whom have opened schools in their own villages or neighbourhoods. They act as role models; many of the current students claim that they joined the madrasa because they were influenced by these *muballighas*. After completing this course, the students who wish to do so have the right to take part, as external candidates, in the final exams of the secular higher secondary school.[13]

The third course, which lasts two years, is a proper madrasa curriculum that prepares the students for the degrees of *fazil-i Arabi* and *sultan al-afazil*. The holders of the latter degree can obtain a statement that states that it is the equivalent of an M.A. in Arabic or Islamic Studies from the University of Panjab.[14] After they pass an examination that tests their didactic abilities at the Allama Iqbal Open University, they are also allowed to teach these subjects in government schools. During the past decade, 140 students have obtained the degree of *sultan al-afazil*, and many of them have in fact become teachers.

The course is traditional in content: it is based on the *dars-i nizami*, that has constituted the standard curriculum of south Asian madrasas since the mid-eighteenth century, along with some specifically Shi'i texts prescribed by the Shi'a madrasa board (Wifaq al-Madaris al-Shi'a).[15] The students must also acquire a solid, passive knowledge of Arabic, which is taught by a Lebanese woman married to a Pakistani cleric who lived in Syria for 17 years, studying at the Imam Khomeini madrasa in Damascus. Language classes are also traditional and consist of the memorisation of *nahw* (morphology) and *sarf* (syntax) textbooks. Persian is also taught, using more modern textbooks published in Iran, but the students do not acquire more than a passive knowledge of this language either.

The fourth course, which lasts another two years, leads to the *'alima* degree. The program of study includes the methods of *tabligh*, or teaching and research with an emphasis on *munazara* (theological debate). This course is primarily for students who wish to continue on to more advanced studies in Iran. It prepares them for the entrance exam of the Jami'at al-Zahra in Qom, where they will study for at least another two years. In the past decade, 38 graduates of this course have been admitted to the Qom; 22 of them have returned to Pakistan since completing their studies. Some of them are directors of madrasas in Pakistan now; the majority have become well-known preachers, whose *majalis* attract large crowds. They have experienced a definite rise in social status and prestige due to their stay in Qom.

Rajoa Sadat

Rajoa Sadat is a Shi'i village in Punjab, situated close to the road linking Faisalabad to Chiniot, built around the shrine of a local Shi'i saint, Shah Daulat Bukhari. As the name of the village indicates (*sadat* being the Arabic plural of *sayyid*), the majority of the inhabitants are *sayyids*, and most of these *sayyid* families are large landowners, whose land is cultivated by peasants who live in the same and surrounding villages. These landlord families have strong connections to Iran, where many of the men have gone for religious studies; some of them have been commuting between Iran and their own villages for the last 12 to 15 years.

In September 2005, I visited a girls' madrasa here that was founded in 2002 by a young university-educated member of one of these landholding *sayyid* families. The madrasa then had 125 students, who were living in two large but dilapidated houses donated by one of the *sayyid* families, and the school appeared to be operating on a very modest budget. However, a huge new building was under construction near the entrance to the village on a piece of land donated by another feudal family. According to the director of the madrasa, once this building is completed it will accommodate 1,500 students. He claimed that the demand for the type of education the school provides is very high; at present many prospective students cannot be admitted because of a lack of space. Currently, the staff of the madrasa consists of only two female teachers and the (male) director. Both teachers are married to clerics, and both have spent over 10 years studying in Qom. They are assisted in their teaching by the more advanced students, who instruct the younger ones. For subjects such as *hifz* (memorisation of the Qur'an) and *tajwid* (its proper articulation) they also use video and audio cassettes.

The madrasa is located in a rural environment, although less isolated than the one in Pakki Shah Mardan, and the girls who are admitted after completing their matriculation (the secondary school exam taken at the end of the 10th grade) are from rural backgrounds, mostly from villages in south and central Punjab. Few of them belong to religious families and many of them admit that they chose a religious education after hearing the *muballighas* preach in their villages during Ramazan and Muharram.

Unlike the one in Pakki Shah Mardan, this madrasa does not focus on the training of *zakiras* or preparing girls for higher educations in Qom, but focuses on providing a basic religious education and promoting values. There is a section for *hifz* and a short course for *muballighas*. As the director stated, most of the girls do not complete the five-year madrasa course, and for them *tarbiyat* (moral disciplining and training to be good wives and mothers) is more important than *ta'alim* (textbook learning). Girls take courses in the madrasa for one or two years prior to their marriage because a girl with some education gained in a madrasa has more value on the marriage market.

The madrasa has no fixed syllabus and no exams. Its objective is, in the director's words, to enable girls to develop their capacities (prayer technique, recitation of the Qur'an and perhaps leading a *majlis*) and to change their personalities so that upon their return to their own villages they will be 'vehicles of silent *tabligh*' and by their example bring about a 'social revolution' to their environment. Furthermore, the director believes that it is more important to teach girls how to raise their children and resolve conflicts with their mothers-in-law than to immerse them in *fiqh* or complex Arabic grammar, which will be of little use to them in their daily lives. Education should be relevant to the students' lives, and the students are expected to live their lives within these limited horizons.

Jami'at al-Muntazar

The third women's madrasa I visited is the girls section in the Jami'at al-Muntazar in Lahore, the most prestigious Shi'i madrasa of Pakistan. This is the major intellectual centre of Pakistan's Shi'a community, and the Wifaq al-Madaris al-Shi'a (Council of Shi'i madrasas), the institution in charge of religious studies which organises exams and issues degrees, is based here. Unlike the earlier two, this madrasa primarily recruits students with an urban background, and modernising Iranian influences even more strongly felt here.

The girls' division was established in 1988, by Safdar Hussain Najafi. Originally based in another neighbourhood in Lahore, it recently moved to the main campus in Model Town for security reasons. At the time of my visit in September 2005, there were 38 students, who had been admitted upon completing their matriculation or intermediate levels, i.e., after 10 to 12 years of general education. Only about one-quarter of them came from Lahore, two were from northern Pakistan (Gilgit), while the remainder came from central and south Punjab, and Jhang and Multan were especially well-represented. For some of the students, the madrasa diploma is a goal in itself – it greatly increases their value on the marriage market – while many others have academic ambitions. Several of the girls, besides pursuing religious studies at the madrasa, were also preparing to take the state F.A. or B.A. exams as external candidates; one of them, in fact, had just passed her M.A.

The atmosphere in the Jami'at al-Muntazar is strikingly different from the other two madrasas I visited. This is an elite institution, more strongly 'Iranianised' than the others, and it caters to an urban middle-class public. The girls wear neat uniforms consisting of white *shalwar-qameez* with *dupattas* of different colours for each of the four grades. The syllabus is very similar to the one at the seminary in Qom, with an emphasis on the Arabic language. Unlike the other madrasas, however, *hifz* is not taught here, nor is there a department for training *muballighat*.[16] Their basic four-month course, which is similar to successful courses elsewhere, seldom attracts any students – another indication that this madrasa serves a different type of public, one with higher academic ambitions.

Most of the girls want to continue their studies in Qom, which is, along with Najaf, the main centre of Shi'i learning in the world. Every year, a committee from Qom visits Pakistan's best madrasas to select students; however, the number invited to Qom is not high, two per year from this particular madrasa, for instance. Those fortunate enough to be selected join a remarkable transnational scholarly network that brings them into contact with colleagues from all over the world.

Iran: The Jami'at al-Zahra in Qom

The madrasa Jami'at al-Zahra in Qom, the first women's madrasa there, was inaugurated in 1984 and the foreign students department was established two years later.[17] In February 2004, the madrasa moved to more spacious premises on a new campus, which continues to expand. At the time of my visit in November 2004, there were some 200 girls studying in this madrasa, from some 40 different countries. The 60 or so Pakistanis comprised the largest contingent among them, followed by 20 to 25 Indian Shi'is, with a smaller number of British Muslims of Pakistani background, many of whom were Gujaratis. Another conspicuous group consisted of some ten French-speaking *ithna'ashari* Khojas from Madagascar.[18] More surprising was the presence of a number of Sunni students, notably from China, Tajikistan and various African countries. The director of the madrasa told me that the demand from China is overwhelming and there would be many more Chinese students if the admission policies were less restrictive. The same is true of Pakistanis: many more capable students are eager to study in Qom than the school can accommodate.

Most of the Pakistani students at the Jami'at al-Zahra hailed from the Punjab (Lahore and Islamabad/Rawalpindi) or from Karachi and many belonged to clerical (*ruhani*) families. Most of them had completed four years of study in a Pakistani madrasa before coming to Qom. I found a few students among them whom I had first met in Pakki Shah Mardan, three years earlier. There were also a number of students from well-to-do, secular-minded urban families. They were the first in their families to receive higher religious educations, and some of them had had to struggle hard to overcome their parents' reluctance to let them follow this path.

The students at the Jami'at al-Zahra are not the first Pakistani women to study at Qom. Several Pakistani women had already done so before the madrasa was established. One of them (whom I also met in Qom), in fact, even acquired the title of *mujtahida*, meaning she had completed the highest level of education available. This woman, from a Muhajir family in Karachi, had first arrived in Qom in 1982, after her marriage to a Pakistani cleric who was studying in Qom then (and who is now an influential Shi'i personality in Karachi, where he directs a cultural centre with close links to Iran, and a part-time resident of Qom, where he is the director of a research institute). At that time, there was no madrasa for girls and she followed a very heavy traditional program of studies for nine years, being tutored in her teachers' private homes. She remembers that the relationship between the (female) teachers and students was very convivial, and the students were highly motivated. Several of the Pakistani women who were studying in Iran in those early days, she claims, have upon their return established their own women's madrasas in Pakistan, and many others have become madrasa teachers. None of those who have completed their studies in Qom have become simple housewives; they are all active in public life. They enjoy prestige and most earn considerable incomes.

The Jami'at al-Zahra has set itself the task of producing a Shi'i female elite in a competitive environment, and it is very selective in the recruitment of foreign students. Those who are selected, however, pay nothing. They must be in the 17-25 age bracket, unmarried, and have at least the equivalent of a Pakistani F.A. or F.Sc. diploma.[19] In fact, the girls I spoke with found the level of teaching so demanding that they thought a B.A. degree would actually be a better preparation. The complete course for foreign students lasts five years and is divided into an introductory year and two higher levels. The students are evaluated at the end of each year, and admission to the second level is not automatic even for those who have passed their exams; only the best students are allowed to proceed with their studies.

Foreign students begin with preparatory coursework, the first four months of which are used to acquire a working knowledge of Persian. For

Urdu speakers this appears to be sufficient; to my surprise the Pakistani girls were even speaking Persian among themselves. Those who did not study in a madrasa in their own countries before coming to Qom have to follow this up with an intensive basic course in religious subjects that takes another six months. The other students take exams and, if successful, are admitted directly to the first level of the general course (*dawra-i 'umumi*).

The curriculum has been revised and modernised over the past few years, following the appointment of Sheikh Mohammad Ali Shomali as the director of the madrasa. Shomali had graduated in Western philosophy at Tehran University, alongside his religious studies in Qom and had gone on to obtain a Ph.D. in philosophy from Manchester University. Of the various subjects, great importance is given to *fiqh*, philosophy, pedagogy and educational theory and practice. The textbooks used here are mostly modern texts, unlike in Pakistan. The works of Ayatullah Mutahhari, in particular, have a prominent place in the syllabus.[20] There is also a strong emphasis on Arabic (20 credits out of 77 for the first level), which appears to present the greatest degree of difficulty for many students. They express their frustration at not being able to speak the language despite the amount of teaching devoted to it. In an attempt to improve their mastery of the language, some of the Pakistani women living in Qom with their families have arranged to be tutored in spoken Arabic by Iraqi women at home.

During the second level, comprising the final two years of the five-year course, the emphasis is on the methodology of critical textual studies. The students can choose between two educational profiles at this level: knowledge of Shi'a doctrine and ethics or the teaching of Islam. They have to write more than a dozen research papers and a dissertation to obtain their degree (*tahsilat-i takmili*). Upon completion, they are expected to return to their home countries. The madrasa is not meant to produce Islamic scholars who will remain in Qom but rather highly qualified teachers who will go back to their countries of origin to become agents of *tabligh*. Some of the most successful students, who are still under the age of 23 when they pass their *tahsilat-i takmili* exams, are allowed to pursue an advanced M.A.-level course. Two advanced course programmes have recently been introduced that specialise in Islamic spirituality and Shi'a studies (the history and sociology of Shi'ism), respectively. Most of the students in these programmes, however, are semi-permanent residents of Qom, who live there with their husbands or parents.

Besides the five-year course, the Jami'at al-Zahra also offers three- to six-week summer courses that are very popular with the students from Pakistan and the Pakistani diaspora. A six-week course in 2004 was attended by 34 girls from Karachi. There are also teacher-training courses, and a basic one-year course. A knowledge of Persian is not required for these shorter courses; the lectures are in English or Arabic, or even French, depending on the audience. Unlike the five-year course, however, these short courses are not offered free of charge.

The madrasa offers the Pakistani students a cosmopolitan environment and a relative freedom that contrasts starkly with their situation at home. Their stay in Qom means a temporary escape from the stifling control of families and neighbours. Many also commented on the freedom of movement that women enjoy in Iran, unlike the situation in Pakistan. Moreover, coming from a country where Shi'is feel constantly threatened, have to maintain a low profile and sometimes even hide their religious affiliations, it was a liberating experience for them to live in a Shi'i environment. One would expect that the cosmopolitan composition of the student population would be conducive to the strengthening of transnational connections, but as the largest national group, the Pakistanis, who constitute one-third of the total student population, tend to keep to themselves and do not mix much with the other students – and notably not with the Indians. The students whom I interviewed had no idea of how many Indian students were enrolled at the madrasa.[21] However, the years spent at the Jami'at al-Zahra have a profound effect on the world views and attitudes of these students, who eventually return to their homes as different persons, eager to reform their own communities.

The Jami'at al-Zahra and its relation with the growing number of Shi'i women's madrasas outside Iran exemplify the new pragmatic policy adopted by Iran under the reformist presidency of Mohammad Khatami (1997-2005). Iran's previous policy of attempting to export the revolution had proved counter-productive and led to widespread sectarian violence, in Pakistan and elsewhere. The reformist policy consists of attempting to create a transnational Shi'i elite in the madrasas of Qom while simultaneously stimulating the development of networks among the graduates.

The Pakistani women who graduate from Qom are part of this new elite, a self-consciously new type of Shi'i women. They have adopted the Iranian style of dress (a long raincoat and headscarf) that has become a symbol of modernity among young urban Shi'i women in Pakistan. Their studies have earned them a considerable amount of prestige, and a level of religious authority that is also recognised by their male counterparts. Moreover, to a certain extent, these female scholars represent a form of Islamic feminism, based on a deconstruction of the Qur'an and of the *hadith* with a view to improving women's rights. Islam, as they preach it, is not a religion of fear, of strict rules and severe punishments, but one of simple principles of belief and conduct in one's everyday life. In their public discussions, they explain details of belief but also address the practical and mundane matters that women face in their daily lives, from health and child care to the psychology of education.

The moderately reformist trend that these women ulama represent is often seen as a threat to the cultural specificities of popular south Asian Shi'ism and they are sometimes branded by conservatives as 'Wahhabis,' who want to destroy the very foundation of Shi'ism as it has developed over the centuries in South Asia. Some of them have understood that Shi'ism can only exist if it is rooted in a particular culture and they have developed a hybrid style of *majlis* in which the sermon uses a rational language and spreads a reformist message, whereas the part dealing with *masa'ib* remains very traditional. The moderate reformism of these women ulama have at times provoked violent reactions. In February 2005, a reformist *zakira* originally from Pakistan but resident in Kenya, who had been invited to Bombay for Muharram, was expelled after she criticised some of the local traditions before an audience of 400 women, inviting them to reject these 'deviant' practices.

Conclusion

The development of women's madrasas catering to young Shi'i women in Pakistan, and the emergence of a new, female, scholarly network with Qom as its prestigious centre, was due to a change in Iranian foreign policy. The efforts of the 1980s to export revolutionary ideology had created a negative backlash among Pakistan's Sunni population and led to violent clashes between Sunnis and Shi'is. After the death of Khomeini, and especially under the presidency of Khatami, Iran began to concentrate its efforts on the education of a new transnational Shi'i elite. The presence of women within this elite of religious scholars was not new in Iran, but it was further strengthened after the revolution. In countries like Pakistan, the availability of higher religious education to women at special women's madrasas constituted a minor revolution. These madrasas form an effective channel for the transmission of religious reform into conservative environments as well as a means of stimulating social mobility and greater autonomy among these 'new Shi'i women.'

Notes

1 This chapter presents the preliminary findings of a research project that is still in progress. It is based on fieldwork in Pakistan (July 2001, December 2004 and September 2005) and in Qom (November 2004). In Pakistan, I visited three madrasas: Jami'at Khadijat al-Kubra in Pakki Shah Mardan (Mianwali), Rajoa Sadat (Chiniot) and Jami'at al-Muntazar (Lahore). In Qom, I visited Jami'at al-Zahra, a madrasa for foreign female students, where roughly one-third of the students were from Pakistan. An earlier version of this was published in French as 'Madrasas de femmes entre le Pakistan et Qom', in: Sabrina Mervin (ed.), *Les mondes chiites et l'Iran*, Paris: Karthala, 2007, pp. 287-300.

2 No actual statistics exist, but these figures are commonly given in official Pakistani publications. With 25 to 30 million, this is the second largest Shi'i community after Iran.

3 See, for details, Derryl N. Maclean, *Religion and Society in Arab Sind*. Leiden: Brill, 1989.

4 Cf. 'Multan' and 'Karmati', *Encyclopaedia of Islam*, 2nd ed.

5 Vernon James Schubel, *Religious Performance in Contemporary Islam. Shi'i Devotional Rituals in South Asia*. Columbia: University of South Carolina Press, 1990; David Pinault, *The Shiites: Ritual and Popular Piety in a Muslim Community*. London: I.B.Tauris, 1992; David Pinault, *Horse of Karbala: Muslim Devotional Life in India*. New York: Palgrave, 2001.

6 See the chapter 'Women and the making of Shi'ism' in Juan Cole, *Sacred Space and Holy War: The Politics, Culture and History of Shi'ite Islam*. London: I.B.Tauris, 2002, pp. 138-160. The quoted passage is found on pp. 150-1.

7 As elsewhere, south Asian *sayyid* families have a strict code of status maintenance that forbids women to marry non-*sayyids*.

8 Allama Hussaini, a Pashtun *'alim* from Parachinar, who studied in Najaf and Qom, was the wakil (representative) of Khomeini in Pakistan. He was the leader of the Shi'i political movement Tahrik-i Nifaz-i Fiqh-i Ja'fariya (later renamed Tahrik-i Ja'fariya Pakistan) from 1984 until August 1988, when he was assassinated. He transformed this originally religious movement into a political party and became an inspiration for the Shi'a students' movement and the leader of the 'Iranianised' group among the Pakistani Shi'i clergy. He was succeeded as the leader of the Tahrik by Allama Sayyid Ali Naqvi.

9 These numbers are based on my observations during my visit in December 2004.

10 Pakistan has such an umbrella organisation, responsible for maintaining standards of education in the madrasas of each of the major denominations,: Deobandis, Barelwis, Ahl-i Hadith, Jama'at-i Islami and Shi'a. See Jamal Malik, *Colonialization of Islam: Dissolution of traditional institutions in Pakistan*. New Delhi : Manohar, 1996, passim.

11 The video cassettes in circulation are exclusively of male preachers and *zakirs*, because the public visibility of women to male audiences is a controversial

matter in pious circles. However, audio cassettes of female preachers and *zakiras* do exist.

12 On women's *majalis* as they are organised in Peshawar, see: Mary Elaine Hegland, 'The power paradox in Muslim women's majales: North-West Pakistani mourning rituals as sites of contestation over religious politics, ethnicity, and gender', *Signs: Journal of Women in Culture and Society* 23, 1998, 391-428 ; and idem, 'Flagellation and fundamentalism: (trans)forming meaning, identity, and gender through Pakistani women's rituals of mourning', *American Ethnologist* 25, 1998, 240-266.

13 This concerns the F.A. and F.Sc. exams (of the arts and science majors, respectively), which are taken at the end of the 12th year.

14 The madrasa reform proposed by the government of Pakistan in 1980 entailed among other things a rule of equivalence that gave the highest degrees of madrasa education parity with the M.A. degree in Islamic or Arabic studies at one of the universities. Most universities, incidentally, rejected this idea of equivalence. See: Malik, *Colonialization of Islam*, pp. 140-1.

15 The *dars-i nizami* owes its name to the scholar Maulana Nizamuddin Sihalvi of Lucknow. It has remained, with some revisions, the standard curriculum not only of Sunni, but also of Shi'i madrasas in India and Pakistan.

16 *Hifz*, or memorisation of the Qur'an, is only in demand in rural areas. Students interested in *hifz* would not apply to the Jami'at al-Muntazar. The training of *muballighat* is not considered as an academic discipline here; one of the teachers told me that this is not a skill that can be imparted through formal teaching; it takes much more than one year of on-the-job training to become a *muballigha*.

17 There is another madrasa for foreign women in Qom named Bint al-Huda, where the emphasis is more on the Arabic language. According to Pakistani sources, circa 25 Pakistani students were studying at the Bint al-Huda in 2005. Most of the students in this madrasa were Iraqis and many of them appear to have returned to Iraq after the fall of Saddam Hussain.

18 Most of the Khojas are Nizari Isma'ilis, but in the early nineteenth century, part of the community converted to Twelver Shi'ism. There are sizeable *ithna'ashari* Khoja communities in both South Asia and among the diaspora (East Africa, Europe).

19 Other rules apply for long-term foreign residents of Qom. Married women up to the age of 35 can be admitted; the madrasa even offers a day-care centre for their young children.

20 The curriculum lists numerous works by Ayatullah Murtaza Mutahhari, on philosophy and the fundamentals of Shi'ism.

21 This is true for the students at the madrasa. The Pakistanis who have settled in Qom as long-time residents, however, have developed wide-ranging contacts with Shi'i residents of Indian origin, and the common Shi'i and Urdu identity appears to be overriding national affiliation.

5 The Uncertain Fate of Southeast Asian Students in the Madrasas of Pakistan

Farish A. Noor

Pakistan's Madrasas and the Phobia of Foreign Students[1]

In the wake of the attacks on the United States of America on 11 September 2001; the US-led invasions of Afghanistan in 2002, and the bombings in London in July 2005, Pakistan has emerged on the international stage as both a crisis-riddled country where radical religious politics has gone out of control and – at the same time – as a key ally in Washington's 'war on terror'.

The ambivalent image of Pakistan as a strategic frontline state has been reflected upon by scholars and media commentators alike and this ambivalence has been projected upon the country's madrasas as well.[2] Since the 1980s, Pakistan has witnessed a boom in the madrasa sector, with hundreds of new madrasas being created along the Afghan-Pakistani border; mainly to provide rudimentary education for the thousands of Afghan refugee children who had fled their country, but also to train many of the young boys in the ways of warfare and to produce the rank-and-file of the Mujahidin who would later return to Afghanistan to take part in the Afghan jihad against the Soviets. Later in the 1990s, many of these madrasas would also be used to recruit and train the Taliban who would also play a key role in the politics of Afghanistan and Central Asia.[3] Following the discovery that several of the London bombers of 2005 had travelled to Pakistan and studied at madrasas there, another concern was raised: namely that of foreign students who travel from one country to another in search of Islamic education and what might happen to them in the madrasas they visit. Again, there were calls for the Pakistani government to take decisive steps in controlling the activities in the madrasas, monitoring their links with radical Islamist groups as well as the movement of students between them.

Long before the latest wave of measures to control the madrasas of Pakistan, the Pakistani government had already embarked on an ambitious reform process to regulate, control and monitor the activities of the country's madrasas as well as the movement of students between them. This was one of the stated goals of General Pervez Musharraf's government, which came to power in October 1999 after toppling the government of Nawaz Sharif and the Pakistan Muslim League (PMS-NS). Upon assuming control of the country, General Pervez Musharraf has tried to improve his international image by wearing his 'moderate' Islamic credentials on his sleeves. In response to pressure from the American government and local Pakistani NGOs, on 12 January 2002 he banned six of the major jihadi militant organisations based in Pakistan, namely the *Lashkar-i Tayyiba* (LT), *Sipah-i Sahaba-i Pakistan* (SSP), *Lashkar-i Jhangvi* (LJ), *Jaish-i Muhammad* (JM), *Tahrik-i Jafariya Pakistan* (TJP) and *Jama'at al-Furqan*.

This crackdown on the radical Islamist militias was accompanied by other measures that were also meant to improve Pakistan's image as a country worthy of investment. These measures included (1) the reform of the madrasa educational system, (2) closer regulation and control of the entry and circulation of students within the madrasa network, (3) promotion of literacy and education among girls, (4) guaranteeing equal access to education and other social services to women, (5) an anti-corruption campaign that targets the corrupt Pakistani businessmen and companies who are said to have transferred their earnings and savings abroad. While the anti-corruption measures were pursued publicly with the arrest of several prominent businessmen and attempts to repatriate their capital from overseas, the reform of the madrasas proved to be the most difficult task of all.

The changes proposed for the madrasa system in Pakistan have been the most comprehensive and taxing, as they came at a time when the country's madrasas felt that they were under pressure to reform solely for the sake of placating American foreign policy and to improve the image of the Musharraf government. They were also made in the context of a country that spends circa 2 per cent of its annual gross national product on education, and where the national literacy rate was estimated at circa 40 per cent at best.[4] The reform measures included the following:[5]

1. The establishment of a national roster for all madrasas in the country, under the Pakistani Central Board of Religious Schools;
2. The declaration of assets on the part of the trustees, organisers and administrators of the madrasas themselves. This will allow the authorities to ascertain their level of development and competence and help deliver the government-allocated funding and support to the most needy madrasas;
3. Actions taken against foreign funders and NGOs suspected of having links or sympathies with radical Islamist groups abroad;[6]
4. Declaration of identity of the trustees, administrators and teaching staff of the madrasas, enabling the government to identify the political affiliation of each institution and its links to the various political parties and Islamist movements in the country;
5. Improvement and modernisation of the curricula of the madrasas, to ensure that 50% of subjects taught will be compatible with that of the mainstream national education system that is on offer in state schools.

It should be noted, however, that since 2002, the Musharraf government's reforms have not gone a long way as alluded to in the 2007 report on the country's madrasas done by the International Crisis Group (ICG).[7] Underlying the madrasa reform project and reports such as the one released by the ICG is the assumption that too many of the country's madrasas have fallen under the control of violent militant groups that seek to use them as recruitment and training bases. Related to this is the claim that many of the foreign students studying there have come to Pakistan with the intention of joining radical groups.[8] Long before the controversy over foreign students was stoked in the aftermath of the London bombings of 2005, Pakistani authorities had already cracked down on the numbers of foreign students from other parts of Asia in the country's madrasas.

It was against this backdrop of paranoia, media hype and growing insecurity in Pakistan that between 20 and 23 September 2003 a series of arrests took place at a number of madrasas in Karachi. Those arrested were all foreign students from Southeast Asia, notably Malaysia, Indonesia and Myanmar (Burma).

During the initial wave of arrests that took place in September 2003 at the Jami'at Abu Bakr and Jami'at al-Dirasat al-Islamiyya madrasas in Karachi, Pakistan's President-General Pervez Musharraf was abroad on a trip to the US. Washington had put a considerable amount of pressure on Islamabad to force it to comply with its demands to crack down on the madrasas. This demand led to the arrest of the Indonesians and Malaysians, whom they accused of being part of a clandestine cell belonging to the nebulous Jama'ah Islamiyyah group operating in Indonesia, Singapore and Malaysia – an underground movement which, we are told, wanted to establish a Pan-Islamic state that spans all of maritime Southeast Asia.

It later turned out that on the day of the arrests at the Jami'at al-Dirasat al-Islamiyya madrasa, the madrasa's 'guest of honour' was none other than Hafeez Muhammad Saeed, leader of the Jama'at al-Da'wa, which is linked to the militant jihadi group Lashkar-i Tayyiba.[9] Following the Presidential decree of 2002 that banned many of Pakistan's radical militant groups, Hafeez Saeed was a wanted man. However, no attempts were made to arrest Hafeez Saeed when the police entered the madrasa: instead, the authorities swooped down on its Malaysian and Indonesian students.

To gain a better understanding of the events that took place in the Jami'at Abu Bakr and Jami'at al-Dirasat al-Islamiyya madrasas in September 2003, I contacted the spokesman for the Jama'at al-Da'wa movement, Yahya Mujahid who informed me that 'the madrasas in Karachi where the foreign students were arrested had nothing to do with the Jama'at al-Da'wa. Despite what the media claims, the Jami'at Abu Bakr madrasa is not under Jama'at al-Da'wa control. It was actually a madrasa run by the Ahl-i Hadith movement'.[10] Although the Jama'at al-Da'wa emerged from the Ahl-i Hadith movement, Yahya Mujahid insisted that the two were separate institutions with separate leaders and membership structures. Furthermore, Yahya insisted that both the Karachi madrasas had come under the control of the banned Jama'at al-Da'wa movement only *after* the Malaysian and Indonesian students had registered there and began their studies, which would suggest that they did not know of the Jama'at al-Da'wa's presence at either madrasa prior to their enrolment there.

Yet, this was not the only high-profile arrest involving Southeast Asian students studying in a Pakistani madrasa. Earlier in 2001, the Malaysian government had arrested a number of Malaysian Islamist activists, including Nik Adli Nik Aziz, son of Nik Aziz Nik Mat, the *murshid al-'am* (spiritual leader) of the Pan-Malaysian Islamic party (PAS) on the charge that he was the leader of an underground militant movement known as the Kumpulan Mujahidin Malaysia (KMM, Malaysian Mujahidin Group). It was claimed that

Nik Adli had been radicalised during his studies in Pakistan.[11] He had studied at the Jami'at al-Dirasat al-Islamiyya in Karachi and the Ma'had Salman in Peshawar before travelling on to Afghanistan. During the time of the crackdown in Karachi a number of foreign students were residing in the two madrasas. The Jami'at Abu Bakr madrasa was home to 62 Afghan, 68 Thai, 15 Malaysian, 9 Indonesian, 17 Ugandan and 7 Somalian students – however, it should be noted that Southeast Asian students were dispersed all over Pakistan's madrasas, and there were also Southeast Asian students in India's madrasas. (Nik Adli's younger brother, Nik Abduh, who had studied at Deoband's Dar al-'Ulum in India, however, was not arrested.)

The arrest and deportation of the Malaysian and Indonesian students in Karachi marked a significant step in the breaking down of the centuries-old student exchange network between South and Southeast Asia. Its implications were twofold: To further reinforce the image of the madrasas as 'dens of terrorism'; and to also reinforce the image of foreign students as dangerous individuals who may be up to no good. The aim of this paper is to balance this view by looking at other madrasas in Pakistan with student exchange programmes and to examine how some of the madrasas have opted for a process of modernisation and reform on their own terms to not only offer a better education, but also to help create a transnational network of religiously-conscious students who may later become part of the global Islamist network.

Pakistan's Madrasas: Interface for Transcultural Production of Knowledge or Transit Points for a Global Network of Terror?

> "Pakistan is no longer a safe place for foreign students studying in our madrasas."
> *Mufti Muhammad Jamil of the* Wifaq al-Madaris, *in* Newsline, *October 2003*

As a result of the crackdown on foreign students in the religious schools of Pakistan, a large number of these students have been forced to return to their home countries or have simply relocated to other Islamic educational institutions in India or the Middle East.

Media hype aside, it should be noted that much of what has been said and written about Pakistan's madrasas has come from media personalities or so-called 'anti-terror experts'. Yet few of these media practitioners, technocrats or 'securocrats' have actually conducted any sustained research or fieldwork in the affected region. Practically none of the security personnel or security experts in Southeast Asia have offered any direct evidence, gained from close-proximity fieldwork or direct interviews with the madrasa community itself, to back up any of their claims.

To further complicate matters, there is precious little documentation on the madrasa community in Pakistan itself. It is difficult, if not impossible, as the 2007 ICG report testifies, to get a figure for the total number of madrasas currently operating in Pakistan.[12] According to the Pakistani monthly *Newsline* (October 2003), in the province of Sindh alone there were said to be 1,248 madrasas with 869 located in the bustling and overcrowded provincial capital of Karachi. The Karachi madrasas are said to have more than 200,000 students, of whom some 10,000 are foreigners from all over the world. In the Hyderabad region, there are approximately 260 madrasas with 30,000 students; while the Sukkur region has 115 madrasas with a total of 9,000 students.[13]

An official figure does not exist and a definitive figure cannot be reached because many of these institutions may also serve as mosques, refugee camps, welfare aid centres, *imambargas* (Shia ritual convention halls), Sufi shrines and so on. The Wifaq al-Madaris (Pakistani Central Board of Religious Schools) estimates that 10,000 madrasas are registered while there may be another 10,000-15,000 that operate outside their control. *Newsline* estimated that circa 700,000 students may be enrolled in the Pakistan's madrasas at any one time, with some 15,000 of them being foreign students from around the world.[14]

The madrasa educational system is not a homogenous phenomenon. Since the nineteenth century, the Indian subcontinent has been home to a myriad of Islamic educational initiatives, ranging from the modernist-reformist Aligarh Muslim University that was founded by Syed Ahmad Khan to the Dar al-Ulum Deoband madrasa that was founded by Maulana Muhammad Qasim Nanotawi and Maulana Rashid Ahmad Gangohi. Many well-known Muslim leaders in Malaysia and Indonesia have travelled to the Indian subcontinent to further their Islamic educations there, including Dr. Burhanuddin al-Helmy, who was the third President of the Pan-Malaysian Islamic Party (PAS), who had studied at Aligarh and Tuan Guru Nik Aziz Nik Mat, the spiritual leader of PAS and a Deoband graduate. But thanks to the virtual hegemony of the global 'war on terror' discourse, the word 'madrasa' has now entered the arena of public discourse and has been conflated with all kinds of religious extremism and violence. To balance the negative depiction and stereotyping of the madrasa as the 'bastion of ossified traditionalism' or '*jihadi* factories', we shall now turn to another Pakistani madrasa – the Syed Maudoodi International Islamic Educational Institute (SMII) – as an example of a modern madrasa institution that has played an important role in the formation of Islamist cadres and intellectuals in Pakistan and beyond.

'Knowledge is my Weapon': *The Syed Maudoodi International Islamic Educational Institute as a Modern Madrasa*

> "Back in Malaysia they are all busy watching the television. It is not as bad in Pakistan as the TV reports make it out to be. From what I hear, back in Malaysia, every time there is a television report on the *Taliban* they also show images of madrasas. Now parents are scared to send their children to Pakistan, and our numbers are diminishing. Since 11 September there are very few (Malaysian) students left here." [15]
>
> *Mohammad Amin, Malaysian student leader at the Syed Maudoodi Islamic Institute*

The Syed Maudoodi International Islamic Educational Institute (SMII) is the foremost Islamic educational institute linked to, and patronised by, the Jama'at-i Islami party of Pakistan. While the Jama'at-i Islami is known to have more than 100 madrasas under its control, with 41 of them located along the Afghan-Pakistani border, the SMII remains its most well-known and prestigious institution.[16]

The Jama'at-i Islami was founded in pre-partition India in 1941 by Syed Abul Alaa Maudoodi; following the partition of India and Pakistan it was divided into two, and after the break-up of Pakistan three, mutually independent sister organisations in Pakistan, India and Bangladesh. But it was in Pakistan that the Jama'at-i Islami really developed into a political party with political ambitions, and today it stands as one of the most prominent Islamist parties in the country with close links to other internationally-known Islamist movements such as the Muslim Brotherhood of Egypt. Nasr (1994) has described the Jama'at-i Islami as a modern Islamist party with a somewhat elitist approach towards the building of a strong base of cadres, and which seeks to transform Pakistan into an Islamic state via both the political and educational processes.[17] As the Jama'at's flagship educational institute of international standing, the Syed Maudoodi International Islamic Educational Institute that is named after the founder-leader of the Jama'at was originally founded within the confines of the headquarters of the Jama'at-i Islami known as the Mansoora complex in Lahore.

Mansoora is located on Multan road, which is off Lahore's main roadway, on the outer fringes of the northern part of the city. The complex is a self-contained (though not self-supporting) community set within an enclave of its own. Established in 1974, it signifies how the Jama'at-i Islami would like to see the rest of Pakistan governed. Approximately 500 party members live in 150 houses on some 50 acres of land.[18] Individual members own 25 acres, while the other 25 acres are owned and rented out by the *Majlis-i Ahya al-Islam* (Organisation for the Revival of Islam). The Mansoora complex is linked to the Syed Maudoodi Institute as well as the Markaz Ulum al-Islamiya (Islamic Research Centre), the Mansoora Model Schools and College, and the Jam'iyat al-Muhsinat (Society of Benefactors). Medical facilities are provided for residents and non-residents alike at the 80-bed Mansoorah Hospital. Security is maintained by a private Jama'at-run security force that is armed. The main feature that dominates the landscape is the mosque, whose minaret towers above all the rest. The central inner courtyard is named after a martyr of the Jama'at, Hafeez Muhammad Yusuf, who was killed just outside the gates during a protest against the government of Nawaz Sharif in 1998.

The SMII lies just off Wahdat Road, around the corner from Mansoora, a distance of less than one kilometre away. It can be reached on foot in about 20 minutes. The SMII was established in 1982, while the founder of the Jama'at-i Islami, Syed Abul Alaa Maudoodi, was still alive. Maudoodi was given the King Faisal Award by the government of Saudi Arabia for his service to Islam. With this money, he and the leaders of the Jama'at then established the SMII in 1982.

The first chairman of the SMII was Maulana Khalid Ahmed Hamdi. During that time, the SMII was located within the Mansoora complex on Multan Road itself. The lack of land and the non-availability of a permanent teaching staff meant that the SMII could only offer madrasa education to a small number of students. All of the SMII students in the 1980s were Pakistanis.

There was no foreign recruitment during this time. The SMII was only moved to its present location on Wahdat Road in 1986, when the Jama'at-i Islami managed to purchase more land there. The SMII was officially inaugurated in 1986 and its opening was conducted by the then Amir of the Jama'at-i Islami, Mian Tufayl Muhammad, who was the second Amir of the Jama'at following the death of Maudoodi.

At present, the SMII's Principal is the retired Brigadier Professor Omar Farooq Dogar, who leads the institution's staff of teachers and who is himself a member of the Jama'at. Since the late 1980s, the Jama'at-i Islami has been strengthening its contact and co-operation with other Islamist movements and parties in Asia and the Arab world, and its main contact in Southeast Asia is the Pan-Malaysian Islamic Party (PAS).[19] Since the late 1980s, PAS has been sending students to SMII via the Jama'at-i Islami. Malaysian and ASEAN students who go to SMII have their study and living costs paid for by the Jama'at, which, in turn, received donations and financial support from local Pakistani members, foreign supporters and foreign donor nations like Saudi Arabia.

There has never been an attempt made to properly monitor the number of foreign students in attendance at the SMII or other madrasas in Pakistan in the past. During my earlier visit in 2001, I encountered students from Malaysia, Indonesia, Thailand, Philippines, Vietnam, Cambodia, China, as well as Central Asia. A small number of Chinese Muslim students (mostly Uighur) are also enrolled in the SMII, as young students who are learning Arabic and memorising the Qur'an. Many of these students are orphans who have been sent to Pakistan by international Islamic donor agencies and welfare organisations. During my subsequent research trip in 2003 to Mansoora and SMII the total number of Malaysian students there was estimated at around 40. The total number of ASEAN students was approximately 100, with Malaysians making up the largest group. Other ASEAN students include Indonesians, Southern Thais, Filipinos, Burmese and Chams from Vietnam and Cambodia. It is interesting to note that, according to enrolment records, there have been no students from Singapore.

The number of ASEAN students at the SMII has now been dramatically reduced thanks to increased surveillance and control at immigration posts. Prior to September 2001, a significant number of foreign students came to Pakistan on tourist visas, and simply overstayed their visas until the time came for them to return. With the imposition of new restrictions on Pakistan by the US, and the introduction of new border control methods and public monitoring facilities instituted with US support, the numbers of foreign students entering the country have been dramatically reduced: Since 2002-2003, there have been fewer Malaysian students in Pakistan and there were no Malaysian students at all in attendance during the 2003-2004 academic year. During my last visit to the SMII in February-March 2004, it was discovered that the number of ASEAN students still studying there has been reduced to only seven Malaysian, three Indonesian and 15 Thai students, from what was once one of the biggest foreign student groups at the SMII.[20]

The debate on Madrasa Reform and the formal curriculum of the SMII

Due to its acknowledged linkage to the Jama'at-i Islami and other foreign Islamist parties and movements, the SMII has had to be very selective in its teaching and recruitment methods of local and foreign students. Between 2001 to 2004, there were significant improvements in the quality and content of the teaching provided at the SMII. These changes have brought the SMII curricula up to a par with that of mainstream educational institutes and the SMII has been granted an official certificate of approval and recognition by the Interior Ministry and the Pakistan Madrasa Education Board, which falls under jurisdiction of the Pakistani Ministry of Religious Affairs, Zakat and Ushr.[21] The SMII's teachers, however, insist that these reforms have more to do with their own desire to provide a modern form of Islamic education that is comprehensive and which equips their students with all the tools necessary to live in the modern age. All of the teachers I spoke to expressed their concerns that the reform measures proposed by the Musharraf government were meant to dilute and 'secularise' the Islamic curricula .

Today, the SMII uses the same techniques and borrows from the curricula of Punjab University based in Lahore. In its teaching outline, the directors of the SMII refer to the following goals:

1. To teach Muslim youth from throughout the Muslim world and from O levels to the B.A. (Bachelors of Arts) level;
2. To educate Muslims about the concepts of Islam and their meaning, ostensibly 'free of sectarian differences' and 'without following any particular *mazhab* (school of jurisprudence)';

3. To train students in research work and techniques;
4. To train students to be fluent in English and Arabic, up to the point where they can speak and translate in both languages;
5. To train students to be cadres of the world-wide Islamist movement so that they can be Islamist leaders in their home countries;
6. To train students in good conduct and the moral values of Islam;
7. To train them in communication skills like public speaking, debating and polemics.

Since the instituted changes to the madrasa educational system, the SMII now teaches a combination of strictly religious and non-religious subjects. The non-religious component of the curricula (i.e., sciences and humanities, including non-religious approaches to the study of the Muslim world) comprises 50% of SMII curriculum. It should be noted that while improvements and adaptations continue, the SMII has *always* taught a combination of Islamic and non-religious subjects.

The non-religious subjects taught at SMII include:

- English (up to B.A. level);
- Economics;
- Political science;
- Sociology;
- Psychology;
- Geography of the Muslim world;
- History of the Muslim world;
- Current Affairs and Contemporary Islamist Movements;
- Comparative Religion (covering the Abrahamic religions: Judaism, Christianity and Islam);
- Computer skills.

All of the non-religious subjects are taught in English and some are taught at a rudimentary level. The textbooks for courses like political theory, sociology and psychology are taken from or based on the teaching material used at Punjab University. For the courses on current affairs and contemporary Islamist movements, the works of Syed Abul Alaa Maudoodi, founder of the Jama'at-I Islami, serve as the core texts. Apart from these subjects that are deemed non-religious, the SMII also teaches religious subjects that are offered by many other madrasas in Pakistan. These religious subjects include:

- Qur'anic studies;
- *hadith* studies;
- *fiqh* (Islamic jurisprudence);
- *'aqida* (doctrine);
- *akhlaq* (ethics and morals); and
- the history of Islamic political and social movements.

All of the religious subjects are taught in Arabic and the texts are derived from the material that has been used at the SMII since its formation in 1982. It is important to note that there has been little development or modification of the religious component of the curriculum at SMII since my first visit in 2001. As far as the range of religious subjects taught at the SMII is concerned, the institution's curriculum is based on the *dars-i nizami* curriculum that was set at the Farangi Mahal madrasa of Lucknow during the time of the Moghul Emperor Aurangzeb. Furthermore, the SMII has also taught a number of non-religious subjects which conforms to the Wifaq al-Madaris's goal of introducing scientific subjects to the madrasa curriculum in Pakistan.

Students at the SMII can begin at the primary level as *hafiz* (memorisers of the Qu'ran). During my visits there I encountered students as young as seven years of age doing precisely that, and, upon a successful completion, will earn the title of *hafiz*. The core text for the four-year standard course taught at the Institute is *Fiqh al-sunna* (Jurisprudence according to the *sunna* of the Prophet) by the Egyptian author Sayyid Sabiq.[22] This book was written upon the request of Sabiq's mentor and teacher, Hasan al-Banna, who was the founder of the Muslim Brotherhood (al-Ikhwan al-Muslimun). Unlike earlier *fiqh* works, that commonly restricted their discussion to one of the four major *mazhabs* or schools of Sunni legal thought, the *Fiqh al-sunna* transcends the *mazhab* system by presenting the reader with a series of legal questions and situations, each of which is addressed by recourse to legal opinion of the different Sunni schools. Sabiq then compares and contrasts the similarities and differences between the four major legal schools, giving final authority to the *sunna* of the Prophet as it is laid down in the *hadith*. Sabiq thus managed to do something that had never been done before: he compared the differences between the schools of thought and then granted final authority to the tradition of the Prophet alone. By independently seeking different comparative opinions by consulting the different schools of thought, Sabiq introduced the practice of *ijtihad* (independent reasoning) to solve legal questions, albeit with the *hadith* as the final arbiter.

The bulk of the religious education conducted at the SMII institute is made up of Qur'anic and *hadith* studies, exegesis (*tafsir*), Arabic language training, history (*tarikh*) and jurisprudence (*fiqh*). It is interesting to note that the Urdu language is not taught at the Institute – though students pick it up incidentally in their discussions with each other – while Arabic and English are the main languages used for daily instruction in the religious and non-religious subjects respectively. This in effect means that the foreign students are not easily able to converse with the local Pakistani community, an observation I made during my trips to the SMII and which has also been remarked upon elsewhere in the reports on foreign students in Pakistan.[23] The effect of this policy is that it engenders solidarity and a group-feeling among the foreign students and creates a linguistic community of its own, as we shall show below. By forcing the students (including the Pakistanis) to speak Arabic, the students at Mansoora quickly learn the meaning of Islamic brotherhood and a strong sense of camaraderie develops. (Incidentally, the Jama'at are not unique in their insistence on Arabic as the sole medium of religious instruction and communication. The same approach is adopted by the Jam'iyat-ul-Ulama-i Islam (JUI), the Deobandi ulama association, in their madrasas throughout the country).

Indoctrination, both formal and informal, at the SMII

In the course of fieldwork carried out in Pakistan between February and March 2004, I observed how the SMII was run: There was a clearly-defined chain of command and authority with Prof. Farooq Dogar as its head; its teaching modules and syllabus have been established and are abided by; the teachers are hired on a contractual basis and there are established rules of conduct, academic performance and entry requirements for its students. Furthermore the SMII's use of Arabic and English; the teaching of social sciences and humanities; the provision of computers and computer literacy classes, etc. are all designed to produce students whose religious educational backgrounds are supplemented with a working hands-on knowledge of the modern tools of the age we live in (communications, media, etc.)

However, it should also be noted that the SMII does not disguise the fact that it is fundamentally an *elitist* institution and that its aim is to produce cadres for the Islamist movement both in Pakistan and abroad, according to the Jama'at-i Islami's stated goal of 'spearheading the global Islamic revolution'.[24] From the moment the visitor walks into the compound of the impressive Mansoora complex, he/she is presented with a bold statement of the Jama'at's vision for Pakistan and the Muslim world at large. The private compound of the Mansoora complex further adds a touch of exclusivity and prestige to the SMII, which is already considered an elite madrasa in Pakistan and abroad and has undertaken the goal of producing ideologues and leaders for the Islamist movement world-wide.

Thus it should not come as a surprise that a considerable degree of ideological indoctrination also takes place in the SMII, which takes place under the direction of the institute's directors as well as the ideologues and leaders of the Jama'at-i Islami. Ideological indoctrination occurs in the teaching of non-religious subjects in the SMII curricula via the inculcation of the ideas and values of the Jama'at-i Islami. This is specifically done via the choice of subjects and teaching methods. History and geography are taught from a Muslim standpoint, and history and geography primarily cover the Muslim world. Comparative religion, meanwhile, concentrates on proving the validity of Islam and the supremacy of Islamic ideas, culture and civilisation over other religious and belief systems.

The ideas and values of the Jama'at-i Islami are communicated via the study of Current Affairs and Islamist movements world-wide. The ideas and teachings of Syed Abul Alaa Maudoodi, the founder of the Jama'at, are disseminated and taught to the students, who are expected to understand and reproduce these ideas during their course work and studies. For this purpose, the SMII uses many of Maudoodi's works such as *The Role of Muslim Students in the Reconstruction of the Islamic World* (*Dawr al-Talabah fi Bina Mustaqbal al-'Alam al-Islami*), *The Finality of Prophethood* (*Khatm-i Nabuwwat*, a refutation of the teachings of the Qadiyani Ahmadiyya), *Purdah and the Status of Women in Islam*, etc. as the standard teaching material. Other textual sources come from Maudoodi's collected works and his exegesis of the Qur'an, entitled the *Tanzim al-Qur'an*. It is important to note that while the SMII offers a course in the history of Islamist movements world-wide, this subject is also taught from the exclusive point of view of the Jama'at-i Islami itself. There is little exposure to other Islamist movements and currents of thought that are contrary to that of the Jama'at.

Besides the teaching of religious and non-religious subjects, the SMII also focuses extensively on the enforcement of discipline and moral character; encouraging group activities and developing solidarity and camaraderie among the boys. The inculcation of group identity and fellowship is done via sports and other forms of extra-curricular activity. Under the direction of the retired Brigadier Omar Farooq Dogar, individual discipline and collective group activity are stressed as important elements in the process of creating upright and resourceful Muslims, sports features prominently in the daily lives of the students. In this respect, the Jama'at-i Islami is similar to other Islamist movements such as the Muslim Brotherhood of Egypt and the Partai Keadilan Sejahtera (PKS) of Indonesia. All boys are expected to take part in games as part of their educational experience and sports are compulsory for all fit students. Sports include cricket, football, netball, badminton, volleyball, *kabadi* (a popular South Asian sport) and *sepak takraw* (a Southeast Asian sport introduced and played by students from Malaysia and Indonesia). Chess is also listed among the sports.

The SMII's extra-curricular activities are extensive and the institute's directors are proud of the students' achievements to date: The SMII football team won the all-Punjab tournament in 2003, while the Malaysian and Indonesian boys seem to be the best at badminton. Sporting activities contribute to credit points in the overall student's performance assessment and medals and prizes are awarded for high achievers. The SMII campus is divided into schools like in the English public school system, with different blocks being divided into different School Houses. Apart from sports, all students are also obliged to take part in public speaking, debates and quizzes. Prizes and credit points are also awarded for these activities and contribute to a student's academic credits.

Besides the formal modes of discipline and indoctrination that accompany the educational process at the SMII, students of the institute are also exposed to the activities and ideas promulgated by other movements linked to the Jama'at-i Islami, notably the student wing of the Jama'at, the Jam'iyat-i Talaba-i Islam (JTI), which is known for both its confrontational tactics and violent rhetoric. During the 1970s and 1980s, the JTI was responsible for some of the violence that took place on the campuses of the country, such as Punjab University, where the youth wings of the various Islamist and non-religious parties were engaged in a violent turf war to gain control of the campus.[25] In the course of my fieldwork in Pakistan during February and March of 2004, I also visited the city of Peshawar in the Northwest Frontier Province, where I witnessed a somewhat violent demonstration by members of the JTI who set out to tear down and deface posters and publicity ads featuring images of women not wearing the veil. This demonstration was carried out in the name of 'public decency' as the JTI insisted that such ads were obscene.

The JTI are and have always been active in the SMII, recruiting new members and followers among both local and foreign students there. The JTI also hold regular weekly meetings and rallies in Mansoora's mosque and in the various public speaking halls in and around the Mansoora complex. Most of their public talks are on contentious issues such as the conflict in Kashmir and the necessity of *jihad* against the enemies of Islam. However, it should be added that it is not known whether any of the ASEAN students have been enrolled in the JTI or if any of them have actively participated in their activities.

The Southeast Asian students at the SMII: An overview

> 'Why are they targeting us? All the foreign boys are good boys, they work and study hard, and they haven't done anything illegal.'
>
> *Interview with Brigadier (rtd.) Prof. Omar Farooq Dogar, Principal of SMII, 26 March 2004.*

No comprehensive survey of the foreign students in attendance at the SMII has ever been done. During my visit there in March 2004, I was informed by Professor Farooq Dogar that many of the Chinese boys who were enrolled in the *hafiz* course were orphans who had been rescued from China by various Islamist NGOs and relief organisations. There were no African Muslim students to be seen, although as we have noted above, there were a fair number of Southeast Asian students in attendance – at least until the early 2000s anyway.

Most of the Malaysian students at the SMII were admitted as a result of a complicated and competitive selection process that began in Malaysia. Many of them were graduates of the Madrasa of Kampung Rusila, which is located in the northeastern Malaysian state of Trengganu. This madrasa is run by the President of the Pan-Malaysian Islamic Party (PAS), Tuan Guru Hadi Awang. The most promising graduates of Madrasa Rusila are given the chance to continue their studies abroad at other famous madrasas, the SMII being one of them. The cost of studying at the SMII is borne by the SMII itself, and the Malaysian students are only expected to cover their travel costs to Pakistan. It is not known if this arrangement is unique between the SMII and the Madrasa Rusila, the Jama'at-i Islami and PAS. But what is clear is that most of the Malaysian students at the SMII come from families that support the Pan-Malaysian Islamic party.

Life for the foreign students on campus is competitive and challenging in many ways: For most of the ASEAN students this is their first time away from home and they are expected to cope with living, working and studying on their own in a new environment that is alien to what they were accustomed to. Living under the protection and patronage of the SMII and the Jama'at-i Islami means that foreign students are sheltered from the complex internal conflicts and internecine struggles between the rival Islamist movements in Pakistan. But this sheltered environment has also incurred its price, including a lack of exposure to daily events in the country and the alternative currents of Islamist political thinking in Pakistan and the rest of the world.

Furthermore, it should be noted that the SMII, like many other madrasas in the Muslim world, is an all-male environment where men and boys are not exposed to members of the opposite sex and have very little with the outside world. Contact with females is strictly forbidden, which means that the boys at the SMII have had little chance to interact with Pakistani girls. In the course of my interviews with some of the Malaysian and Indonesian students, several of them noted that this was their first time in a foreign country where contact with the locals was kept to a minimum. Needless to say, their lack of knowledge of Urdu, coupled with the restrictions on their movements outside the SMII and their lack of exposure to women meant that few of them have had any opportunity to form any kind of relationships with Pakistani women. There has not been a single documented case of a Malaysian or Indonesian student marrying a Pakistani woman and settling down in Pakistan.

Inter-personal contacts among the SMII students also contribute to the creation of a common group identity and unity of purpose among the students there. The international profile of the SMII's student body is meant to favour the establishment of lasting relationships between students from various nations. The use of English and Arabic also encourages them to communicate in a neutral language that is not their mother tongue, and their common learning of these two foreign languages means that bonds of commonality and feelings of solidarity are bound to develop. I should point out, however, that on the two occasions when I was invited to speak to the students at both the SMII and Mansoora my lectures were delivered in English (for the benefit of the Jama'at leaders who were also present), and in the course of the discussions that followed it was not clear to what extent my lectures in English were understood by the Southeast Asian students. In the course of my private discussions with the boys from Malaysia, Thailand and Indonesia it was clear that they preferred to talk in Bahasa Malaysia or Bahasa Indonesia rather than English.

Further studies should be done to establish the extent to which SMII graduates maintain their contacts with one another when they return to their mother countries. Though contacts between ASEAN students with their non-ASEAN (African, Arab, European and South Asian) counterparts seem negligible, it was clear that strong bonds of solidarity have developed among the Malaysian, Thai and Indonesian students. During the course of my interviews in 2004, I did not come across a single instance of an ASEAN student who had established long-term contact with students from Africa or the Arab states. This does not mean that these contacts have never occurred, but it would suggest that they are rare in comparison to the contacts established among the ASEAN students themselves.

Compared to the Malaysian students, many of whom came from families who are active supporters of the Pan-Malaysian Islamic Party (PAS), the Thai and Indonesian students seemed to have more varied backgrounds. Many of the Thai-Muslim students came from the southern Thai province of Patani and spoke Malay in the same dialect as their Kelantanese schoolmates and friends. Apart from language, cultural affinity was also evident in the games they preferred to play like *sepak takraw*, a popular sport in many parts of Southeast Asia but particularly in the region between the northern Malaysian peninsula and the southern Thai provinces. The Malaysian and Thai boys often cooked together, sometimes in the company of their Indonesian schools mates. The most common complaint among them was the lack of rice in the daily meals offered by the madrasa's kitchens.

The Thai students we interviewed did not admit to belonging to 'political' families while the Indonesians admitted it readily. What is clear, however, is that, like the Malaysian students, their SMII studies were paid for by the institution and the Jama'at, the only financial burden being their travel costs to and from Pakistan.

Because most of these students seemed to come from poorer families, few of them have had the opportunity to return their homes in Malaysia, Indonesia or Thailand during the holidays. Most of the students I met in 2004 were in the final years of their studies and they often complained of homesickness; a factor that was further aggravated by the diminishing numbers of foreign and especially Southeast Asians students at the SMII. During the few breaks in the academic year, students were taken on trips to sites within Pakistan, again at SMII expense. In the 2003-2004 academic year, the Southeast Asian students were taken on two school outings: One was a weekend tour of Lahore to visit the sites of the old Moghul Empire such as the Red Mosque; and the second was a longer trip to Kashmir to 'see the mountains'.

A common concern among the students I met at SMII was what their fate would be upon their return to their home countries. Although television and newspapers are not allowed in the SMII, students have access to newspapers and magazines outside the madrasa during their daily lunch-breaks. Many of them were aware of the news in their own countries and knew of the arrest of Malaysian and Indonesian students in Karachi in 2003. The arrest of the Malaysian Islamist Nik Adli Nik Aziz earlier in 2001, as we have mentioned above, set the stage for the stigmatisation of Malaysian students studying in Pakistan's madrasas. The SMII was also tainted by its association with another famous graduate, Ja'far Umar Thalib, who studied briefly at the SMII in 1987 before going on to Afghanistan to join the Afghan *jihad* against the Soviets. Ja'far Umar Thalib later returned to Indonesia to establish the militant group Laskar Jihad, that was actively involved in the Muslim-Christian conflict in the Moluccas.[26]

The Southeast Asian students at the SMII were not only cognisant of political developments in Pakistan, but in their home countries as well. Thanks to the availability of computers and the Internet, students could keep in contact with their families and friends back home. Mobile phones were also permitted for foreign students and all of the students I met had mobile phones with Pakistani phone numbers. Despite the institution's relative isolation, they were not cut off from the outside world, and despite restrictions on popular media and entertainment, the foreign students were very well informed about developments around the world. This became obvious in the discussions I had with the Malaysian students who were fully updated on the developments within the Malaysian Islamic Party (PAS) and the internal politics of PAS as well as Malaysia.

Notwithstanding the media attention paid to Pakistan's *madrasas*, most of the SMII's teachers and students wished to be left alone to pursue their studies uninterrupted. The SMII's Principal, Prof. Farooq Dogar, added that 'the Malaysian, Thai and Indonesian students are among the best students we have from overseas. They work hard, speak Arabic fluently, and always finish among the top of their classes. So why is the media and government targeting us all the time?'[27] The Principal noted that the Southeast Asian students were the best in Arabic, Qu'ran and *Hadith*, and excelled in sports like badminton. Moreover, he also noted that the Malaysians, Thais and Indonesians were the most disciplined and rule-abiding students of the SMII and no serious cases of unruly behaviour had ever been reported among them.[28]

The major complication faced by the Malaysian students in particular is the obvious association between the SMII and its parent party, the Jama'at-i Islami. Due to the fact that most of the Malaysian students I met at the SMII were from families that supported the Pan-Malaysian Islamic Party (PAS) and had graduated from the Madrasa Rusila which has always been a PAS madrasa and the headquarters for Tuan Guru Hadi Awang, the party's leader, the political connection between the two parties and their respective educational institutions are rather clear for all to see.

It should, however, be stressed that the SMII also stands a world apart from the Jami'at Abu Bakr and Jami'at al-Dirasat al-Islamiyya madrasas in Karachi where the arrest of ASEAN students took place in September 2003. The SMII has instead managed to secure the recognition of the Pakistani government and Pakistani universities such as Punjab University, by expanding its curriculum to include non-religious subjects. Furthermore, the SMII has always been transparent about its teaching activities and its enrolment procedures, which is one of the reasons why research on and in this institution could be carried out with relative ease compared to the more opaque madrasas in places like Karachi. Some of the SMII's activities, such as the annual awards-presentation day, which I attended, are carried out in the public domain such as public parks or the main courtyard of the

Jama'at's Mansoora complex, where outsiders – including the media and political figures – are invited to attend as guests of honour. Furthermore, the SMII's enrolment process has always been transparent and regulated. Meanwhile, Malaysian students are admitted to the school upon formal completion of their basic studies in madrasas in Malaysia.

While the SMII cannot be seen as representative of all madrasas, neither can or should the Jami'at Abu Bakr and Jami'at al-Dirasat al-Islamiyya madrasas be. The fact is that the thousands of madrasas that dot Pakistan's landscape today cannot be reduced to a single stereotype.

One thing, however, is certain: Life at the SMII is characterised less by violence and militancy than the daily humdrum of laborious study. The SMII is far from the clichéd stereotype of the madrasa as a '*jihadi* factory' or centre for the training of militants, and stands out as a modern madrasa – albeit with a religious curriculum every bit as conservative as other institutions of its ilk – with modern facilities and high expectations imposed on its students. The students themselves do not conform to the stereotype of the semi-literate fanatic currently beloved by the popular media, which posits the grossly exaggerated picture of madrasa students being radical conservatives *in toto*.[29] If anything, the SMII and its student body is more like a conservative English public boys' school or a Catholic missionary school, producing students who are expected to one day rise to leadership positions in their respective societies. And English public schools, we should remember, are not noted for their open-mindedness either.

The Uncertain Fate of ASEAN Students in the Madrasas of Pakistan in the Age of the 'War on Terror'

"Since 11 September, the Americans have realised their mistake and suddenly they are calling these groups terrorists. Everyone is shifting the blame on the other: Washington wants to blame Pakistan, so Islamabad is now putting pressure on the *jihadi* groups. But these groups have become entrenched and they have gone mainstream... They are not willing to close their doors and so when the pressure is on they sacrifice a few of their followers as scapegoats. The only innocent ones in this whole scenario are the foreign students themselves, who are young, naïve, innocent and vulnerable. They are the real victims."
Interview with Ahmed Rashid, Lahore, March 2004

While there are indeed madrasas in Pakistan that are linked to radical militant groups where violent hate-discourse is being taught and hatred of non-Muslims is being preached,[30] I have also tried to balance this view with an account of another type of madrasa where religious education leads not to the creation of violent militants but rather professional, educated members of an Islamist movement. The findings offered here are far from exhaustive. Nor do I claim that the SMII model disproves the allegation that *some* madrasas may be engaged in radical activities such as the training of future *jihadi* militants. It is, however, possible to end with the following conclusions:

Firstly, the case of the Jami‘at Abu Bakr and Jami‘at al-Dirasat al-Islamiyya madrasas in Karachi show that some madrasas are public institutions that are both rooted in society and open to the shifts and changes occurring in the social milieu around them. The case of the two madrasas where the Malaysian and Indonesian students were arrested in 2003 demonstrate that the control of the madrasas can and often does pass from one group to another, particularly in the case of newer, lesser-known madrasas that rely on public financial contributions for their support. This dispels the notion that madrasas are static institutions, permanently under the control of particular groups/movements. Thus we must admit that there are other madrasas that have been run by various other types of groups at different times, such as the Jami‘at Abu Bakr and Jami‘at al-Dirasat al-Islamiyya madrasas in Karachi.

The bogeyman of the itinerant madrasa student continues to tarnish the image of foreign students in the madrasas of Pakistan, however. In the wake of the London bombings of 2005, in August of that same year, President Musharraf announced that henceforth student visas would no longer be extended to foreign students who come to study in the country's madrasas. This, in effect, has brought to an end the long-established global network of itinerant scholars and students who have travelled across Asia over the centuries. And as we have already noted earlier, by the early 2000s, the enrolment of foreign students in institutions like the SMII has come to a standstill.

Secondly, it has to be noted that while some madrasas *do* engage in forms of violent sectarian politics, there are also elite madrasas that are more inclined towards political education. The SMII – like its patron organisation the Jama‘at-i Islami – does not disguise its pretensions to elite and exclusive status. The Jama'at has always presented itself as a selective organisation that is solely preoccupied with the task of creating Islamist cadres, leaders and intellectuals to lead the global Islamist movement and the institutions that have come under its patronage reflect this elitist outlook and its values. Another grander project, the university city of Qurtuba that was modelled on the Oxbridge system in the UK and is to be built near the Pakistani capital of Islamabad, reflects this same concern for exclusivity and prestige.

It is this desire to remain at the forefront of Islamic education that partly accounts for the Jama'at-i Islami's willingness to address the issues and concerns of the times, and this is reflected in the broader teaching curriculum at the SMII and the use of modern technologies such as computers and computer training. The SMII is cognisant of the growing concern about the viability of madrasa degrees and awards, and has consistently upgraded and improved its teaching methods to ensure that its graduates receive a well-rounded education and that they are taught social sciences like economics, political theory and history as well. The SMII is also aware of the stigma and misconceptions that have surrounded the madrasa system over the years, and thus the focus on sports and extra-curricular activities is obviously designed to counter the negative stereotype of madrasas as institutions of rote learning that offers students few opportunities for social activities.

None of this should distract us from the fact that the SMII, like its other madrasa counterparts, is primarily a religious school with an undisguised political-ideological agenda. The social activities, extra-curricular events, extensive promotion of sports on its campus, etc. are all intended to create a class of disciplined Islamist cadres who are united in their singular vision as future leaders of the Islamist movement and the Muslim *umma* by extension. Though on a superficial basis the trappings of the SMII may resemble that of an English public boys school (complete with its cricket field, sports events, public speaking contests and trophy room brimming with cups and medals) the net result is the creation of a body of students who are actively encouraged to internalise the ideology of the Jama'at-i Islami and to exhibit these values in their future careers.

From a Foucauldian perspective, the regime of education and discipline that characterises the SMII is thoroughly modern, and aimed at the production of cadres shaped by a singular political and religious vision of the world. It is a form of modern education aimed at ensuring the unity of dispersion of the Jama'at's ideas, which can only be achieved after the individual characteristics of each student are controlled, regimented and subsumed beneath the collective identity of the greater student body and the institution itself. Those who fear the Jama'at-i Islami and what it stands for may balk at the thought of the SMII being the engine of reproduction for the party, but they cannot deny the thoroughly *modern* mode of ideological reproduction that takes place in its most prestigious educational institution.

Notes

1 The author would like to thank Ejaz Haider, Najam Sethi, Ahmed Rashid, Prof. Khalid Masud and Prof. Muhammad Waseem. Much of the material and information that went into writing this paper was collected during the months of February and March 2004, while the writer was engaged in fieldwork in Pakistan that was supported by the Zentrum Moderner Orient (ZMO), Berlin. The author would also like to thank Ayub Munir and Abdul Ghaffar Aziz of the Jama'at-i Islami, Prof. Omar Farooq Dogar of the Syed Maudoodi International Educational Institute (SMII) and the students of this institute for their co-operation and consent to be interviewed in the course of the author's research work.

2 See, for instance: Ahmed Rashid, *Taliban: Islam, Oil and the New Great Game in Central Asia*. London: I.B. Tauris, 2000; Zahid Hussain, *Frontline Pakistan: The Struggle with Militant Islam*. New York: Columbia University Press, 2007.

3 For more on the role of the Pakistani madrasas in the training of the Mujahidin and later the Taliban, see: Peter W. Singer, 'Pakistan's Madrassahs: Ensuring a System of Education Not Jihad', Washington, DC: Brookings Institute Policy Paper no. 14, November 2001; International Crisis Group (ICG), 'Pakistan: Madrasas, Extremism and the Military', Asia Report no. 36, Brussels, 29 July 2002; International Crisis Group, 'Pakistan: Karachi's Madrasas and Violent Extremism', Asia Report no. 130, Brussels, 29 March 2007; and the books by Ahmed Rashid and Zahid Hussain mentioned in the preceding note.

4 Singer, 'Pakistan's Madrassahs', pp. 2-3.

5 See the Pakistani monthly *Newsline*, October 2003. The reform measures were also discussed in the ICG report 'Pakistan: Madrasas, Extremism and the Military', pp. 19-27.

6 Thus far, Pakistani authorities have taken steps to stop the funding of Pakistani madrasas by Arab NGOs and funding bodies such as the Lajnat al-Da'wa al-Islamiyya based in Kuwait; the Qatar Charity Association based in Qatar and the Islamic Relief Agency based in Saudi Arabia (International Crisis Group, 'Pakistan: Madrasas, Extremism and the Military', p. 22).

7 International Crisis Group, 'Pakistan: Karachi's Madrasas and Violent Extremism'. The authors of the report noted that many of the proposed reforms have not been effective and that in places such as Karachi the madrasas are still run by radical religious groups beyond state control (pp. 2-3).

8 International Crisis Group, 'Pakistan: Madrasas, Extremism and the Military', pp. 22-23.

9 The Lashkar-i Tayyiba was founded in 1993 and its origins go back to the Ahl-i Hadith movement that began in India in the early 19th century. In 1994, a separate Islamic college was set up by the Ahl-i Hadith movement in Muridke, where the Lashkar was based, and attracted students from all over the world. By 2001, the organisation had built circa 130 schools, with 15,000 students and more than 800 teachers. After the Afghan conflict came to an end in 1992, the

Lashkar redirected its military efforts against India and focused their attention on Kashmir in particular.

10 Interview with Yahya Mujahid, spokesman for the Jama'at al-Da'wa, arranged by the offices of the *Pakistan Daily Times*, March 2004.

11 See: Farish A. Noor, *Islam Embedded: The Historical Development of the Pan-Malaysian Islamic Party (PAS), 1951-2003*. Kuala Lumpur: Malaysian Sociological Research Institute (MSRI), 2004, pp. 663-664, n. 120.

12 International Crisis Group, 'Pakistan: Karachi's madrasas', p. 5.

13 The Pakistani monthly *Newsline*, October 2003.

14 Ibid.

15 Original in Kelantanese Malay: 'Kok Malaysia demo ashik menonton TV. Tapi apa yang digambarkan di kaca TV di Malaysia itu tak seburuk dengan apa yang berlaku di Pakistan. Apa yang ambo dengar di Malaysia ialah tiap-tiap kali ada gambor Taliban, dikaitkan pulo dengan gambor madrasah. Jadi ibubapa pun takut hantar anak demo ke Pakistan, hingga sekarang tidak ada lagi pelajar dari sana. Jadi selepas 11 September mereka tak datang ke sini lagi.' Interview with Muhammad Amin, Leader of the Malaysian Students at the Syed Maudoodi International Islamic Educational Institute (SMII), Lahore, March 2004.

16 International Crisis Group, 'Pakistan: Madrasas, Extremism and the Military', p. 12.

17 For the most comprehensive account of the history of the Jama'at-i Islami, see: Seyyed Vali Reza Nasr, *The Vanguard of the Islamic Revolution: The Jama'at-i Islami of Pakistan*. London: I.B.Tauris, 1994.

18 Measured in local terms, the total area amounts to 400 *kanals* of land, with 1 *kanal* being the equivalent of 0.125 acres.

19 For an account of the historical development of PAS and its links to the Jama'at-i Islami, see Noor, *Islam Embedded*.

20 Of the seven Malaysian students at the SMII then, three were from Kelantan, two from Kedah, one from Selangor and one from Johor. Ten of the Thai students were from the southern Thai province of Patani (neighbouring Kelantan, in Northeastern Malaysia) and the rest were from Bangkok.

21 See: Pakistan Madrasah Education Board (Ministry of Religious Affairs, Zakat and Ushr, Pakistan) document F. no. 7(4) 2003/PMEB, re: Equivalence Sanad/Certificate. According to this document 'the Equivalence Committee of the Pakistan Madrasah Education Board at its meeting on 26 June 2003 has decided to recognise the B.A. degree entitled '*Shahadat ul Aalia*' awarded by the Syed Maudoodi Islamic Educational Institute, Wahdat Road, Lahore, as equivalent to a B.A. degree' (signed Dr. Zaitoon Begum, Acting Secretary, Pakistan Madrasah Education Board).

22 Sayyid Sabiq was a follower and student of Hassan al-Banna. Though a conservative at heart, Sabiq was an activist in his actions. He took part in the Palestinian struggle along with the *Mujahidin* in the 1940s and later spent

much of his life travelling and teaching in various universities and colleges in the Muslim world. He travelled to the Soviet Union to report on the conditions faced by Muslims under Communism and was an advocate of Muslim political rights. In his later years, he taught at both Al-Azhar University in Cairo and Umm Al-Qura University in Mecca. His *Fiqh al-sunna* has emerged as a standard text in reformist, non-*mazhab* Islamic teaching institutions all over the Sunni Muslim world.

23 International Crisis Group, 'Pakistan: Madrasas, Extremism and the Military'. In the case of Arab students in Pakistan, for instance, this report notes that 'The Arabs differ from the Pakistanis and Afghanis in many respects. They do not mingle well with the locals, not least due to the language barrier' (p. 23).

24 Nasr, *Vanguard of the Islamic Revolution*.

25 International Crisis Group, 'Pakistan: Madrasas, Extremism and the Military', pp. 11-12.

26 See: Noorhaidi Hasan, *Laskar Jihad: Islam, Militancy and the Quest for Identity in Post New-Order Indonesia*. Ithaca, NY: Cornell Southeast Asia Program, 2006; John T. Sidel, *Riots, Pogroms, Jihad: Religious Violence in Indonesia*. Ithaca, NY and London: Cornell University Press, 2006.

27 See: Farish A. Noor, *Quran and Cricket: Touring the Madrasas of Pakistan*. Kuala Lumpur: Off the Edge, 2004.

28 Ibid.

29 Peter W. Singer, for instance, makes a rather sweeping statement when he writes of the madrasa students as 'graduates who have no acquaintance with needed subjects like economics, science or computing' and 'students (who are) unable to multiply, find their nation on the map, and are ignorant of basic events in human history such as the moon landing' (Singer, 'Pakistan's Madrassahs', pp. 5, 3).

30 The 2007 ICG report 'Pakistan: Karachi's Madrasas and Violent Extremism' lists several of the madrasas of Karachi that are openly linked to the more radical and sectarian trends of the Deobandi school, as well as militant outfits such as the Lashkar-i Tayyiba (pp. 4-9).

6 Muslim Education in China

Chinese *Madrasas* and Linkages to Islamic Schools Abroad

Jackie Armijo

Introduction

This chapter looks at two aspects of Muslim life in China: the development of Chinese Muslim schools, with a special emphasis on girls' schools; and the linkages and networks of Chinese Muslim students who have travelled abroad to further their Islamic educations. The data presented here was collected over a period of five years of fieldwork carried out in southwest China among Muslims while researching the early history of Islam in this region. The aim is to show how the development of Muslim educational institutions in China and linkages to Muslim educational centres abroad has helped to give the Muslims of China a sense of identity in the context of a Muslim-minority country where Muslims have come under considerable pressure to assimilate to the dominant culture of the non-Muslim Han Chinese.

Muslim identity politics in China is linked to the development of the Muslim educational sector in many ways. Across the province of Yunnan, for instance, there is currently a tremendous revival in Islamic education. Virtually every mosque offers Qur'anic classes for children, known as *kuttab* in the Muslim Middle East, as well classes for older people who were denied the chance to study when they were younger. In Yunnan alone, at least 12 full-time independent Islamic colleges or *madrasas* have been established over the past ten years. These schools offer a full curriculum including classes on the Qur'an, *hadith*, *tafsir*, *fiqh*, Islamic history, Arabic grammar, and the Chinese language. At present, most of the textbooks used for the traditional Islamic sciences are from Saudi Arabia, the Arabic language textbooks from the Foreign Language Institute in Beijing, the Islamic history texts are translated from the Arabic, and the texts on the history of Islam in China are currently being published. Many of the graduates from these colleges go on to teach in smaller schools and establish new schools throughout the country (except for Xinjiang).[1] Recently, growing numbers have chosen to continue their Islamic studies overseas.

Another visible feature of Muslim life in China today is the growing networks of students and teachers as they pursue their studies and travel to different regions to offer their services as teachers. I met Muslims from all over China who had travelled to the far southwest to continue their studies and teach, and Muslims from the southwest who had travelled to distant regions for the same purpose. One of the many important consequences of these networks is that even in the most remote and impoverished Muslim villages one encounters people who are well informed about local, provincial, national, and even international affairs.

Muslims in China: A Historical Overview

With a Muslim population of 20 million, China today has a larger Muslim population than most of the Arab countries of the Middle East. The Muslims of China are divided into 10 different ethnic groups, nine of which are concentrated in the northwest, while the tenth and largest group, known as the Hui, is spread throughout the entire country. In addition to being the largest group, the Hui are unique in that they are also the most assimilated. Descendants of Arab and Persian immigrants who came to China during the earliest period of Islam and in larger numbers during the Mongol Yuan dynasty (1274-1368), over the centuries the Hui adapted to whichever region or community they settled in. In the majority of cases, that has meant adapting to the dominant Han Chinese culture: speaking Chinese, wearing traditional-style Chinese clothing, and practising all manner of social customs except those that contravened Islamic practices. However, if the Hui community settled in a minority region of China, such as Tibet, or among the Dai, Bai, or Yi of southwest China, or among the Mongols of northeastern China, they assimilated into those communities and cultures.

According to the 2000 China national census, the Hui population of China is approximately 9.2 million while the Uighur number 8.6 million. The other Muslim populations are: Kazak 1.3 million; Dongxiang 400,000; Kirghiz 171,000; Salar 90,000; Tajik 41,000; Uzbek 14,000; Baonan 13,000; and Tatar 5,000. The concentration of China's Muslims across the country has also changed due to demographic and political factors. In Xinjiang, the Uighurs, who at the time of the establishment of the People's Republic of China (1949) made up 90% of the population of the province, now make up less than 45%, with Han Chinese migrants from other parts of China making up the remainder. The overwhelming majority of Muslims are Sunni and they follow the Hanafi school of law.

There have been Muslims in China since shortly after the advent of Islam. During the period of the Mongol Yuan dynasty (1274-1368), hundreds of thousands of Muslims from Central and Western Asia were both forcibly moved to China or migrated there to assist the Mongols in the establishment of an imperial dynasty. However, during the Ming dynasty (1366-1644), Muslims together with other foreigners who had settled in China were subject to new laws requiring them to dress like the Chinese, adopt Chinese surnames, speak Chinese, and essentially become Chinese. In the mid-seventeenth century, the Qing dynasty (1644-1911) was established, marking the beginning of a period of unparalleled growth and expansion. Travel restrictions were lifted, and China's Muslims were once again allowed to make the pilgrimage to Mecca and study in the major centres of learning in the Islamic world. However, this period also witnessed unparalleled violence against China's Muslims. The collapse of the Qing dynasty in 1911 saw a period of political unrest and social chaos that eventually led to the creation of two powerful political groups: the Nationalists of the Guomindang (known as the KMT) and the Chinese Communist Party (CCP).

During the ensuing years of civil war between the CCP and KMT, both parties sought the support of the nation's largest minority groups, including the Muslims of China. Many of the Hui chose to support the Communists, and in the initial period of the People's Republic of China, the Hui and other Muslim minority peoples enjoyed a period of religious freedom.[2] However, during subsequent political campaigns, culminating in the Cultural

Revolution (1966-1976), the Muslims of China found their religion outlawed, their religious leaders persecuted, imprisoned and even killed, and their mosques defiled, if not destroyed.

In the years immediately following the Cultural Revolution, the Muslims of China lost no time in rebuilding their devastated communities. Their first priority was to rebuild their damaged mosques, thereby allowing communities to create a space in which they could once again pray together, but also so that the mosques could reassert their role as centres of Islamic learning.

As Muslim communities sought ways to revive their traditions of Islamic learning, the state also began to establish Islamic colleges around the country.[3] These schools were administered by the Islamic Association of China, which is part of the state's central Religious Affairs Bureau. Spread out in different regions of China, these schools were fully funded and controlled by the state: teacher appointments, student selection, curriculum, course materials, etc., were all decided by government officials. In addition to offering the traditional courses in Arabic and the Islamic sciences, these schools also required that students take courses in patriotism.[4] Although these schools play an important role in educating Chinese Muslims, as they fall under the control of the state, they are not held in universal high regard. Some Muslims are wary of any institution that falls under such direct government control. As independent Islamic schools have been set up throughout China, the importance of the role of the state schools has diminished. However, given that they are able to offer scholarships to students in need, and continue to attract excellent teachers and students, they continue to play an important role.

Meanwhile, in addition to the independent Islamic schools that have been set up, communities have also organised Islamic pre-school programmes, after-school and summer school programmes for primary and secondary students, day-time programmes for the elderly, as well as evening and weekend programmes for working adults eager to gain knowledge and a deeper understanding of Islam. These efforts represent some of the most important ways in which Muslim communities are reviving their religious identity.

Early Islamic Education in Southwest China

Islamic education traditions in different parts of China evolved in different ways, reflecting local histories. The case of Yunnan is one of the more important and influential. First settled by Muslims from Central and Western Asia in the Yuan period (1274-1368), Yunnan has for centuries attracted Muslim students from throughout the country and region. As early as the Ming period (1368-1644), Muslim scholars from Yunnan were invited to teach in other parts of China, and scholars from outside were invited to teach in Yunnan, thus creating networks linking the Muslims of Yunnan with Muslims in the rest of China and Southeast Asia. Throughout this period, Islamic education took place in mosques and was known as *jingtang jiaoyu* (education in the Hall of the Classics).

While Islamic education in other parts of China has always concentrated on the study of Arabic, Persian and Islam, in Yunnan the tradition has been one of *Zhong-Ah bing shou* (side-by-side Chinese and Arabic education). In the past, this consisted of intensive instruction in classical Chinese, whereas today it includes the study of modern Chinese with Chinese history and culture, together with Arabic language and Islamic Studies.

A Tale of Two Schools

In southwest China, two of the most interesting schools happen to be an independent girls school in an extremely impoverished region of northeastern Yunnan province and an independent Islamic college outside Dali in western Yunnan.

In 1998, I visited the girls school established in 1985 outside Zhaotong and was believed to be the first girls school in southwest China. Although it was still quite a modest affair, it had a compound with several small buildings attached to it. The head teacher spoke of the ongoing difficulties of teaching in such an impoverished community and the growing numbers of students who were not even literate in Chinese. As a result, more class time was being allocated for Chinese language classes. The school did not charge fees and it provided boarding facilities for students who lived far away. Funding for the school came from the local communities, but also from regular contributions in wealthier Muslim communities in other parts of the province.

In 2001, I learned more about the history of the school when Salima, the young woman who had founded it in 1985, returned to Yunnan after studying in Pakistan for 10 years. She had grown up in a religious family and had decided when she was young that she wanted to study Islam. In 1981, at the age of 16, she left home to enrol in the mosque school in Shadian, a two-day bus ride away. There were 100 students in the school, 20 of whom were female. She completed her studies two years later, and though she had wanted to travel to northwest China to continue her studies at a women's Islamic school in Gansu, she instead returned to Zhaotong and began teaching at a small mosque school. During this time she learned of the growing need for a school for girls in the region, which is one of the poorest in all of China. She developed a plan for a girls school and presented it at a meeting of representatives from ten mosques. Although a few were opposed to the idea, she was able to convince most of them of the need for a girls school and the mosques found a small two-room school house which opened its doors in 1985.

Although nine years of education is required for all children in China, and is supposed to be free, central government support of education has decreased dramatically over the past twenty years. As a result, local schools have had to institute various fees in order to cover educational expenses. In impoverished areas like Zhaotong the result has been that parents end up sending only one child to school and preference is invariably for boys.

The Zhaotong girls school quickly attracted some 80 students, overwhelming the tiny school house, with students sitting on the floor and standing during classes. Most of the students were 16 or 17 years old, although some were in their twenties. In addition to the basics of Islam, Salima also taught basic language skills as many of the students had not completed their public school studies. She also quickly realised that there was a tremendous need for health and hygiene classes as many students were woefully ignorant of the most basic understanding of these issues. After an exhausting first year of teaching by herself, she enlisted the help of four of the more advanced students from her first class to teach additional classes the second year. In the third year, 19 students graduated, and four of them were immediately recruited by mosques to start girls schools. That summer she decided to travel around China to visit other Muslim communities that had established girls' schools, as well as share her experiences of setting up a school in one of the poorest regions in China. She returned for a fourth year (1987-89), but then decided at the end of the school year that it was time to further her own studies. She was able to find financial assistance that allowed her to study Arabic at a well-known foreign language university in Beijing, and while there she learned of a delegation from a Pakistani Islamic college that was recruiting students. Salima passed the exam, and, after much difficulty obtaining a passport, left for Pakistan on 1 January 1990. She was the first female Chinese student to study at the International Islamic University in Islamabad, Pakistan. At that time, there were already about 30 male Chinese students studying in Islamabad and a similar number in Karachi. She ended up staying in Pakistan for ten years, completing a bachelor's and master's degree. Her thesis compared Islam to Confucianism. Upon returning to Kunming in 2000, she and her husband decided to teach at the government-run Kunming Islamic College, which was founded in 1987.

The outstanding feature of the Zhaotong girls' school is its emphasis on girls' education, as well as giving Muslim women the right to teach Islam. However, it is not a unique example of a Muslim girls' school: of the twelve major independent Islamic schools I visited in Yunnan, four are for women only, and most of the other schools, while predominantly male, do allow women to attend.

The female graduates of these schools have taken a very active role in promoting the study of Islam among other Muslims. Most become teachers themselves upon graduation, either working in Islamic schools that are already established or helping to establish new schools in poor and remote regions. Several recent graduates have also established Islamic pre-schools and after-schools for Muslim children.

The women with whom I spoke to in these schools expressed the importance of Islam in their lives, their commitment to Islamic education, and their determination to educate others. I met several young women who, upon graduation from Islamic colleges, had volunteered to teach in remote impoverished villages, isolated from friends and family. I also met several exceptionally strong-willed women who had established independent Islamic girls' schools. One spoke of the fundamental role women played in society and the importance of the role of education; for as she put it, 'Educate a man, educate an individual; educate a woman, educate a nation.' She explained the various ways in which a young woman's education could have a positive influence not only on her own life, but also later on the lives and social well-being of her children and grandchildren, and eventually the entire community.

In addition to playing an important role in the revival of Islamic education throughout China, in certain regions of the country, Chinese Muslim women also have the unique opportunity to serve as imams in women's mosques. In the Hui communities of the Central Plain provinces of Henan, Shandong, Anhui, Hebei, and Shaanxi, there is a long history of women's mosques and women have traditionally served as imams there.[5] According to one prominent expert of Islamic law, Khaled Abou El Fadl, the tradition of female imams in China is a remnant of a practice that existed in the earliest days of Islam but was gradually undermined by traditional Arab patriarchal values together with those of other cultures encountered as Islam spread.[6] As growing numbers of Muslims travel to different regions of China to further their Islamic studies, more and more women are being exposed to these traditions found in Central China. Research by French scholar Elisabeth Allès shows that the practice of women's mosques has recently spread to other regions of China, as students who have studied in places where they are common return to their home communities.[7] And as female imams from this region travel to other areas to further their own studies, they introduce the concept of women serving as imams (within women's mosques). According to a Chinese press report, there are now women imams in Ningxia, which shares with Gansu the reputation of being home to the most conservative Muslims in China, especially when it comes to issues related to gender.[8]

Apart from the girls' school at Zhaotong, another highly respected Islamic school in Yunnan is the Wuliqiao Islamic College. It was established in 1991 by several retired Hui public school teachers. Although at that time there was already the government Islamic college in Kunming, a group of Hui educators decided there would be several advantages to having an independent private school. For one, every aspect of the teaching and administration of the state Islamic college was controlled by government officials: from faculty and student selection to curriculum and textbooks. Many were surprised that the government approved the independent school at that time. However, the fact that the founding faculty consisted of retired Hui school teachers who had dozens of years experience teaching in the public school system no doubt helped their cause.

The school opened in the autumn of 1991, with an enrolment of 60 students (50 male, 10 female) from throughout China. That the school was able to attract students from such a range of places in its first year is evidence of the complex networks of communication linking Muslim communities across China. The school made two decisions early on that proved somewhat controversial. The first was that all classes would be co-educational. Having taught in public schools for years, the faculty were confident that the students would benefit from mixed classes, and that they would not be distracted from their studies. The second proved somewhat more controversial. Early on, a decision had been made to focus on Chinese language studies in addition to Islamic studies. Although in other regions of China, especially the northwest, Muslim communities have been reluctant to study Chinese language and civilisation as they are seen as somehow undermining Islamic traditions and values, in Yunnan they have always practised a form of Islamic education known as *Zhong-Ah bing shou*, as was mentioned above. However, when the headmaster chose a Han Chinese rather than a Hui as the Chinese language studies teacher, the decision was not universally accepted.[9] However, headmaster Na Wenbo stood by his decision, and the Chinese language teacher proved to be an outstanding teacher who respected the school's values.

Another interesting characteristic of the school was its decision very early on to recruit young people who it believed would not only be outstanding teachers upon graduation, but also people who were committed to teaching fellow Muslims about Islam. Many of the graduates I interviewed expressed their commitment to spreading Islam to Muslim communities who had not been exposed to Islam.

The commitment of Na Wenbo and his colleagues to the establishment of the school and selection of outstanding faculty and students did not end there. An equal amount of consideration went into the placement of graduates upon completion of their studies. The headmaster himself travelled to Muslim communities throughout southwest China, identifying areas with the greatest need for Islamic studies teachers, noting the atmosphere and local conditions as well as the needs of the community. He then carefully matched these criteria with the abilities, interests, and personalities of the graduating students who wanted to teach. Students would then be assigned two-year teaching posts. However, before the graduation ceremony and before the final decision was made on assignments, students were expected to spend one month teaching in their assigned communities. At the end of this month they were asked if they were committed to spending two years teaching in that community, and only then was the final assignment made. This method proved extremely effective, and the graduates with whom I spoke were satisfied with their assignments.

The Complementarity of Secular and Religious Education

Apart from Chinese Muslims studying in *madrasas* in places like Yunnan, there are also a considerable number of Chinese Muslim students who study in the local universities and who form Muslim student associations to promote and encourage the study and practice of Islam. There are four universities in the Northern district of the city of Kunming. Muslim students at each of these institutions have joined together to organise classes as well as other activities. The Muslim students often come together to provide for needs that are specific to their religious community. A few years ago they set an initiative to make fasting during Ramadan more convenient for Muslim students. Although all large college and university campuses have Muslim cafeterias their hours of operation do not necessarily correspond with fasting times during Ramadan, and it becomes difficult, if not impossible, to get a proper early morning meal. The students located an apartment nearby, rented it, and set up a kitchen. This same group also organised a series of events including a public celebration of Eid al-Fitr that helped educate non-Muslim students about Islam.

Students who were active in this group expressed their commitment to both religious and secular education. For example, one student who had majored in English literature was planning to return home and teach English in a local Islamic college, whereas another English literature major chose to teach English at a public university with a large Muslim student population. A student with a degree in information science from a highly respected science and technology college was planning to leave for Malaysia upon graduation to join the Islamic studies programme at the International Islamic University of Malaysia. When asked why, he replied, 'My years of studying science and technology have made it clear to me that science and technology are not what the people of China need, they need an understanding of God.'[10]

Expanding Networks

In the course of my research it became clear that many Muslim villagers I met were informed not only about the situation of Muslims living in other parts of China, but also about the latest issues concerning Muslim communities throughout the world. This phenomenon was, in part, a result of the large number of Chinese Muslims travelling to different regions of China to study, but also because of the increasing numbers of students who chose to study overseas. In addition to the growing number of Islamic schools in China, the past few years have also seen a dramatic increase in the number of Chinese Muslim students studying overseas. Although no official records are kept, it is estimated that a total of between 500 and 1,000 Chinese Muslims are presently studying in Egypt, Syria, Pakistan, Iran, Saudi Arabia, Libya, the Sudan, Turkey, Malaysia, and Indonesia. Al-Azhar has the largest number, with approximately 300 students. Most of the students are sponsored by their families and communities, and receive small stipends from the Islamic university they end up attending. The students I interviewed at Al-Azhar in 1999 spoke of how difficult it was to adapt to the lifestyle of such a crowded and overwhelming city, but they were also very cognisant of the importance of Al-Azhar and its role in Islamic history. Some, however, expressed their disillusionment with the realities of living in a modern Muslim society. For the Muslims of China, who have always been a small minority in a sea of Han Chinese and who have survived for centuries isolated from the rest of the Islamic world, often experiencing intense periods of persecution, the idealistic expectations they have of Islamic countries can serve as the source of disappointment.

Initial Impacts: Scarves, Mosque Architectural Styles and Gender Roles

The most visible influence of the growing numbers of Muslims studying overseas is the rapidly increasing number of women wearing headscarves.

Although there had been a tradition of headscarves among different Muslim communities, they had almost all died out and only elderly women were seen wearing scarves. Now, however, many more women wear scarves, not in one of the traditional Chinese styles, but a modified version of the style worn in Malaysia.[11]

The potential impact of overseas studies is also evident in the rapidly changing attitude towards the traditional mosque architecture of China. Strongly influenced by the design of Buddhist temples, mosques are often almost indistinguishable from temples from the outside, but upon closer examination one sees how they reflect an extraordinary blend of two very distinct traditions that have evolved over time. Some mosques, like the Huajue in Xi'an, have been preserved and are well maintained by their congregations. But other mosques dating back to the Ming and Qing periods have been torn down and replaced with what can best be described as 'neo-pseudo-Middle Eastern' style mosques. When questioned about their decision to tear down ancient mosques, most community members point to the need to build mosques that are more 'authentic' and less Chinese. That a loose interpretation of an architectural style from the Middle East should be held up as more 'authentic' is just one of the ways in which unconscious assumptions about the purity of Islam in the heartland is perpetuated. Although the destruction of these traditional mosques is a devastating loss to the cultural history of Muslims in China, both old and young Muslims assured me of the benefits of their wonderful newly constructed concrete and tile 'modern' mosques. In at least some instances, students returning from their studies overseas played a role in the community's decision to tear down and rebuild a mosque. Thus far, most of the mosques that have been torn down are in towns and villages with the necessary funds to carry out such a major project. Older mosques in more remote and impoverished regions are much more likely to escape this fate.

In Kunming, the most obvious example of this phenomenon can be seen at the South City Mosque. This new mosque, which replaced an older one, is a white tile two-story building with no evidence of traditional Chinese Muslim architectural details. Even the calligraphy on the front is not traditional Chinese Islamic calligraphy but instead one of the standard forms common in the Middle East. What makes the building that much more awkward is the fact that it has been squeezed behind a large commercial building that was built for income generation to help pay back the loan used to build the mosque. The commercial building is eight stories high and has several large domes on top, as a token reminder of its Islamic identity. The original mosque dated back to the Ming period but had been seriously damaged during the Cultural Revolution. The young imam who helped design the new mosque had studied overseas.

However, at least in Kunming, during a period in the past few years when several mosque communities had to decide on the style during the rebuilding a centuries' old mosque in disrepair, the community chose to rebuild it in a style that was as close to the original as possible. The most important example is that of the Shunchengjie mosque. Originally built during the Ming dynasty, the mosque has been repaired several times over the centuries. However, in 2004, the community chose to rebuild it in the original style, using as many traditional building methods and building materials as possible. As this was the largest and most prominent Muslim community in the region, they were able to shoulder the huge expense of this method of construction. The newly completed mosque looks almost identical to the original. Ironically, during the time the mosque was being rebuilt, the city of Kunming was in the process of tearing down the large Muslim neighbourhood that surrounded the mosque. While it was once surrounded by dozens of Muslim restaurants, food stalls, and speciality stores, not to mention thousands of Muslim homes, the mosque is now located next to a high-rise apartment building and a huge construction site.

Another of the outcomes of this newly emerging network of Chinese Muslim students studying in Muslim countries abroad and returning to China is the change in gender relations and the role of Muslim women in the community. Despite the active role played by many Muslim women in different parts of China, there is anecdotal evidence that male students studying in schools in Saudi Arabia may, upon their return, have a negative impact on the role of Chinese Muslim women in their communities. During one of my interviews, I met a young woman living in a city in northwestern China who had helped establish a large Islamic women's school based in a mosque and attended by over 500 students ranging in age from 5 to 80. She had also organised a wide range of development projects to assist Muslims living in the most impoverished villages in the region. She mentioned that she started an advanced Islamic studies degree in Malaysia, but had to drop out because her husband, who was already studying in Saudi Arabia when she received her scholarship, was not pleased with her going overseas to study. When he learned that classes at the Islamic University in Malaysia were coeducational he demanded her return to China.

I asked several dozen Chinese Muslims, both in China and overseas, how they would interpret this story. The majority felt it would only affect students who were enrolled in the Wahhabi-controlled schools in Saudi Arabia who might adopt this type of attitude toward women (generally referred to as *zhongnan, qingnu*, 'valuing men and belittling women'). Students from Yunnan maintained that although they believed Muslims from northwestern China (who seemed to be fairly patriarchal to begin with, as a result of the influence of more traditional Han Chinese attitudes regarding women in that region of China) might be susceptible to this type of indoctrination regarding gender roles, they were quite adamant that Muslims from Yunnan would not allow themselves to be manipulated in this way.

In addition to the Saudi Arabian government's sponsorship of dozens of students in Saudi Arabia every year, individual Saudis also travel to China on a fairly regular basis to conduct intensive Islamic studies workshops. In Yunnan, for example, for the past several years, Saudi religious scholars have organised one-week workshops in towns relatively distant from the provincial capital of Kunming. To the best of my knowledge, there have never been any workshops in the capital, nor are these classes sanctioned by the authorities. In fact, there is a law that forbids the Hui from inviting foreign Muslims to teach Arabic and religious studies. Although the Dai (a minority related to the Thai) in southern Yunnan, who are Buddhist, have been able to sponsor monks from Thailand to teach classes in their recently revived temples, no foreign Muslims have been allowed to teach in any of the newly established Islamic schools.

Perhaps as a response to these workshops, a group of moderate Muslims in Yunnan, including several who have studied overseas, have started more elaborate workshops that sometimes last as long as two weeks. Young Muslims, mostly college students, are invited to take part in workshops that are led by a series of religious teachers, with expertise in various subjects. The college students are allowed to bring non-Muslim friends who have expressed an interest in Islam, and in the past, some of them have ended up converting during the workshop. During the workshop retreat in the summer of 2002, there was a clear and obvious government surveillance presence at the event and efforts to discover the identities of those who attended were obvious.

Naqshbandi Influence

The Chinese government has for decades been sending students to study Arabic in many of the major public universities in the Middle East, to prepare them for careers as future government officials and diplomats. More recently, independent students have also been allowed to study abroad, and Chinese Muslims have been studying in various centres of Islamic learning. One of the first independent groups of students to be allowed to study overseas was sent to Abu Nur Islamic College in Damascus, the school established and led by the late Naqshbandi shaykh and chief mufti of Syria, Shaykh Ahmad Kaftaru, which draws large numbers of students from all over Asia.[12] This group consisted of ten men, who are now among the most respected young Muslim scholars of their generation. At present, there are over 100 Hui studying at the Abu Nur.[13] They study a general *madrasa* curriculum, with a special focus on *fiqh*, but because of Kaftaru's position as a leading Naqshbandiyya shaykh, most of them also become acquainted with the practices of this Sufi order. They do not, however, actively teach Sufism upon their return to China. One of the imams commented that what he learned about Naqshbandi Sufi philosophy he kept close to his heart for himself. And what he learned of more traditional Islamic philosophy he shared with his students. He avoided getting into any arguments about religious interpretations, and found himself frequently remembering the advice of Shaykh Kaftaru to 'be a doctor, not a lawyer.'

This imam was also one of the very few who was able to find a place within the traditional Muslim religious leadership almost immediately upon his return. In most of the areas that I visited, I learned that the young men were usually not welcomed into the religious leadership upon their return from their studies overseas. Thus, I was surprised that within months of his return, he had been appointed a teacher at one of the major mosques in Kunming. He said that the elders had told him that they were making an exception for him, and although they were very impressed with him, they were going to keep an eye on him. Religious leaders told me that although they had confidence in the religious knowledge of those who had studied overseas, they were not confident of their knowledge of the Muslim communities in China. Thus, they were not considered qualified to hold leadership positions within these communities, and thus they first had to prove their understanding of Islam as practised in China.

There are, in fact, only a handful of relatively young imams who have studied overseas and who are also held in high regard by Muslims in China. This small group, which travelled abroad in 1990, were the first in post-1949 China to pursue their studies overseas. They were among the few who had managed to attain a high level of Islamic learning even though all forms of Islamic education had been forbidden for decades. As a result, they were already well versed in traditional Chinese Islamic thought by the time they first went overseas, and upon their return this group was consequently accorded special status.

I wish to conclude this chapter with some observations on contemporary trends that are still very fragmentary but, in the absence of more systematic studies, may nonetheless be of interest. They concern how surprisingly appreciative China's Sunni Muslims are about the education they received in Shi'i Iran, and the negative impact of the 'war on terror' on the widening of their transnational horizons.

Iranian Influence

In 1999, I met a young Hui woman in Damascus who had completed her studies in Iran and had thereafter returned to China. She said that, of the original group of students, that she was the only who had decided to stay in Iran for several years after her graduation. She spoke very highly of the education she had received there, the living conditions, and the way her and her fellow students had been treated. The program there is fully funded by the Iranian government, and thus the living situations are quite comfortable. She noted that many from this first group of students strongly encouraged their siblings, friends, and even their parents to come study there. She said that by the end of her six-year stay in Iran, the number of Hui students had increased dramatically.[14]

The only other similar graduate I interviewed had returned to Yunnan a couple of years after graduation and was teaching Persian at the provincial university. He had been asked by educational leaders in Yunnan and Iran to organise a series of student exchanges between the two universities. He spoke very candidly about his Islamic education and his treatment by fellow Muslims upon his return. He felt strongly that those who had studied in Iran had received an outstanding Islamic education that was perhaps superior to the education that others received. In addition to studying the major works of Shi'a thought, they also studied the four traditional Sunni Islamic legal schools and the major works of Sunni religious thought. Moreover, in addition to learning Persian, students were also expected to learn Arabic. As for his own religious views, he identified himself as Muslim, without distinguishing between Sunni or Shi'a. He also spoke of encountering suspicion from fellow Muslims in China when they learned he had received his training in Iran. This surprised me because most Chinese Muslims I know are unaware of any major sectarian differences among Muslims, and it is highly likely that this new prejudice against Shi'ism has to do with the views of those returning from their studies at the Islamic University of Medina in Saudi Arabia.

The Impact of the 'War on Terror' on Religious Education in China and the Case of Xinjiang

China, like numerous other nations, was quick to jump on the 'war on terror' bandwagon in order to justify and expand domestic policies that further restricted the lives of its Muslim minorities. Throughout China, Muslims found it more difficult to obtain the passports that were necessary to travel overseas to continue their studies, or to take part in the *hajj*. Moreover, new government programmes were established for imams to insure that they had a 'correct' understanding of the role of the state vis-à-vis religion, and the role of religion vis-à-vis society. These policies to restrict and control the practice and study of Islam in China have in the post-9/11 era been taken to near draconian levels in Xinjiang.

For reasons both unclear and unjustified, the Chinese government has chosen to conflate the practice of Islam with Uighur separatist movements in Xinjiang. As China's largest province and the one with the most important natural resources in terms of oil and natural gas, it has been the focus of major national development projects. However, according to the Uighurs, those who have benefited the most from these development projects have been the immigrant Han Chinese and not the local population. Beginning in the 1980s, there were a series of violent clashes between Uighur nationalist groups and government forces. Most of these clashes were in response to government efforts to control religious practice, but were also due to the growing resentment of the unequal distribution of benefits from both the development projects and the extraction of local natural resources. However, there have been no serious incidents since 1998, even though there are now literally thousands of violent demonstrations every year throughout the rest of China.

The most important difference between Xinjiang and the rest of China is the absence of any form of independent Islamic education. There are no pre-school, after-school, or summer programmes of study for children and no classes for adults or the elderly. There is only one officially sanctioned Islamic training school for imams in the provincial capital, and it is closely monitored by government officials. The government appears especially concerned that children are not exposed to religious teaching or practices. Children are forbidden from attending Islamic studies classes even after regular school hours. There are signs posted on mosques stating that no one under 18 years of age may enter. According to a recent Human Rights Watch study, parents reported that they were afraid to even speak to their own children about religion.[15] When some parents decided to send their children abroad or to other parts of China to receive an Islamic education, that was effectively prohibited as well, since it would now require government permission, which would most certainly not be granted and would expose families to being classified as 'separatists'.

Moreover, China's increased restrictions on the lives of Muslims in the aftermath of 9/11, together with tighter surveillance of all religious activity throughout the country, has heightened Chinese Muslims' feelings of identity and solidarity with Muslims around the world. Moreover, the government has also made it significantly more difficult for Hui students to study abroad by frequently refusing to issue passports to Chinese Muslims. As religion (in the case of Muslims) is conflated with ethnicity in China, and all official identification documents list a person's ethnicity, it is quite easy for the government to control the issuance of passports to Muslims.

As a result of these measures, the number of students able to study overseas has levelled off, and it will probably decline as well. However, according to some of those who have completed their studies and returned to teach in established Islamic colleges in China, there is, in fact, no longer that much need for Chinese Muslims to study overseas as there are now enough teachers with sufficient training in China that it has become more attractive for students to just continue their advanced Islamic education in China.

Conclusion

The tradition of the 'search for knowledge' has played a primary role in the history of Muslim society world-wide, and China is no exception. I have tried to show how the quest for Muslim education in China has been linked to the struggle for a distinct Muslim identity, and at the same time, has also opened up alternative avenues for Muslim women in particular as well as itinerant students who have travelled abroad. The search for knowledge has been facilitated by both more efficient means of travel as well as the establishment of international centres of Islamic learning that seek to educate Muslims from around the world. My own research has concentrated on the recent re-emergence of traditional Islamic educational projects in China, and the growing role of students travelling overseas to complete their training. It is through examining their experiences of living amongst other Muslims with their different societies and communities (although their experiences are actually fairly similar as well) that I seek to represent ways in which identities are shaped and reshaped, and the potential impact of these changes on their communities upon their return home. The Muslim emphasis on education, both secular and religious, is not a surprise. As other minority groups who have survived the vicissitudes of state persecution over time, they have learned that the only thing that cannot be taken away from them is their education.

Notes

1 The situation in Xinjiang, in northwestern China, is so different from the rest of China that it will be dealt with separately. For a variety of historical, geographic and political reasons, the state has always maintained a much stricter level of control over all aspects of Muslims' lives there.

2 For a comprehensive overview of Islamic education efforts in China in this period, see Leïla Chérif-Chebbi, "Brothers and Comrades: Muslim Fundamentalists and Communists Allied for the Transmission of Islamic Knowledge in China," in: Stéphane Dudoignon (ed.) *Devout Societies vs. Impious States? Transmitting Islamic Learning in Russia, Central Asia and China, through the Twentieth Century*, Berlin: Klaus Schwarz Verlag, 2004, pp. 61-90.

3 The first of these schools was established in Beijing, in 1955; later, government madrasas were set up in Xi'an, Shenyang, Xining, Lanzhou, Yinchuan, Urumqi, Zhengzhou, and Kunming.

4 A common slogan seen in many mosques and government Islamic schools is '*ai guo; ai jiao*' or 'love your country; love your religion;' the point is that you should remember that your country comes first.

5 For a comprehensive overview of the role of women's mosques in China, see Maria Jaschok and Shui Jingjun, *The History of Women's Mosques in Chinese Islam: A Mosque of their Own*, Richmond, Surrey: Curzon Press, 2000.

6 Professor Abou El Fadl also goes on to express the hope that 'perhaps, from the margins of Islam, the great tradition of women jurists might be rekindled.' Lousia Lim, 'Chinese Muslims Forge Isolated Path', BBC News, 15 September 2004.

7 Elisabeth Allès, 'Chinese Muslim Women: From Autonomy to Dependence', in: Stéphane Dudoignon (ed.) *Devout Societies vs. Impious States?*, pp. 91-103.

8 'First Generation of Female Imams Emerges in Western China', Xinhua News Service, 24 August 2003.

9 Many Hui in the community felt strongly that only Muslim teachers should be allowed to teach in the Islamic college. Perhaps some felt that because so much had already been taken away from the Muslims by the government, they should be allowed one institution that was entirely their own. Also, since Muslims have suffered through long periods of persecution over the centuries in China, as well as more systematic racism and discrimination in more recent times, some of the Hui were reluctant to trust a Han teacher to respect their values and traditions.

10 Although one might interpret this statement as a plan to proselytise among non-Muslims, in fact, I found no Muslims who were actively seeking to convert others. What I did hear was stories of young people who had been raised as Han Chinese, only to find out by accident that they were in fact Hui or part Hui. Because of government persecution over time, many Muslims simply abandoned their faith. Several teachers who taught evening Islamic and Arabic classes told me about students coming to their classes to learn more about a

faith they had only just discovered they had some connection with. There were also other cases of young people with no connection to Islam who suddenly became interested, but cases like these were much less common.

11 This style of headscarf is especially popular in the southwestern part of China. One explanation provided by a local imam from Kunming was that when large groups of Muslims from Yunnan began going on *hajj*, many travelled via Thailand and while there they were provided with headscarves from Malaysia. Upon their return to Yunnan after their *hajj* they simply started wearing their newly acquired headscarves, and these ultimately became popular.

12 Shaykh Ahmad Kaftaru, who died in 2004, was for many years a pivotal figure in president Hafez Asad's policy towards Islam. See Annabelle Böttcher, *Syrische Religionspolitik unter Asad*, Freiburg im Breisgau: Arnold-Bergstraesser-Institut, 1998, and Leif Stenberg, 'Naqshbandiyya in Damascus: strategies to establish and strengthen the order in a changing society', in: E. Özdalga (ed.), *Naqshbandis in Western and Central Asia*, Istanbul: Swedish Research Institute in Istanbul, 1999, pp. 101-116.

13 I visited Damascus in 1999 and 2004 and interviewed several of the Hui studying at the Abu Nur Institute at that time. Moreover, I have also interviewed imams who had returned to teach in China after completing their studies at Abu Nur.

14 See also the observations on foreign students in Qom by Mariam Abou Zahab in this volume (editors' note).

15 Human Rights Watch, 'Devastating Blows: Religious Repression of Uighurs in Xinjiang', *Human Rights Watch*, vol. 17, no. 2 (2005).

7 From Pondok to Parliament

The Role Played by the Religious Schools of Malaysia in the Development of the Pan-Malaysian Islamic Party (PAS)

Farish A. Noor

The *pondok* or madrasa has for centuries been a core institution of Malay society, as the centre where the indigenous elite were trained. The *pondok* school takes its name from the dormitories in which the students (predominantly male) live, often simple huts clustered around the home of the teacher or teachers. In the past, states like Kelantan, Trengganu and Patani (which today is a province in Southern Thailand) were known for their *pondoks* that produced successive generations of Muslim scholars who in turn contributed to the Malay world of letters. *Pondok* schools also played an important role in the development of early Muslim political consciousness and were instrumental in the early stages of the anti-colonial struggle in Malaya, much in the same way that madrasas did in many other colonised Muslim societies in the nineteenth and twentieth centuries.

This chapter looks at the phenomenon of the *pondok* schools of Malaysia with reference to the Pan-Malaysian Islamic Party (PAS), that was formed in 1951.[1] It will consider the development of both the Malaysian Islamic party and the network of *pondok* schools from which it emerged, and which it later nurtured and developed as its political power base. It has to be noted from the outset that the *pondok* schools of Malaysia have been the subject of intense debate since the beginning of the twentieth century, and that until today there are those in Malaysia – notably the leaders of the ruling United Malays National Organisation (UMNO) party – who regard these institutions with some degree of suspicion, branding them as schools that teach a conservative interpretation of Islam. The Malaysian government has been particularly critical of those *pondoks* and madrasas that are known to have links with PAS, and the criticism of PAS's madrasas and *pondoks* as training centres for potential radical militants and as institutions that preach hate against the state has remained a constant leitmotif in Malaysian politics until the present day while the country is under the leadership of Mahathir's successor, Prime Minister Abdullah Ahmad Badawi.[2]

Since the events of 11 September 2001, many Muslim countries have redoubled their efforts to control, monitor and even shut down these institutions that have been cast in a negative light, as bastions of conservative Muslim thinking and training centres for violent Islamist groups. Reports by various intelligence agencies and research centres have pointed to the alleged links between these religious schools and militant Muslim organisations, and the South Asian Analysis Group's (SAAG) report in 2004, for instance, went as far as claiming that at least 167 Malaysian students were enrolled in the militant-linked madrasas of Pakistan in 2002.[3] Consequently, since 2001, the Malaysian government, both under Prime Minister Mahathir Mohamad (1981-2003) and Abdullah Ahmad Badawi (since 2003), has tried, time and again, to control the development and proliferation of these institutions.[4]

Notwithstanding the media hype over the network of *pondok* schools in the country, the Malaysian government's apparent concern over the *pondoks* and madrasas of Malaysia has more to do with the fact that many of them were formed by and supported by the Malaysian Islamic party today. In the Malaysian context, therefore, discussion of the alleged 'threat' represented by some *pondok* schools is a loaded one, where the real issue is not the existence of religious schools (that have existed for centuries, in any case) but rather the political challenge posed by PAS. This party was formed in 1951 and has evolved into an Islamist party that explicitly calls for the transformation of Malaysia into an Islamic state and which enjoys considerable support among Malay Muslims. However, PAS has since the late 1990s also adapted itself to the realities of multiracial, multicultural and multi-confessional Malaysia where circa 40% of the population are non-Malays and non-Muslims. Over the past two years (2005-7), PAS has instituted a series of important changes in its outlook and self-representation, reaching out to non-Malays and non-Muslims across the country as well as the new breed of urban-based Malay-Muslim professionals.

Notwithstanding the new urbane look of the Malaysian Islamic party, one should not overlook the fact that the party's emergence on the local political scene was largely aided and abetted by its links to more traditional Muslim educational institutions, the *sekolah pondok* and madrasa system in Malaysia. In order to get a better insight into PAS's historical links to the latter, we begin with a cursory overview of the development of the Muslim educational system in British Malaya from the late nineteenth century onwards, which sets the scene for the subsequent emergence of PAS.

The Madrasa and Political Mobilisation in Colonial Malaya

The mode of British colonial rule in Malaysia (then known as British Malaya) was complex, combining various forms of direct and indirect rule.[5] While attempting to create a colonial import-substitution economy based on a pluralistic economic system, the British colonial administrators were also cognisant of the fact that the society they had colonised was deeply influenced by Islam, which had arrived in the Malay archipelago and taken root in the thirteenth century.[6]

Fearful of the prospect of causing a nation-wide Malay-Muslim backlash against Western colonial rule, the British – while seeking to expand their economic interests and exploitative practices – tried to maintain some semblance of traditional Malay-Muslim identity as well. Hence, there was little interference on their part in the areas of Malay religion and customs, and few attempts were made to control the development of the *pondoks* and madrasas of the Malay kingdoms across the Peninsula.

That the Malay-Muslim community had to be pacified and possibly coopted into the colonial economic-political apparatus was evident then for it was during the period of the late-nineteenth century that opposition to the British and their mode of colonial rule first emerged among the Malay and Peranakan (Indian-Malay or Arab-Malay) Muslims of Malaya.[7] Caught between a secular mode of governance in the Straits Settlements and the conservative mode of feudal governance in the Malay kingdoms, many of the younger generation of Malay and Peranakan Muslims began to organise themselves into political associations and movements that sought the betterment of Muslims via education. This loosely assembled group was called the '*Kaum Muda*' (Younger Generation) who were opposed to the conservative ways of the '*Kaum Tua*' (Older Generation).

During this period the *pondoks* and madrasas of Malaya were among the first centres of political mobilisation for the new generation of the *Kaum Muda* reformers, mostly Malay and Peranakan Muslims who had grown up in the British colonial settlements of Penang, Malacca and Singapore. Unlike the native subjects of the Malay kingdoms, these urban-based Malay and Peranakan Muslims did not live under the influence of courtly protocol or customary *adat* law. They were shaped by the values and lifestyle of a modern, cosmopolitan mercantile community where economic and political success was the key to survival.

Among the influential figures of the *Kaum Muda* were Sumatra-born Sheikh Mohamad Tahir Jalaluddin al-Azhari and Malacca-born Syed Sheikh Ahmad al-Hadi. Both were regarded as representatives of the *Kaum Muda* generation and they were very attracted to the reformist and modernist ideas then in vogue in the Muslim world. Interestingly, it was during the British colonial era that the *pondoks* and madrasas of the Kaum Muda reformers became more closely connected to other institutions of learning abroad, thanks to the development of modern transport and communications. The spread of modernist ideas was facilitated by the advances in modern transport and communications made possible by the opening of the Suez Canal. Like other reformers of the Malay world, men like Sheikh Mohamad Tahir had travelled to the Arab lands and studied in Mecca and at al-Azhar University in Cairo. With other prominent Malay-Muslim reformers such as Sheikh Muhammad Basyuni Imran of Sambas, these reform-minded Islamists studied with Malay-Muslim ulama and scholars already based in Mecca. It was also during their travels to the Arab countries that the *Kaum Muda* reformers were first exposed to the ideas of the Egyptian scholar and disciple of Muhammad Abduh, Rashid Rida.[8]

As a result of colonial intervention and the introduction of new transport, communication and media technologies, the form and content of teaching that took place in the more modern *pondoks* and madrasas of the *Kaum Muda* reformers began to change as well. Some of these reformers founded new religious schools of their own: Syed Sheikh al-Hadi was the most active in setting up reform-minded modern madrasas in the Crown

Colonies of Penang, Malacca and Singapore. Among the numerous madrasas he set up were Madrasah al-Iqbal al Islamiyyah in Singapore, Madrasah al-Hadi in Malacca and Madrasah al-Mashoor al-Islamiyyah in Penang. Many of these madrasas also served as printing presses and publication houses where new books and journals promoting the cause of reform were published and disseminated. On 23 July 1906, Sheikh Mohamad Tahir established his own reformist magazine *al-Imam* (the Leader), modelled on the reformist publication *al-Manar* (the Beacon) published in Cairo by Rashid Rida. Among the more popular and influential of the journals then were *al-Imam* (published by Sheikh Mohamad Tahir and Syed Sheikh al-Hadi in Singapore), *Al-Ikhwan* (published by Syed Sheikh al-Hadi in Penang), *Seruan Azhar* (published by Kesatuan Jamiah al-Khairiah (Malay Students Association of al-Azhar, Cairo), *Pilihan Timur* (published by Indonesian students at al-Azhar, Cairo) and the teachers' magazine, *Majalah Guru*. Through the educational efforts of Sheikh Mohamad Tahir and Syed Sheikh al-Hadi, the modern reformist ideas of the new generation of Muslim thinkers like Muhammad Abduh and Rashid Rida were introduced to the Malay-Muslims of the peninsula.

Thus, in the early twentieth century, the colony of British Malaya was witnessing the development of a relatively new phenomenon: modernist-inspired *pondoks* and madrasas that set themselves up as alternative sources of Islamic teaching that were more inclined towards political mobilisation and developing the political clout of the Muslims of Malaya. By the 1930s, a period characterised by global economic depression and a period when the economic strength of the Malay-Muslim rubber planters and rice farmers was at its weakest these modern *pondoks* and madrasas took the plunge and entered the world of politics. Foremost in the emerging nationalist struggle in Malaya was a madrasa in the village of Gunung Semanggul in Northern Perak, called Ma'ahad al-Ehya as-Sharif, that had come under the control of the Kaum Muda.[9] The Ma'ahad al-Ehya was set up on 15 April 1934. It was built on the foundations of an older educational establishment, the Sekolah Pondok al-Rahmaniah, founded by Ustaz Haji Abdul Rahman bin Mahmud, who had studied in Mecca as well as al-Azhar University, Cairo.

The earlier Sekolah Pondok al-Rahmaniah was a more traditional and conservative institution that offered basic religious education and classes in Arabic and Islamic history. But as Nabir Abdullah (1976) notes, by the early 1930s, the teachers of Sekolah al-Rahmaniah felt that it was time to expand its services and facilities. They were readers of reformist magazines and journals like *Seruan Azhar, Pilihan Timur* and *al-Ikhwan* published by reformist thinkers like Syed Sheikh al-Hadi in Penang. They decided to turn their school into a modern madrasa. Discipline at the revamped reformist madrasa was strict. Ustaz Sheikh Abu Bakar al-Bakir, the first principal, required that all students wear white uniforms and the black felt *songkok* (not the white skull cap, *kepiah*, associated with traditional *pondok* schools), shave their heads and work six days a week. The school taught a combination of religious and worldly subjects, including art, music, world literature as well as Indian, Chinese and European culture and civilisation. This madrasa was one of the few religious educational establishments with a special department for female students. (There were not as many girls as boys; by the late 1930s, the female enrolment was circa 30.)

Many students of the madrasa became activists who later joined *Sahabat Pena* (Pen Pals Association) as well as other Malay associations in the 1930s. On 1 January 1940, the madrasa formed a company of its own, the Persatuan al-Ehya as-Sharif Berhad, with 1,786 members. Within a year the company's membership rose to 3,258. In the 1940s, the school became the focal point of many Malay-Muslim political activities from which the country's first Islamic party, *Hizbul Muslimin*, was to emerge.[10]

In March 1947, the Malay National Party of Malaya (Partai Kebangsaan Melayu Malaya, PKMM) under the leadership of Dr. Burhanuddin al-Helmy sponsored the first Pan-Malayan Islamic conference at the Ma'ahad al-Ehya as-Sharif. The madrasa was then run by Ustaz Sheikh Abu Bakar al-Bakir, who was also one of the PKMM's founders. The conference set out to address the economic problems faced by the Malay-Muslims. It was meant to bring together the more politically active and progressive Islamic movements and thinkers in the country. As a result of this conference, the *Majlis Agama Tertinggi* (Supreme Religious Council, MATA) of Malaya was created. At the second MATA conference on 17 March 1948, the *Partai Orang Muslimin Malaya (Hizbul Muslimin)* was formed, after the second Pan-Malayan Islamic conference declared that MATA should be reorganised as an Islamic political party. The *Hizbul Muslimin* put forward the claim that Malaya should be independent and that the country should be governed according to Islamic law.[11]

However, the *Hizbul Muslimin* was not destined to last long. The British colonial authorities who had returned to Malaya after the Second World War were already engaged in a low-level conflict with the Malayan Communist Party (MCP) and were also wary of the *Hizbul Muslimin*, fearing that its links with the left-wing Malay nationalists and the Islamic movements of Indonesia might make it a powerful force in Malay political circles. In a report entitled 'Effect of Action by Government in Malaya to Counteract Malayan Communist Party Plans', issued in August 1948, the Malayan Security Service claimed that the MCP had 'made a further approach to the Malays under the religious cloak of the Supreme Islamic Council and later the pseudo-political party *Hasbul Muslimin* (sic).'[12]

By late 1948, growing political tension in the colony led to the declaration of a state of emergency and the banning of the Malayan Communist Party. Also on the list of banned parties was the *Hizbul Muslimin*, whose leaders were arrested. Their detention spelled the end of the Ma'ahad al-Ehya as-Sharif madrasa, because colonial authorities had also arrested and detained the party's president Ustaz Abu Bakar and six other leaders. These arrests adversely affected the educational and political activities at the Ma'ahad. Nearly half the students left as there were no longer enough teachers. It was from this period onwards that the *pondoks* and madrasas of Malaya came under the scrutiny of the Malayan security services, for it was now clear that these religious schools could also play a role in the politics of the colony.

Despite the arrests of the teachers at the Ma'ahad al-Ehya as-Sharif, the madrasas and *pondoks* of Malaya continued to flourish throughout the late 1940s and 1950s. In summing up the early history of these institutions in Malaya, it can be said that as a result of the colonial encounter a new type of modernist, politically-inclined *pondok* system had developed in Malaya, running parallel to their more traditional and conservative counterparts. The links of the Ma'ahad al-Ehya as-Sharif to the country's first Islamic party demonstrated that *pondoks* and madrasas were not solely educational institutions and that they could also play a role in the political lives of Muslims. It was therefore not surprising that the development of the country's second (and longest-lasting) Islamic party PAS took place in the bosom of the country's *pondok* and madrasa network as well.

The Founding of PAS and its Links to the Pondok and Madrasa Network of Malaysia

The nucleus of the Pan-Malaysian Islamic Party actually lay in the Bureau of Religious Affairs of the ethno-nationalist Malay party, the United Malays National Organisation (UMNO) that was founded in 1946 by a coalition of nationalist Malay organisations at the peak of the struggle against British colonial rule.[13] At that time, UMNO's bureau of religious affairs was dominated by Malay-Muslim imams and teachers of *pondok* and madrasa schools, and many of their concerns (such as the need to develop Islamic education in Malaya) reflected their own professional interests in keeping the *pondok* system alive in the country. But deep-rooted ideological differences between the *ulama* and political elite of UMNO eventually led to the split between the two factions and the emergence of PAS on 24 November 1951.

PAS's close links to the world of Muslim education was evident in the name of the organisation itself. When it was formed in 1951, PAS was then called the *Persatuan Alim Ulama Sa-Malaya* (Organisation of Muslim Scholars of Malaya) and it was led by Haji Fuad Hassan, who was the head of the UMNO party's bureau of religious affairs. The party's first official headquarters was based at the Madrasah al-Masriyyah at Bukit Mertajam in Penang, an old establishment that had been founded by Sheikh Salleh Masri in 1906, and which happened to be the madrasa where Fuad Hassan himself had studied. At the second PAS General Assembly, held in 1952 at another madrasa in Bukit Mertajam, Penang – the Madrasah Da'irat al-Ma'arif al-Wathaniah that was founded by Sheikh Ahmad Badawi (father of the current Prime Minister of Malaysia, Abdullah Ahmad Badawi) – the party established its youth wing known as the *Dewan Pemuda PAS*. Later the party's youth wing would open its own offices at a third madrasa, the Madrasah Khairiyyah at Pokok Sena in Kedah. During PAS's early years, many of its leaders and members happened to be religious teachers, imams and *lebais* at the madrasas, *pondoks* and mosques of the northern Malay states, and it was no accident that PAS's opponents referred to the party as one of the three P's: *Padi, Pondok, PAS* (rice fields, *pondoks*, and PAS).

From its earliest days, PAS's leaders were keen to develop their contacts and links to Malaysia's *pondok* and madrasa network. In the period 1956-1969, Dr. Burhanuddin al-Helmy and Dr. Zulkiflee Muhammad – both of whom were the products of both religious and as secular educations – were the leaders largely responsible for turning PAS into a political party with a rationalised organisational structure, a chain of command and links with other Islamic parties and movements abroad. Cognisant of the fact that the new Islamic party was desperately in need of funding and manpower, PAS leaders like Dr. Burhanuddin and Dr. Zulkiflee turned to the *pondoks* and madrasas for help. It was during this period that PAS began to develop its sub-elite strata of party-political functionaries consisting of PAS-supporting ulama, imams, *gurus* and *dakwah* missionaries.

In the 1960s, PAS began to lay down its foundations of a cadre system by developing its network of Islamic schools. Through their contacts in the *pondoks* and madrasas that dotted the Malay Peninsula, the PAS was able to spread its message quickly, effectively and most important of all, cheaply. Under the leadership of Dr. Burhanuddin al-Helmy, PAS developed into an Islamist party that was both nationalist and anti-imperialist in its outlook. The party articulated concerns related to economic independence, the struggle against colonialism and neo-colonial hegemony, as well as the need to promote a dynamic and issue-based form of popular Islam. But in 1969, Dr. Burhanuddin passed away after being detained without a trial by the Malaysian government. PAS then came under the leadership of Mohamad Asri Muda, who was a staunch defender of Malay rights and privileges.

The period of Asri Muda's leadership of PAS was a highly controversial one. In Malaysian political circles, he was known as a fervent Malay ethnonationalist as well as one of the few upcoming Malay-Muslim politicians whose educational background was entirely local. In his youth he had studied at both the madrasas and Malay vernacular schools of Kelantan and neighbouring states.[14] Between 1970 to 1982, Asri Muda turned PAS into an ethno-centric Malay-Muslim party that was concerned with the promotion of the status of Malay-Muslims in Malaysia.

It was during Asri Muda's time that PAS's power base was rooted in the northeastern state of Kelantan, and it was in Kelantan that Asri worked hardest to secure PAS's organic links with the *pondok* and madrasa network. The predominantly Malay state of Kelantan was, at that time, one of the most remote and isolated states on the peninsula and was viewed with a mixture of curiosity and contempt by the elites in the capital, Kuala Lumpur. But despite the relatively low level of development, Kelantan was known as a centre of Islamic learning, earning it the reputation of being both the heart of Malay culture on the peninsula and as the *serambi Mekah* (porch of Mecca). Kelantan was also closely linked to the Malay community of Patani to the north, which had once been a Malay kingdom but had been incorporated into the state of Thailand (formerly Siam) after the Anglo-Siamese treaty of 1909. Both Kelantan and Patani had been at the forefront of Muslim education and like Kelantan, Patani was also known for its extensive *pondok* school network.[15]

Soon afterwards, Asri was able to expand his local support base when he was given the opportunity to set up party branches in the predominantly Malay state of Trengganu, directly to the south of Kelantan. Besides lectures given at mosques, *surau* and madrasas, they also used the more informal modes of communication used by Islamist movements in other parts of the world. Like Hassan al-Banna, the founder of the Muslim Brotherhood in Egypt, Asri Muda preferred winning new supporters via informal personal contacts at places such as coffee shops.

Meanwhile, Kelantan's southern neighbour, Trengganu, also had a reputation as a centre for Islamic learning. While Kelantan was known as the *serambi Mekah*, Trengganu proudly declared itself the *serambi Madinah* (porch of Medina) in the peninsula. The first PAS branch in Trengganu was set up in 1956 in Dungun under Asri's personal direction. Henceforth, Asri concentrated most of his efforts on the northern states of Kelantan and Trengganu, working closely with his lieutenants and trying to convert the local imams and *pondok* teachers to PAS's cause. Asri realised that when one dealt with the local *guru* of the *pondok* schools and madrasas he had to adopt a very different approach. The local imams and gurus of Kelantan and Trengganu were not particularly happy with PAS's success, as it represented a threat to the *status quo ante*. Traditionally, the state's gurus and imams were respected and revered men of learning, but they kept their distance from the world of politics. Winzeler (1975), among others, has noted that the gurus of Kelantan were generally conservative and traditional in their outlook, belonging to the more reactionary *Kaum Tua* generation.[16] They shied away from politics and were reluctant to embrace any kind of Islamist movement that called for socio-political reform. Some were also supporters of the traditional establishment, which was identified with the Kelantan royal family and UMNO, under Tunku Abdul Rahman. Asri knew that he had to win the support of this vital local constituency if he was to win control of Kelantan for good. To win over these conservative and recalcitrant religious functionaries and leaders, Asri needed to adapt his own Islamist discourse to emphasise both his Islamist and his Malay-centric nationalist concerns.

Through the careful cultivation of personal client networks with the local religious teachers and patronage of the *pondoks* and madrasas of Kelantan and Trengganu, Asri Muda managed to secure their loyalty and support during the elections of 1959 right up to 1969. During the 1959 elections, PAS's election campaign in the states of Kelantan and Trengganu was aided and abetted by the state's religious teachers and schools, helping the party rise to power in both states for the first time ever. This made PAS the first Islamist party in Asia to be legally elected into office.

The close co-operation between PAS and the religious schools network continued right up to the late 1960s, which allowed PAS to again win big in both states during the 1969 elections. The results of these elections, however, were nullified as a result of the declaration of a state of National Emergency in May 1969 by the UMNO-led government, which had lost considerable support across the country.

Economic and Structural Change in the 1970s and its Impact on PAS and the Pondok Network

It is evident that the existence and development of the *pondoks* and madrasas of Malaysia were determined by various political-economic factors and the changes that took place in Malay-Muslim society as a result of structural-economic changes as well. Earlier we argued that *pondoks* and madrasas existed in the Malay world well before the coming of Western colonial rule, though the encounter with Western colonialism did ultimately force some of the *pondoks* and madrasas of Malaysia to adapt to the political and economic realities of the times. That the *Kaum Muda's* modern *pondoks* and madrasas emerged in the 1920s was to be expected, considering the migration of Muslims to the Crown Colonies of Penang, Malacca and Singapore whose political economies were very different from that of the traditional agrarian feudal economies of the Malay kingdoms. The different socio-economic realities of the Crown Colonies opened up new opportunities for the economic and political mobilisation of Malayan Muslims, which also led to the emergence of these new modern *pondoks* and madrasas that were interested in issues of economic and political emancipation.

By the 1970s, Malaysia was beginning to undergo more radical socio-economic changes that likewise affected the development of the *pondoks* and madrasas and their place in Malaysian society. Thanks to economic and demographic factors brought about by Malaysia's economic development and the transition to a more urban-based polity, the country's religious schools were gradually sidelined by the rise of the nation's new urban-based universities. By 1969, Malaysia was witnessing the emergence of new Islamist actors and agents on the national scene, mainly the urban and campus-based Islamist student movements such as the *Angkatan Belia Islam Malaysia* (Malaysian Islamic Youth Movement, ABIM) and the Sufi-inspired traditionalist-mystical *Darul Arqam* movement.[17]

ABIM and the Darul Arqam movement were both campus-based, urban organisations that were symptomatic of the changes taking place in Malaysia and in Malay-Muslim society at the time. The introduction of the New Economic Policy (NEP), which sought to improve the economic lot of the Malays, coupled with the creation of new industrial zones on the west coast of the Malaysian Peninsula and the opening of new urban settlements meant an expansion of the urban services sector, which led to more rural youth migrating to the cities for educational and work opportunities while the Malay hinterland was slowly but eventually significantly depopulated. As a result of the gradual urbanisation of the Malay community, the religious schools of Kelantan and Trengganu shrunk in size, numbers and importance; only to be overshadowed by the new modern universities, Islamic colleges and the International Islamic University that was founded in Kuala Lumpur in 1982.

The gradual socio-economic changes that were taking place in the Malay community meant that both PAS and UMNO had to adapt to the developments among their primary political constituency. By the 1970s and 1980s, the UMNO-led government was already trying to reform Malaysia's *pondoks* and madrasas by bringing some of them under state control and patronage. PAS in its turn sought to maintain its links with the *pondok* network by sponsoring religious schools of their own, and providing opportunities for the best graduates of these *pondoks* and madrasas to continue their studies in the religious schools of Pakistan and India. By 1980, about 14% of Malaysia's total student population was estimated to be engaged in Islamic studies in the strict sense.[18] But both the UMNO-led government and PAS were aware of the political potential of the religious schools, and, furthermore, the Iranian revolution of 1979 had demonstrated how students, when indoctrinated and mobilised, could be a potent force.

PAS was then under the leadership of Haji Yusof Rawa, who was of ulama background and who led the so-called 'ulama faction' that had grown in power within the party. Yusof Rawa was himself a product of religious education in Malaysia's madrasas and was later a student at several Islamic madrasas and colleges in Cairo and Mecca. Yusof Rawa had come under the influence of the Muslim Brotherhood during his studies in Egypt, and it was he who re-oriented PAS's struggle and brought it in line with other Islamist movements and political organisations in the rest of the Islamic world. Borrowing some of the methods of the Muslim Brotherhood, PAS under the leadership of Yusof Rawa introduced the practice of *usrah* (group meetings) in madrasas and mosques intended to bring party members together and to encourage them to understand, develop and propagate the ideology of the party among themselves as well as among non-members. These *usrah* sessions were divided into different types: *usrah* sessions for the party leaders and *usrah* for ordinary members. *Usrah* sessions for the *muslimat* (women members) were also encouraged. On some occasions, the *usrah* was accompanied by a *kenduri* (feast) held in members' homes to which non-members were also invited. These meetings helped to generate a sense of common belonging and fellowship (*ukhuwwah*) among the PAS members and bring them closer together. Apart from *tarbiyah* and *usrah* sessions, Yusof Rawa and PAS's leaders also played an active role in supporting (and often leading) many religious meetings and rituals performed by PAS members. *Qiamulail* (Ar. *qiyam al-layl*, 'rising from sleep in the night') sessions were also held on every Thursday evening.

Yusof Rawa and the other ulama leaders of PAS were instrumental in promoting the *pondoks* and madrasas that served as their political base as well as privately-run educational centres. Besides Yusof Rawa subsequent decades also saw the rise to political prominence of two *pondok*-based ulama, Tuan Guru Nik Aziz Nik Mat in Kelantan and Tuan Guru Hadi Awang in Trengganu. The much-revered Tuan Guru Nik Aziz Nik Mat was based in Kelantan and became the first PAS leader whose education was almost entirely based on the traditional *pondok* and madrasa system. His father, Ustaz Nik Mat Alim, had his own religious school, the Sekolah Agama Darul

Anwar, and, in his youth, Nik Aziz was sent away to study in various famous traditional *pondoks* in Kelantan and Trengganu, completing his education with a long stay at the Dar al-ʻUlum of Deoband in India. He emerged to play a crucial role in the transmission of the Deobandi concept of education and the Deobandi curriculum amongst the Malay *pondoks*.[19]

Like Yusof Rawa, Nik Aziz's outlook on Islamic education and the role of the *pondoks* and madrasas was shaped in part by his own experience and the teaching he had received abroad in Deoband, India. Upon his return to Malaysia in 1962, Nik Aziz first worked at Tarbiyyah Mardiah Islamic Secondary School. He then began working at his father's school, the Madrasah Darul Anwar. Worried about the prospect of the demise of the *pondoks* and madrasas of Kelantan and equally concerned by the government's constant attempts to reform these institutions, Nik Aziz began to tour the state, giving speeches in which he compared the state of Islamic education in Malaysia with that of other Islamic countries. He argued that Muslims should pay for their own Islamic education, and cited the example of al-Azhar University in Cairo, which was sponsored by public donations. This produced the desired result, and the public began making donations to the Darul Anwar school.

For PAS leaders like Nik Aziz, a religious education was a means for creating a class of spiritually inclined leaders who would safeguard the welfare and concerns of Muslims and see that *shariʻa* law would eventually be implemented in Malaysia.[20] Students of the religious schools were seen as assets in the struggle to promote a stricter adherence to Islam in the country. Another aspect of Deobandi thinking clearly evident in Nik Aziz's style of leadership is the desire to purify Islam and Muslim culture from elements regarded as superstitious (*khurafat*), polytheistic (*shirk*), unlawful innovations (*bidʻa*) and deviant teachings (*ajaran sesat*). Some of the traditional ulama, he argued, were wrong because their scriptural knowledge rested on old Malay textbooks (*kitab Jawi*) that were poorly translated.[21] He insisted that only a thorough campaign to eliminate and remove all of these elements from Malay society could transform them into true Muslims. This brought him into conflict with the traditional ulama of the more traditional madrasas and *pondoks* of Kelantan.

The other PAS leader and *alim* who was noted in his efforts to promote the *pondoks* and madrasas was the Trengganu-based Tuan Guru Hadi Awang, who was strongly entrenched in his Madrasah Rusila in the small coastal town of Rusila (near Marang, Trengganu). Ustaz Hadi Awang had inherited control of the madrasa from his father who was also known as one of the foremost Ustazs in the state. Both of these prominent madrasas were attended by Malay-Muslim children whose families were mainly members or supporters of PAS. In the case of Hadi Awang's Madrasah Rusila, the institution would eventually develop working links with major madrasas abroad such as the Syed Maudoodi International Islamic Institute (SMII) of Lahore that was run by the Pakistani Islamist party, the Jama'at-i Islami. The best graduates of Hadi Awang's Rusila madrasa would be selected to continue their studies at the SMII in Pakistan, which, in turn, further bolstered the links between the two Islamist parties across the Indian Ocean.[22]

However, while PAS leaders like Yusof Rawa, Nik Aziz and Hadi Awang were busy trying to expand and develop the network of *pondoks* and madrasas linked to PAS, other developments in Malaysia further complicated the already complex image of these traditional institutions. The UMNO-led government was relentless in its efforts to cast the PAS-controlled *pondoks* as centres of obscurantist teaching and militant anti-government activity. In 1985, another opportunity to demonise the *pondok* institution arose.

Suppressing the Radical Tendency in PAS: The Memali Massacre

The 1980s witnessed the rapid industrialisation and urbanisation of Malaysia as it was led by the country's fourth Prime Minister, Dr. Mahathir Mohamad. Dr. Mahathir was a modernist at heart who wished to transform Malaysia into a fully-industrialised country. He was also known for his antipathy towards and suspicion of PAS – which he regarded and cast as a fundamentalist party – and its links to Malaysia's *pondoks* and madrasas. Understandably PAS's ulama and teachers of the PAS-controlled *pondoks* regarded Dr. Mahathir as a dangerous secular leader who was keen to radically transform and modernise the madrasas and *pondoks* altogether, in order to deprive the Islamic party of one of its most important support bases and networks.

Throughout the 1980s, the tenor of the strife between UMNO and PAS reached its most virulent peak, with several PAS leaders openly condemning Dr. Mahathir and the UMNO-led government for being secular, Westernised and anti-Islam. Among these scholar-leaders was Ustaz Ibrahim Mahmood, a well-known religious teacher in Kedah, who had studied at various *pondoks* and madrasas in Malaysia and later abroad at places such as the Dar al-'Ulum Deoband in India and al-Azhar University in Cairo, Egypt. Later he completed his studies at the University of Tripoli in Libya, earning him the nickname 'Ibrahim Libya'.

Upon his return to Malaysia, Ibrahim Libya worked for the Malaysian government's Islamic Centre, which was one of the offices linked to the Prime Minister's Department. He soon left government service and joined the opposition PAS instead, and founded his own madrasa, the Madrasah Islahiyyah Diniyyah, in the state of Kedah.[23] The madrasa soon became recognised as one of the most active centres of PAS activities in Kedah, and it was from his madrasa that Ibrahim Libya began to issue his calls for *jihad* against the Malaysian government on the grounds that UMNO, as an ethno-nationalist party, was in fact a secular party opposed to the values and objectives of political Islam. Ibrahim Libya's call for open revolt against the state eventually led to a warrant for his arrest being issued.

On 19 November 1985, the state's security forces surrounded the village of Memali in an attempt to arrest the PAS leader and his followers. In the clash that ensued, Ibrahim Libya and fourteen of his followers were killed. On the same day, a state of emergency was declared in the state of Kedah and restraining orders were imposed in the neighbouring states of Kelantan, Trengganu and Perak. Henceforth, the Malaysian government's relations with PAS's madrasas and *pondoks* became troublesome and difficult, to say the least.

The killings at the Memali madrasa marked the nadir of the UMNO-led government's relations with the *pondok* and madrasa network in Malaysia. PAS, in its turn, used the Memali incident as proof that the Malaysian government was not sincere in its claims that it wanted to promote Islamic education in Malaysia, and reacted to the UMNO-led government's criticisms by further intensifying its support of and co-operation with the *pondok* and madrasa network. During the Federal Elections of 1990, PAS managed to win many of the State Assembly seats and all of Kelantan's Federal seats, thereby wiping out all traces of UMNO influence there. Tuan Guru Nik Aziz was elected as the Chief Minister of Kelantan, the first *ulama* ever to be elected to such a prominent political position.

Having thus risen to power, one of the first things that Tuan Guru Nik Aziz did was to table a financial aid package to the state's madrasas. This was because all Federal government funding to the religious schools in the state had been stopped by the UMNO-led government. In the 1991 Kelantan state budget, the PAS-led government allocated 15 million Ringgit (4 million USD) to the *Yayasan Islam Kelantan* (Kelantan Islamic Foundation), to improve the standard of religious (Islamic) education. State funds were also allocated to *pondok* schools.[24] Tuan Guru Nik Aziz even arranged for the Sultan of Kelantan to tour the *pondok* schools during his birthday celebrations in 1991.[25] These investments paid off very quickly. In 1990, 34,721 students were enrolled in religious schools sponsored by the Yayasan Islam. In 1991, the figure rose to 37,726; in 1992, 39,633; and in 1993, 41,864.[26]

The Future of Malaysia's Madrasas and Pondoks, and Their Relevance to PAS

The future development of Malaysia's madrasas and *pondoks* hangs in the balance as the country continues in its march towards economic development accompanied by massive rural migration to the urban centres and the creation of a new urban-based Malay-Muslim constituency. The question therefore arises: What will the fate of Malaysia's predominantly rural madrasas and *pondoks* be in the long run?

This chapter has focused primarily on the strong historical links between the Pan-Malaysian Islamic party and Malaysia's madrasa and *pondok* networks. As we have shown, PAS's early success would not have been possible without the close co-operation between the Islamist party's leaders and the madrasas and *pondok* schools in the predominantly rural Malay states of the north. From the very beginning, PAS, the party whose leaders and members were originally composed of religious scholars and functionaries, had close links to the religious schools network that spread across Malaysia's Malay-dominated rural hinterland, which has served as its support base and communications centres till this very day. When the party began to adopt hi-tech modes of communication to maintain its links with its members and to spread its message even further, one of the first innovations it introduced was the practice of filming and transmitting the sermons and speeches of the party's *ulama* leaders from the madrasas and *pon-*

doks via the Internet. The Friday sermons and lectures by PAS leaders like Tuan Guru Nik Aziz and Tuan Guru Hadi Awang from their respective madrasas in Kelantan and Trengganu are still being beamed across the planet to their followers and supporters through the party's Web site and other related services such as PAS-TV.

For obvious reasons, PAS is not about to abandon its long-standing relation with Malaysia's *pondok* and madrasa network. Though no definitive statistics are available and little research has been done on the religious schools in Malaysia today,[27] it is estimated that some 125,000 Malaysian boys and girls are enrolled in the country's madrasas and *pondoks*.[28] Furthermore, there is still no definitive register today that includes all of the religious schools in the country; or a register of religious schools that are linked to, and supported by, the Malaysian Islamic party itself. What is clear, however, is that the Malaysian government is now forced to deal with the issue of madrasas and the phenomenon of educational dualism (to borrow Hashim Rosnani's phrase).[29]

The Malaysian government is fully cognisant of the fact that madrasas and *pondoks* are here to stay, and that PAS will continue to nurture its links with these institutions of Muslim learning, and it has since the 1970s attempted to create, fund and develop its own network of state-sponsored Islamic religious primary and secondary schools, Sekolah Rendah Kebangsaan Agama (SRKA) and Sekolah Menengah Kebangsaan Agama (SMKA). While the Malaysian government has been less successful in determining the form and content of the independent madrasas and those that have come under the support and patronage of PAS, it has at least been able to extend its educational reform measures to the SRKAs and SMKAs under its control, where today English has become a compulsory subject for all students.[30] The Malaysian government's concern about what is taught in these *pondoks* and madrasas also extends further abroad, to the point where the Malaysian government has even suggested that it may play a role in improving the teaching curriculum of the madrasas in the troubled Muslim-dominated provinces of Patani, Jala, Satun and Narathiwat in Southern Thailand.[31]

The stakes in the campaign to rein in the *pondoks* and madrasas were raised even higher following the attacks on the United States of America in 2001 and the Malaysian government's tacit endorsement of Washington's global 'War on Terror' that ensued. While the government of Dr. Mahathir

Mohamad was not exactly known for its love of Washington, the advent of the 'War on Terror' allowed the Malaysian government to strategically re-position itself in a favourable light thanks to its own long-standing campaign to weaken the appeal of the Islamists of PAS.

The transnational networks of itinerant scholars and students who move around the world from one madrasa to another was among the first things to be affected by the new of the post-9/11 geo-political realities. By 2002, the Malaysian government was already clamping down on foreign students coming to Malaysia to study in its religious schools, and other Muslim governments followed suit. By 2004, the number of Malaysian (and other Southeast Asian) students in countries like Pakistan, Bangladesh and India had dropped to a trickle and the government of Pakistan refused to offer new student visas to Southeast Asian students who wanted to study in the madrasas there. Furthermore, in January 2002, the Malaysian government ordered its security forces to raid and close down the madrasa of the conservative Indonesian cleric Abu Bakar Ba'asyir (who was on the run from Indonesian authorities and who had been living in exile in Malaysia) that was based in the southern Malaysian state of Johor, bordering Singapore. Though Ba'asyir had no relations or contact whatsoever with PAS, the clampdown on his small madrasa came at a time when all *pondok* and madrasa schools were suspected and this only further exacerbated the negative image of these institutions as a whole.

In 2002, the Malaysian government also suspended funding to 260 madrasas and *pondoks* across the country that were run privately by non-state and non-UMNO trustees and directors, on the grounds that some of them might be directly or indirectly linked to PAS.[32] In 2003, the then Prime Minister Mahathir Mohamad was actively discouraging Malaysian parents from sending their children to *pondok* schools (particularly those with open links to PAS) on the grounds that these schools were 'preaching hate' against the Malaysian government and being used as recruiting grounds for both PAS and other more radical dissident Islamist groups in the country.

Fear and Loathing: The Demonisation of the Pondoks and Madrasas of PAS in Malaysia Today

As we have shown earlier, *pondok* schools and madrasas have existed in Malaysia since before British colonial rule. What is significant, however, is how the impact of Western colonialism gave birth to a new type of *pondok* and madrasa that was not only modern in its teaching methods and curriculum, but also in its political ambitions. A new generation of *kaum muda*-led *pondoks* and madrasas emerged in the early decades of the twentieth century, which were overtly political and played a key role in the political empowerment and mobilisation of the Muslims of Malaya. During the early stages of the anti-colonial struggle in British Malaya, the Malay-Muslim elite were less wary of these politicised *pondoks* and madrasas for the simple reason that their struggle against British colonial rule concurred with the interests of the Malay-Muslim elite who also wanted to see the end of British colonialism in Malaya. Thus the *pondok* and madrasa schools were seen (and characterised) by the Malay elites as generally positive, and were commended for the role they played in preserving Malay-Muslim identity as well as developing the first generation of Malay-Muslim proto-nationalists who later took active part in the anti-colonial struggle in British Malaya.

The view of the *pondoks* and madrasas began to change in the late 1940s, when it became clear that some of these religious schools were aligned to the radical Malay Left who not only wanted independence but also wanted to create an independent Muslim state, which would cater to the interests of the Malay peasantry. By the time the conservative UMNO party was formed (in 1946) and the Malaysian Islamic Party PAS had entered the arena of post-colonial politics (in 1951), PAS's *pondoks* and madrasas were specifically singled out as potential threats to UMNO's political fortunes, and by extension, to the Malaysian state.

As we have shown earlier in this chapter, the UMNO-led Malaysian state's reaction to the *pondok* and madrasa network in Malaysia has been two-fold: On the one hand, the UMNO-governed state has tried to co-opt and patronise non-political *pondoks* and madrasas as their own; while, on the other hand, doing its best to limit the popularity and influence of those religious schools that have come under PAS's influence. This was the background to the numerous attempts at Islamic educational reform in Malaysia during the Mahathir era (1981-2003) and which persists to this very day under the leadership of Prime Minister Abdullah Ahmad Badawi.

This sustained campaign to control the *pondoks* and madrasas of the country has often been couched in a discourse of paternalistic concern for Malaysia's Muslim citizens that posits the view of *pondoks* and madrasas as being, at best, quaint, rustic and traditional institutions that need to be overhauled and reformed: In 2001 the country's Education Minister Musa Muhammad noted that less than 25% of the madrasas and *pondoks*' graduates qualified for admission to the country's universities (as compared to some 90% of secular national school graduates).[33] Shortly after other Malaysian leaders such as Abdul Ghani Othman, Chief Minister of Johor, added that 'there must be a balance between religious education and scientific knowledge so that students from religious schools will not lag behind in the modern world'.[34] Some Malaysian politicians have even suggested that some of the *pondok* schools be re-packaged as potential sites for foreign tourists to visit, in order to get a glimpse of the 'authentic, traditional' life of rural Malays.[35] However, this paternalistic and sometimes patronising discourse of care and control once again reiterates the common jaundiced view (favoured by Malaysia's Western-educated elite) that the *pondok* and madrasa are exotic, outdated institutions that have not kept up with modernity and that if left to their own devices, can only produce poorly-educated graduates whose knowledge skills are useless in a modern industrial economy.

In its attempt to keep the nation's *pondoks* and madrasas under its control, the UMNO-led state has sought to promote the religious schools that have come under its own patronage. With higher-level Islamic education being offered by institutions like the International Islamic University of Malaysia and research on Islamic issues being carried out at institutes such as IKIM and ISTAC, the government-sponsored religious schools (SRKAs and SMKAs) of Malaysia have also received further financial, material and logistical support in the form of higher budget allocations, donations of computers and special promotional campaigns (via the Internet and other forms of communication) to advertise themselves as alternative institutions of Islamic learning to PAS's madrasas and *pondoks*.[36]

In tandem with this paternalistic discourse of care and patronage that posits the stereotypical image of the traditional *pondok* and madrasa as an outdated institution is a more aggressive and sinister discourse of security and anti-terrorism, which puts forward the claim that the *pondoks* and madrasas of PAS in particular have been instrumentalised by the party to create its own pool of fanatical party cadres; and that some of PAS's madrasas may even have links to violent militant groups both inside and outside of the country. As we have shown above, this second discourse has been particularly well served since 11 September 2001 and Washington's unilateral declaration of a 'War on Terror'. The government of Malaysia (like the governments of Pakistan, Indonesia, Egypt, Turkey and many other Muslim countries) seized upon this shift in geo-strategic realities to renew its assault on PAS's *pondoks* and madrasas, this time with the tacit endorsement of Western agencies, governments and media who were likewise worried about the prospect of the rise of militant radical Islam world-wide.

However, this discourse of security-maintenance and terror-prevention also reiterates the trope of the *pondok* or madrasa as an institution that should be kept at arm's length and mistrusted. In the Malaysian context, it also involves the historical erasure of the genuinely emancipatory role played by many of the *pondoks* and madrasas of the past in the anti-colonial struggle for independence (which was indeed a political struggle with radical political objectives).

The fate of the *pondoks* and madrasas of Malaysia today therefore hinges on the twists and turns of geo-politics and how the combined pressure of the discourse of paternalistic education reform as well as the discourse of terror-prevention will be utilised by the UMNO-led state in the future. As we have shown above, this conflict is primarily a political one, which has more to do with the constant battle for Malay-Muslim votes between the two biggest Malay-Muslim parties of Malaysia, UMNO and PAS, than with the teaching of Islam in the Muslim schools themselves. After all, the UMNO-led government has shown that it is more comfortable with the *pondok* and madrasa schools that have come under its control, thereby demonstrating that Islam and Islamic education is not the problem *per se*, but rather PAS and its support of other *pondoks* that have eluded governmental patronage and surveillance. Thus the long-term future of Malaysia's *pondoks* and madrasas will be determined by the outcome of this political contest between UMNO and PAS, as both sides will undoubtedly remain relentless in their claim to be the party that best caters to the needs of Muslim education in Malaysia.

Notes

1 For an account of the emergence and historical development of PAS, see: Farish A. Noor, *Islam Embedded: The Historical Development of the Pan-Malaysian Islamic Party 1951-2003*, 2 vols., Kuala Lumpur: Malaysian Sociological Research Institute, 2004.

2 Farish A. Noor, 'Stirring the "Militant Islam" Bugbear Again?', *Pakistan Daily Times*, 27 June 2007.

3 See: B. Raman, 'Thailand and the International Islamic Front', SAAG paper no. 890, 9 January 2004. The SAAG report of 2004 claimed that 'according to very reliable statistics for 2002, there were 190 students from Southeast Asia in the madrasas of Sindh, Pakistan, of whom 86 were from Malaysia, 82 from Thailand and 22 from Indonesia; 151 in the madrasas of Punjab, of whom 61 were from Malaysia, 49 from Thailand and 41 from Indonesia; and 59 in the madrasas of the Northwest Frontier Province, of whom 21 were from Indonesia, 20 from Malaysia and 18 from Thailand. Thus, there were 167 Malaysians, 149 Thais and 84 Indonesians in the various madrasas of Pakistan then.

4 Jonathan Kent, 'Malaysia's Doubt About Muslim Schools', BBC World Service, 3 April 2003.

5 The encroachment of British colonial rule into the Malay states was carried out slowly and in stages: first through the creation of the Straits Settlements in 1826, then the formation of the (indirectly ruled) Federated Malay States in 1896 and finally the Unfederated Malay States in 1909. In 1867, control of the Straits Settlements was passed over to the Colonial Office in London.

6 On Islam's early arrival in the Malay world, see: S.Q. Fatimi, *Islam Comes to Malaysia*, Singapore: Malaysian Sociological Research Institute, 1963; Syed Naquib Al-Attas, *Preliminary Statement on a General Theory of the Islamization of the Malay-Indonesian Archipelago*, Kuala Lumpur: Dewan Bahasa dan Pustaka, 1963; William R. Roff, 'Patterns of Islamization in Malaysia, 1890s-1990s: exemplars, institutions, and vectors', *Journal of Islamic Studies* 9(2), 1998, 210-228.

7 In the Malaysian context, the term 'Peranakan' refers to those of mixed ancestry, be they of mixed Malay-Arab, Malay-Indian or Malay-Chinese descent.

8 For more on the contact between Muslim thinkers and reformers of Southeast Asia with their counterparts in Egypt and the Arab world, see: Michael Laffan, *Islamic Nationhood and Colonial Indonesia: The Umma Below the Winds*, London: RoutledgeCurzon, 2003.

9 Nabir Haji Abdullah, *Ma'ahad al-Ehya al-Sharif Gunung Semanggul, 1934-1959*, Bangi: Universiti Kebangsaan Malaysia Press, 1976.

10 Abdullah, *Ma'ahad al-Ehya al-Sharif.*

11 The *Hizbul Muslimin* party's founders included Ustaz Abu Bakar al-Bakir (principal of Madrasa Ma'ahad al-Ehya as-Sharif), Ustaz Abdul Rab, Dr. Burhanuddin al-Helmy (leader of the PKMM) and Kyai Masyhur Azahari of the Indonesian Masyumi movement. Other Malay radicals and leftist-nationalists

such as Mohammad Asri Muda, *Hizbul Muslimin's* first secretary, also played a crucial role in its formation and activities.

12 A.J. Stockwell, *British Documents on the End of Empire: Malaya*, part I, London: HMSO, 1995, p. 55.

13 The conservative-nationalist UMNO party has its roots in the First Malay Congress that was held in Kuala Lumpur on 1-4 March 1946. The Congress discussed the plan to form PEKEMBAR (*Persatuan Kebangsaan Melayu Bersatu*), but later opted for the title UMNO (United Malays Nationalist Organisation) instead. On 11 May 1946, the UMNO party was officially launched at the *Istana Besar* (Grand Palace) of Johor Bharu. UMNO's first President was Dato' Onn Jaafar. In the early days, the party was a broad and all-encompassing organisation that included Malay political movements from across the entire political spectrum of the country. Over time, however, the conservative character of UMNO emerged as Leftists and Islamists began to leave the organisation to form parties of their own.

14 After he had completed his basic religious education in Kelantan, Asri Muda worked briefly at the madrasa Ma'ahad al-Ehya of Gunung Semanggul, where he began to formulate his ecumenical ideology of Islamism combined with radical Malay nationalism. When the *Hizbul Muslimin* party was formed in 1948, Asri became its secretary. When PAS was first established in 1951 as the *Persatuan Islam Se-Malaya*, he became one of its first members and, with the help of Osman Abdullah, was made a member of the executive committee. His wife, Ustazah Sakinah, eventually rose to become head of Muslimat PAS, the women's wing.

15 For more on the pondok schools of Patani, see: Hasan Madmarn, *The Pondok and the Madrasah in Patani*, Bangi: Universiti Kebangsaan Press, 1999. Hasan Madmarn notes that until the early 20th century, the pondoks of Patani served as the last bastion of traditional Malay-Muslim culture and identity in the face of successive assimilation policies adopted by the Thai government since the time of King Chulālongkorn right up to the military dictatorship of General Phibun Songkram of the 1930s. Madmarn also notes that the pondoks of Patani were almost universally conservative and aligned themselves with the Kaum Tua conservative tradition, and that their curricula and teaching methods were antiquated and 'medieval' compared to what was taught at the *pondoks* and madrasas of the Kaum Muda reformists (pp. 18-20).

16 Robert L. Winzeler, 'Traditional Islamic Schools in Kelantan', *Journal of the Malaysian Branch of the Royal Asiatic Society* 48 (1975), 99-100.

17 On the emergence of these new Islamic movements, see: Judith Nagata, *The Reflowering of Malaysian Islam*, Vancouver: University of British Columbia Press, 1984; Chandra Muzaffar, *Islamic Resurgence in Malaysia*, Petaling Jaya: Fajar Bakti Press, 1987.

18 Quoted in Shanti Nair, *Islam in Malaysian Foreign Policy*, London: Routledge / Singapore: ISEAS, 1997, p. 116.

19 For more on the life of Nik Aziz Nik Mat, see: Mohammad Sayuti Omar, *Salam Tok Guru: PAS Perintah Kelantan*, Kuala Lumpur: Tinta Merah, 1999.

20 Omar, *Salam Tok Guru*, pp. 36-37.

21 The term *kitab Jawi* refers to Malay-language Islamic books in Arabic script, dealing with doctrine and canonical obligations and containing medieval cosmological and eschatological ideas. See: Mohd. Nor bin Ngah, *Kitab Jawi: Islamic thought of the Malay Muslim scholars*, Singapore: ISEAS, 1983.

22 See also Chapter 5 in this volume.

23 C. N. al-Afghani, *Operasi Kenari: Suatu Hukuman Tampa Bicara*, Kuala Lumpur: Penerbit Pemuda Press, 1990, p. 64.

24 Jamal Mohd. Lukman Sulaiman, *Biografi Tuan Guru Dato' Haji Nik Abdul Aziz*, Kuala Lumpur: Sulfa Press, 1999, p. 141.

25 Sulaiman, *Biografi Tuan Guru Dato' Haji Nik Abdul Aziz*, p. 160.

26 Nik Aziz Nik Mat, *Kelantan: Universiti Politik Terbuka*, Nilam Puri: Ma'ahad ad-Dakwah wal-Imamah, 1995, p. 236 n. 18.

27 One of the research projects currently being undertaken in Malaysia on the subject of madrasas and *pondoks* is the research cluster '*Design of Madrasahs – A Case Study of Madrasahs in Malaysia that are run by Private or Non-Governmental Bodies*'; currently being carried out at Universiti Teknologi Malaysia (UTM) in Johor. (see: http://www.rmc.utm.my/ProjectDir/abstract.asp?vot=71274).

28 Jonathan Kent, 'Malaysia's Doubt About Muslim Schools', BBC World Service, 3 April 2003.

29 See: Hashim Rosnani, *Educational Dualism in Malaysia*, Oxford: Oxford University Press, 1996.

30 Mujtaba Hamdi, 'Madrasas: Lessons from History', SEAPA (Southeast Asian Press Alliance) report, 2003, online at: http://www.seapabkk.org/newdesign/fellowshipsdetail.php?No=674 ; and Eric Teo Chu Cheo, 'Malaysia Gives Islam a Chance to Shine', *Japan Times*, 19 April 2004.

31 That the Malaysian government is worried about the teaching that takes place in the *pondoks* and madrasas of the Muslim provinces in Southern Thailand is understandable considering the escalation of inter-religious violence there between 2002 to the present. During the tenure of Thai Prime Minister Thaksin Shinawatra, the Thai government's relations with the Malay-Muslim minority in Southern Thailand reached an all-time low: Sporadic attacks and bombings led to killings on a weekly basis, causing havoc to local commerce and increasing the political tensions. Allegations of militant training in the *pondoks* of Patani added to the fear that these institutions were guerilla training centres linked to international terrorist organisations. Furthermore, the proximity of Patani to the Malaysian state of Kelantan that is ruled by PAS also meant that there was the danger that alleged Muslim militants from Thailand may seek refuge in Malaysia. On 12 February 2007, the Malaysian Prime Minister Abdullah Ahmad Badawi met with his Thai counterpart Sarayud

Chulanorn to discuss Malaysia sending government-appointed religious teachers to teach at the pondoks of Patani, and to update and modernise the curriculum of its institutions. ('Malaysia and Thailand to Accelerate Development in Border Areas', *Bernama Press*, 12 February 2007, online at: http://www.bernama.com.my/bernama/v3/news.php?id=246401).

32 'International Religious Freedom Report 2004: Malaysia'. United States Department of State, Washington, DC. Online at: http://www.state.gov/g/drl/rls/irf/2004/35405.htm.

33 M. Bakri Musa, 'Meanwhile: Religious schools hinder progress in Malaysia', *International Herald Tribune*, 24 April 2001.

34 Michael Richardson, 'Asians Take a Closer Look at Islamic Schools', *International Herald Tribune*, 12 February 2002.

35 See: 'Call to Upgrade Malaysia's Tourist Homestay Industry', (Bernama News Agency, 28 November 2007, online at: http://web7.bernama.com/events/tmm2007/news.php?id=299194. Ironically perhaps, the suggestion of converting *pondoks* into tourist attractions came from a PAS member of Parliament, Abdul Fatah Harun.

36 One such case being the Muslim religious school affiliated to the Technological University of Malaysia, the Sekolah Agama Universiti Teknologi Malaysia (in the state of Johor) which was supported by government funds when it created its own promotional Web site to attract more students. See: 'UTM Religious School Launches its own Website',*The Star*, 24 April 2007.

8 Traditionalist and Islamist Pesantrens in Contemporary Indonesia

Martin van Bruinessen

Like the madrasas in India and Pakistan, the Indonesian *pesantrens* – religious boarding schools, the local variant of the madrasa – have in recent years drawn some unfriendly attention due to suspicions of their involvement in radical and possibly terrorist activities. The Indonesian authorities did not appear to share those suspicions, certainly not concerning the *pesantren* in general, but those of the Philippines, Singapore, Australia and the US, as well as numerous international journalists have shown grave concern. This was mostly due to the fact that some highly visible terrorism suspects share a connection with one particular *pesantren* in Central Java, the PP (Pondok Pesantren) Al-Mukmin in Ngruki near Solo or with one of a small number of offshoots from this school.[1] Ustad Abu Bakar Ba'asyir, who was one of the founders of this *pesantren* in the early 1960s, returned in 1999, after having spent fourteen years in Malaysian exile. He has been accused of being the spiritual leader of an underground movement known as Jama'ah Islamiyah, which is believed to be active throughout Muslim Southeast Asia and to have carried out a large number of terrorist acts in this region. Several of the perpetrators of the Bali bombing of 12 October 2002, which killed some two hundred people, were associated with a small *pesantren* in East Java where Ngruki graduates gave lessons; all of them held Ba'asyir in high regard as the most learned and disinterested of the ulama.

The links that this particular *pesantren* had to terrorist acts appeared, upon closer inspection, to be more tenuous than had been originally claimed. Furthermore, nothing could be more misleading than to extrapolate from 'Ngruki' to other Indonesian *pesantrens*. The PP Al-Mukmin and the handful of secondary *pesantrens* that it has spawned were established with the express purpose of constituting an alternative to the existing 'traditional' *pesantrens*; its founders were Muslim reformists highly critical of the *pesantren* tradition. The curriculum and the general culture of this *pesantren* make it stand out from the vast majority of *pesantrens* in Java and, for that matter, Southeast Asia as a whole. The *pesantrens* of Java and similar institutions (*surau*, *pondok*) in other parts of Southeast Asia are the centres of rural religious life; they tend to be tradition-oriented and socially conservative, the mainstays of beliefs and practices against which reformists have turned their most fervent efforts. Besides the *pesantren* at Ngruki, there have been a few other attempts to establish alternative types of *pesantren*. Some of these were associated with the reformist movements in Islamic Indonesia, such as Persis and Muhammadiyah; others with various Islamist currents from the past three decades or, most recently, the Saudi-inspired Salafi movement. In general, however, the reformist movements have been associated with 'modern' school types with a heavy emphasis on general, non-religious subjects, oriented towards secular professional careers.

In the first decades of Indonesia's independence, mainstream Islam was conventionally represented as consisting of a 'modernist' and a 'traditionalist' stream, with the associations Muhammadiyah and Nahdlatul Ulama as their major organisational vehicles.[2] 'Modernists' were typically urban and (lower) middle class and sent their children to a modern school; 'traditionalists' were largely rural (or urban lower class) and sent their children to a *pesantren*, where they learned some Arabic and Islamic jurisprudence (*fiqh*) but little or nothing about more general subjects. Muhammadiyah, established in 1912, focused most of its energies on education and welfare, establishing hospitals and modern schools, both modelled on Christian missionary examples. In matters of religious belief and practice it was reformist and fiercely opposed to 'syncretistic' practices such as those surrounding death and the visiting of graves and all other practises for which no precedent could be found in the Qur'an and *hadith*. The Nahdlatul Ulama association (NU) was established in 1926 specifically to protect the institutions and practices that were criticised by the reformists and then actually threatened by the then recent Saudi conquest of Mecca and Medina, the centres of traditional learning.[3] The NU was an association of *kyais* (*pesantren*-based ulama) with a mass following, which after Independence became a political party. In the 1950s, most of its active members only had a *pesantren* education, which at the time did not include many general subjects, so that the party had great difficulty finding qualified personnel to fill positions in the government and bureaucracy to which it was entitled on the basis of its numerical strength. The Ministry of Religious Affairs thus became its only fief in the newly independent Republic of Indonesia.

Between them, Muhammadiyah and Nahdlatul Ulama can lay claim to the loyalties of about half the Indonesian population. In a recent nationwide survey, 42% of the respondents indicated that they felt more or less represented by the NU, 12% by Muhammadiyah.[4] The way the questions were framed suggests, however, that those who identified with the NU did not mean so much the organisation itself as the religious attitudes it is associated with, including an openness to local traditions (and even syncretism), flexibility and tolerance, as opposed to the more principled and puritan, if not fundamentalist, attitudes associated with Muhammadiyah. In the NU's organisation itself, the *pesantren* remains the major institutional prop, and the *ulama* of major *pesantrens* remain the chief authorities.

The Traditional Pesantren: Origins and History

Dutch colonial scholars have wanted to see in the *pesantren* the continuation of pre-Islamic institutions: forest hermitages, *mandala* communities, or centres of transmission of Hindu and Buddhist scriptural knowledge. Although it is not impossible that certain families and certain locales may represent such a continuity, and although there is an obvious similarity in function – some *pesantrens* are more than just centres of scriptural transmission and are actually centres of spiritual and mystical exercises or supernatural healing besides– the *pesantren* tradition as found in twentieth-century Indonesia is of much more recent origin.

Islam began to spread among the indigenous population of Java in the fifteenth century. The earliest mention of a Muslim religious school thus far is in a Dutch East Indies Company document of 1718, that is based on hearsay and refers to the establishment of a 'training school for religious' near Surabaya.[5] The oldest *pesantren* still in existence was established in the late eighteenth century in the village of Tegalsari near Ponorogo in East Java.[6] A survey of indigenous education by Dutch authorities in 1819 found few institutions that we would recognise today as *pesantrens*. Basic religious education was given informally in the mosque or in the private home of someone who was slightly more learned than the people in his surroundings. Some of the more advanced students, the report states, were sent to schools in the Madiun-Ponorogo region (where the said Tegalsari *pesantren* was located). In an 1831 survey, simple Islamic schools are mentioned in the coastal districts of Cirebon, Semarang and Surabaya but there were very few inland. Java appears not yet dotted with *pesantrens* at the time of these surveys, which is quite unlike the situation a century later.[7]

Most of the prestigious old *pesantrens* that still exist do not date further back than the late nineteenth century, and many not even that far.[8] Their founders were usually men who had spent years studying in Mecca or Cairo. Rather than imitating Hindu and Buddhist precursors, these late nineteenth- and early twentieth-century *pesantrens* appeared to be modelled on institutions with which their founders had become familiar during their studies in Arabia: the study circles (*halqa*) in the Great Mosque of Mecca (the Masjid al-Haram), Cairo's Azhar, which had a dormitory assigned to Southeast Asian students (the *riwaq al-Jawa*), and especially the slightly modernised madrasas in Mecca at the time. The most prominent of the latter was the Madrasa Sawlatiyya, which was established by Indian Muslims in 1874 and which also attracted many Indonesian students. In 1934, following an incident in which their national pride was impaired, the Indonesians abandoned this madrasa and founded their own school, Dar al-'Ulum al-Diniyya, which exists to this very day and has been a major centre of orientation for the Indonesian traditional *ulama*.

Some of the founders of the early *pesantrens* may have belonged to families that already enjoyed some religious prestige; others were bright young men who could make the voyage to Mecca due to patronage; others again supported themselves by engaging in trade. By the mid-twentieth century, and perhaps even earlier, we find the *pesantren*-based *ulama* or *kyai*s consolidated into a caste-like rural elite, among whom descent is as important as learning. A *kyai*'s sons shared their father's prestige irrespective of learning; and a bright and learned young man of low descent could only join their ranks by marrying an established *kyai*'s daughter.

The teaching methods in Indonesian *pesantrens* followed those of Mecca and Cairo, and educational reforms in these centres (classrooms, a grading system, changes in curriculum) gradually spread from there to the Indonesian *pesantrens*. The curriculum in Indonesia was very similar to that of other regions where the Shafi'i school is followed: a few basic compendia of Ash'ari doctrine and the major handbooks of Shafi'i *fiqh* were the dominant texts. *Hadith* collections, which are very important to Muslim reformists, until recently hardly figured in the *pesantren* curriculum. When *hadith* were studied at all, it was in the form of such collections as Nawawi's 'Forty Hadith' (*Arba'in*) or his *Riyad al-salihin*, which legitimised popular devotional beliefs and practices the reformists frowned upon. The *pesantren* tradition held devotional practices associated with the veneration of the Prophet and the visiting of graves in high esteem, and many of its teachers were involved in Sufi orders and Islamic healing. The reformist call for a return to the Qur'an and *hadith* (to replace the uncritical following of classical *fiqh* texts) was strongly rejected by the *pesantren* world, but it did have the effect that in the course of the twentieth century the canonical *hadith* collections of Bukhari and Muslim and an increasing range of Qur'anic commentaries became incorporated into the curriculum of many *pesantrens*.[9]

An important aspect of the *pesantren* tradition is the emphasis on the oral transmission of knowledge, even of written texts. In the traditional didactic styles, that are still maintained in many *pesantrens*, the student studies a specific text with a specific teacher, and upon finishing this text may move on to another teacher, at another *pesantren*, to study another text. The student may sit with others in a circle (*halqa*) around the teacher, who reads the text aloud while students read along with him in their own copies of the book. The teacher stops from time to time to comment on a point of syntax or vocabulary, but he seldom if ever offers a critical interpretation or comments on the applicability of the text. In a more individual mode, the student may himself read passages of the text aloud while the teacher listens, questions, and comments on his reading. Both the teacher and the teachings he handed down were treated with great respect, which precluded a critical discussion. The student was aware of being connected to great masters of the past through the chains of oral transmission (*isnad*) of the texts he studied, just like any follower of a Sufi order had a spiritual genealogy (*silsila*) linking him through successive teachers to the order's founder and ultimately to the Prophet. Love and even veneration for the *ulama* of the past was and is an important part of the *pesantren* tradition. Where possible, one was expected to follow their example, especially in legal thought. Reformists criticised *taqlid*, the 'blind' following of the rulings of ulama of the past, and proclaimed the need for independent interpretation, or *ijtihad*, instead.[10] For traditionalists, however, *fiqh* belongs to the essential core of Islam, and *fiqh* is impossible without *taqlid*, following the rulings of the great *ulama* of the past who had developed the Shafi'i *madhhab* or school of *fiqh*.

The debates between reformists and traditionalists, which were at times very heated, revolved around such issues as *taqlid*, rituals for the dead and the visiting of saints' graves, the recitation of devotional texts for 'magical' purposes, etc. Reformists also criticised *pesantren* education for its emphasis on rote learning without critical understanding and the study of post-classical scholastic texts rather than the original sources, Qur'an and *hadith*. Under the influence of such criticism and the demands of a changing labour market, most *pesantrens* introduced changes into their curriculum in the course of the twentieth century. Among the religious subjects, *hadith* and Qur'anic exegesis gradually took a more prominent place; many *pesantrens* added general subjects and organised the curriculum in school classes parallel with those of the public school system.

In Indonesia, the term *madrasa* (spelled as *madrasah* in Indonesian) is reserved for religious schools with classes and a standardised curriculum including mostly general subjects. Government-supervised *madrasas* with 30 percent religious subjects and 70 percent general subjects offer diplomas that give an opening to employment as a religious teacher as well as access to state institutes of higher religious studies (IAIN) and eventually an avenue to a modern career. Many *pesantrens* have adopted the *madrasa* system besides, or sometimes even instead of, more traditional modes of teaching, and have thus to some extent become part of the national education system (although not under the Ministry of Education but that of Religious Affairs).

Those *pesantrens* that maintained the 'traditional' curriculum and methods of teaching came to be known as 'Salafiyah', which may be translated as 'in the way of previous generations'. This term has recently given rise to confusion, when the Saudi-inspired Salafi movement came under suspicion of violent radicalism.[11] Both Salafiyah *pesantrens* and the Salafi movement name themselves after *al-salaf al-salih*, 'the pious predecessors'. But for the latter, these *salaf* are the first three generations of Muslims in the time of the Prophet and for the former the great *ulama* of an idealised, much more recent past. In terms of religious belief and practice, they represent opposite extremes within Indonesian Islam.

Reformist Alternatives to the Traditional Pesantren[12]

As remarked earlier, the major reformist association is the Muhammadiyah, which became best known for its modern schools, that offered a good general curriculum with relatively little time devoted to religious lessons. Students in these schools learned no Arabic. Muhammadiyah people spoke of returning to the Qur'an and *hadith* but most could only read them in translation – and their actual religious reading consisted almost exclusively of contemporary reformist writers. Muhammadiyah established a few *madrasas* to train its own religious teachers, but these remained rather unremarkable institutions.[13]

A more interesting effort to bridge the gap between the Muhammadiyah religious attitude and traditional *pesantren* education resulted in the 'modern *pesantren*' of Gontor in East Java, which was established in 1926. Gontor combined the study of classical texts with modern concepts of education and a reformist spirit; it became the example on which a range of other reformist-oriented schools later modelled themselves.[14] For inspiration, the founders of Gontor not only looked at the reformist trend in Egypt (the Dar al-'Ulum, where Abduh and Rashid Rida were active) but also at more modernist experiments in India, the Anglo-Muslim college of Aligarh and even Rabindranath Tagore's philosophy of education and his Santiniketan experiment. The didactic methods were those of the modern school, and students were obliged to communicate in either Arabic or English, in order to train them in active mastery of these languages. The religious teaching material continued to include some classical *fiqh* texts, notably Ibn Rushd's *Bidayat al-mujtahid*, which compares various legal schools. The *pesantren* of Gontor thus positioned itself ideologically between the NU and Muhammadiyah; some of its graduates became teachers in the NU *pesantrens*, others in Muhammadiyah schools. Several went on to establish their own *pesantrens* on the Gontor model, or to reform an existing one, with their Gontor experience guiding them. Since the 1960s, the school has developed close relations with the Saudi-based Muslim World League (Rabitat al-'Alam al-Islami).

Other reformist associations also established religious schools that were to have a wider influence. Al Irsyad is a social and religious reform movement active among Indonesia's Hadrami community, that broke away from an earlier, more conservative Arab educational association, the Jamiat Khair (al-Jam'iyya al-Khayriyya). Al Irsyad's madrasa in Jakarta, established in 1913, taught a curriculum of religious and general subjects exclusively in Arabic, for which it employed mostly teachers from the Arab Middle East. The school was oriented towards Egyptian reformism; instead of classical *fiqh* texts it placed emphasis on the Qur'an and *hadith*, *usul al-fiqh*, and the works of Abduh and other modern authors. The general subjects (at the secondary school level) included mathematics, Arab history and modern European history.[15] Many graduates of this madrasa spread the reformist message as teachers and preachers beyond Hadrami circles in Indonesia.

Persatuan Islam ('Islamic Union') or Persis, established in Bandung in 1923, was by far the most puritan of Indonesia's reform movements and it developed a religious attitude close to that of Saudi Salafism, although not under any noticeable direct influence from Arabia. Unlike Muhammadiyah, it had little interest in welfare work and it concentrated its efforts on 'correcting' religious belief and practice. The fatwas of its founder, A. Hassan, which referred exclusively to the Qur'an and *hadith* but reflected a rational spirit, found eager readers among reformist-minded Muslims outside Persis as well. Persis ran a well-known school in Bandung, not unlike Muhammadiyah schools but with a stronger emphasis on Qur'an and *hadith* in the religious classes. Towards the end of the colonial period, A. Hassan moved to Bangil in East Java, where he established a *pesantren* (of secondary school level) that was to teach only religious subjects. For a long time, this was the only *pesantren* in Indonesia that was deliberately non-*madhhab* and focused very strongly on the study of *hadith*.[16] This *pesantren* became an important training centre for religious teachers of a strict, puritan stripe.

Independence Movement, Jihad, *and Darul Islam*

Both the reformists and the traditionalists had generally adopted accommodating attitudes towards the Dutch colonial authorities. The Japanese occupation during World War II constituted an important break. The Japanese carried out a programme of politicising and indoctrinating the Indonesian *ulama*, and they created an umbrella organisation in which all Muslim associations were represented.[17] Within days after the Japanese surrender in August 1945, Indonesian nationalist leaders declared independence; when the first Allied troops landed to take control of the country on behalf of the former colonial authorities, they were not welcomed. The highest *ulama* of the NU declared that in the current situation *jihad* was called for, because non-Muslim forces were attempting to occupy independent Muslim territory. *Ulama* of other associations, throughout the country, followed suit with similar declarations of *jihad*. In the following struggle for independence, youth of *pesantren* background, organised in militias called Hizbullah and Sabilillah, played a prominent part.

After four years of intermittent fighting, a split occurred among the Muslim supporters of the independence movement when the nationalist leadership, in negotiations with the Dutch, accepted a temporary military withdrawal from strategically important West Java. The Muslim guerrilla units that refused to withdraw set up their own rudimentary government under the name of Darul Islam. After independence, the Darul Islam refused to recognise the secular republican government in Jakarta, and for more than a decade it continued to control mountainous parts of West Java and to successfully resist all efforts to subdue it. Insurgent movements in Aceh and South Sulawesi joined it.[18] The Darul Islam movement, which also called itself the Islamic State of Indonesia (NII), had a *shari'a* court as its major non-military institution. The political leaders were reformist Muslims, but especially in West Java, it was mostly traditionalist *pesantrens* that provided the movement with its fighting power. In the early 1960s, the movement was finally vanquished and the leaders surrendered or were killed. Decades later, it would become evident that the Darul Islam had continued as an underground movement, maintaining the old network of supporters and recruiting new members.

Initially, the West Javanese Darul Islam appears to have enjoyed quite widespread support, but after the Republican government had won independence, most of the *pesantrens* in the region opted for good relations with this government. The Japanese-created Muslim umbrella organisation, Masyumi, was integrated into the Republic as a major political party. In 1952, the NU broke away from Masyumi to become a separate political party, so that Masyumi became largely (though not exclusively) a Muslim reformist party. In both parties there were individuals who were close to the Darul Islam, but both supported the government's efforts to subdue it.

Integration into the National Education System

Many *pesantrens* nowadays teach a government-approved curriculum consisting of 70% general subjects and 30% religious subjects and are similar to the government-run religious schools known as *madrasa*; they can give their graduates the same *madrasa* diplomas. Insofar as they also offer more intensive religious teaching, this is done at the secondary or higher levels, to students who already have a school diploma. What distinguishes a *pesantren* from a madrasa in the state system is that it is a private enterprise, usually with dormitories where a considerable proportion of the students live, and that education in a *pesantren* usually includes more traditional teaching of classical texts in addition to the state madrasa curriculum. Moreover, most *pesantrens* concentrate on students of secondary and higher levels. A *madrasah ibtida'iyah* is like a primary school; *madrasah tsanawiyah* and *'aliyah* correspond with lower and higher secondary. Some *pesantrens* offer higher levels that may be called *mu'allimin*, i.e., 'teacher training', or *ma'had 'ali*, a name that suggests university level.

A *madrasa* diploma does not give access to a proper university, but after Indonesia's independence, one Institute for Higher Islamic Studies was established that was accessible to *madrasa* graduates. Since the 1960s, the number of such institutes, then called State Institute of Islamic Studies (IAIN) has rapidly increased; there is now one in each provincial capital. As a result of the *madrasa* curriculum and the opportunities provided by the IAINs, most *pesantrens* have become integrated into the national educational system and have to a considerable extent been brought under government control. For a significant part of the population this development opened up a channel for social mobility. *Pesantren* education was cheaper than education in secular schools, whether private or state, and for certain families an education in a religious school was culturally more acceptable than one in a non-religious environment. Numerous IAIN graduates found employment as religious teachers or in clerical positions or other jobs in the vast bureaucracy of the Department of Religious Affairs (which oversees all religious education, administers marriages, runs religious courts, organises the pilgrimage, and administers the collection and distribution of *zakat*). Increasing numbers of successful IAIN graduates have moreover been able to move on to a general university for postgraduate studies (mostly in the humanities or social sciences) and have embarked upon careers outside the religious sphere.

Involvement in Community Development and New Discourses

Some *pesantrens* deliberately refused to adopt the standard *madrasa* curriculum, for a number of different reasons. Some preferred to offer a solid religious curriculum, reading more and more difficult texts than was possible in the standard curriculum – or different religious texts altogether (non-*madhhab* or Salafi texts). Others did not wish their graduates to become civil servants and preferred to teach them more practical knowledge. In the 1970s and 1980s, several *pesantrens* experimented with teaching agricultural or technical skills besides religious subjects. This approach had been pioneered by the 'agriculture *pesantren*' Darul Fallah in Bogor, which was established as early as 1960 by local Masyumi activists, but was soon closed down because it leaders were jailed along with other Masyumi politicians. It reopened in 1967. The curriculum consisted of practical agricultural skills, new technologies, relevant theoretical subjects, and the economic skills needed for small rural enterprises, besides 25% religious subjects. The well-connected leadership of this school found various Western aid agencies interested in supporting this experiment; students came from all over Indonesia, perhaps because of the school's association with respected Masyumi leaders.[19]

The most famous of the *pesantrens* that experimented with rural and community development was that of Pabelan near Yogyakarta, which belonged to the Gontor 'family.' The *kyai* of this *pesantren* insisted on teaching the students self-reliance and refused to give his graduates diplomas in order to prevent them from becoming just civil servants. (Nonetheless, several Pabelan graduates were to have successful academic careers.) Pabelan taught a solid curriculum in Islamic subjects, with a strong emphasis on active command of Arabic, and complemented this with practical training in technical and agricultural skills that could be useful when the students returned to their village.[20] The well-known writer V.S. Naipaul, who visited Pabelan on his 'Islamic journey' in 1980, caustically asked what use it was to teach village boys to become village boys,[21] but other visitors, such as Ivan Illich, were much more upbeat about this 'alternative' type of education.

Many Indonesian social activists believed that it was precisely this type of education that was needed to bring genuine development to the country and not just economic growth that failed to empower the poor.

In the late 1970s and 1980s, co-operation developed between development-oriented NGO activists and a number of *pesantrens*, including Pabelan, whose leading teachers evinced a definite social commitment and the belief in development from below. The inspiration for this co-operation came again from Indian self-reliance movements, from the experiments of Paulo Freire with teaching the Brazilian poor through 'conscientisation', and from the radical critique of established education by thinkers like Ivan Illich. It was, obviously, highly educated activists with international connections who first picked up these ideas, but their choice of the *pesantren* as the focus of their activities made good sense. In Suharto's New Order Indonesia, the government pursued a policy of depoliticisation of the rural population (as well as the poor urban population) and made it illegal for political parties and all sorts of associations to set up branches and have public activities in the countryside. District towns constituted the lowest local level where activities were permitted; reaching out to the rural population was therefore practically impossible for them. *Pesantrens* were virtually the only non-state institutions actually functioning at the grassroots level, which made them appealing to activists who believed in bottom-up development besides or instead of the government's top-down policies.

It was at LP3ES, a development NGO founded by former student activists of reformist Muslim and socialist backgrounds, that the idea of reaching out to the grassroots via the *pesantren* and turning this traditional institution into a vehicle for rural development and empowerment of the poor was first conceived.[22] In order to identify appropriate *pesantrens* and gain access, some people of NU background were recruited to co-ordinate LP3ES's *pesantren* program. Socially committed students of the Bandung Institute of Technology, who were barred from direct political involvement due to new legislation following a wave of student protest in 1978, joined the effort, with various initiatives to bring appropriate technology to the rural poor through the *pesantren*. Western aid agencies – first the German Liberal Party's Friedrich Naumann Foundation, later various other agencies – supported these efforts financially and with expertise.[23] People of *pesantren* background were recruited as mediators, and gradually a group of experienced activists emerged within the conservative NU that acted as an increasingly effective lobby for a reorientation of this organisation.

In 1984, an important NU congress decided that 'social activities', meaning relief and development work, would be one of the organisation's top priorities, and it established several affiliated NGOs that were to engage in these activities.[24] The following two decades saw a dramatic increase in NGO activity in and around the *pesantrens*, which at least provided a considerable number of *pesantren* graduates with employment and training in various practical skills. Many *pesantrens* that had been isolated and self-contained were opened up to the outside world through these activities; broadening the worldviews of both teachers and students. It is harder to assess the impact of these activities on the welfare of the poor rural population, however, and opinions on the economic success of the programs are divided.[25]

The integration of the *pesantren* into the national education system also had another interesting consequence: the emergence of a dynamic and rapidly growing circle of young Muslim intellectuals of *pesantren* background, who, while studying at IAINs, were exposed to a range of other intellectual influences that included social science, philosophy, theology of liberation and Marxism. Partly overlapping with the environment of NGO activists, this diffuse group of young people, sometimes dubbed the 'progressive traditionalists', were one of the most surprising and interesting phenomena of the late 1980s and 1990s.[26]

Islam Against the New Order

The developments sketched so far took place in the most visible part of the religious spectrum, among groups and prominent individuals who were acceptable into the New Order government and who themselves agreed in principle, even if critically, with its policies. There were other circles that had a more antagonistic relationship with the regime and resented its policies of social and religious engineering. Two broad groups stand out. One consisted of the most outspoken leaders of the former Masyumi party, who were reformist Muslims with a religious orientation and a liberal democratic political style. The party had clashed with Sukarno over the president's authoritarian style and its leaders had taken part in an American-supported regional rebellion in the late 1950s, after which the party was dissolved. Suharto never allowed the party to resurface and mistrusted its most prominent leaders, the best known of whom was Mohammad Natsir. Natsir and friends established an association for *da'wa* (religious propagation), the Dewan Dakwah Islamiyah Indonesia (DDII), with the intention of changing society and the state by changing individual people's attitudes, transforming them into better Muslims.

The other group, which was even less visible, consisted of an underground network of Islamic activists who strove to turn Indonesia into an Islamic state. The network consisted of the remnants of the Darul Islam movement, which had from 1949 until 1962 been in control of parts of West Java, South Sulawesi and Aceh and as the 'Islamic State and Army of Indonesia' (NII/TII) challenged the Republican government. At the grassroots level, there had always been close relationships between the Masyumi following and that of Darul Islam, but the leadership of both had always been antagonistic to one another. Masyumi considered the Republic as legitimate and Natsir once served as a prime minister; the Darul Islam resented Masyumi's political support for the military operations aiming to destroy it.

The Darul Islam was a home-grown movement and never had international contacts worth mentioning. Masyumi had been more internationally oriented, and the DDII developed especially close contacts with the Arabian Peninsula. It became the preferred Indonesian partner of the Saudi-sponsored Muslim World League (Rabitat al-'Alam al-Islamiyya), of which Mohammad Natsir was a founding member and long-time vice-president. The DDII was the intermediary through which the ideas of the Egyptian Muslim Brotherhood (many of whose activists had taken refuge in Saudi Arabia and the other Gulf states) first reached Indonesia. It published several seminal texts in translation and was instrumental in introducing Brotherhood-style mobilisation and moral training on university campuses.[27] The DDII has fallen increasingly under Salafi ('Wahhabi') influence since the 1980s.[28]

The *pesantren* at Gontor was ideologically close to the DDII. Like the Dewan itself, it developed increasingly close relations with the Muslim World League, which may have contributed to an increasingly more 'puritan' attitude than in other *pesantrens*. It appears however that the DDII leadership was disappointed with Gontor because it produced alumni who adopted much more liberal religious views and politically accommodating attitudes than what the DDII had hoped for – Nurcholish Madjid, who in

1970 called for secularisation and opposed the idea of Islamic parties, being the most prominent example.[29]

The DDII maintained close relations with the 'agricultural *pesantren*' Darul Fallah in Bogor, whose leading *kyai*, Sholeh Iskandar, had always been a loyal Masyumi supporter and a man of moderate views who was much loved and respected by the population of the region. Like many other West Javanese *kyais*, Sholeh Iskandar had chosen to remain in Masyumi when the Nahdlatul Ulama organisation, with all the Central and East Javanese *kyais*, broke away from it to establish an independent party. In 1972, Sholeh Iskandar and a handful of other prominent West Javanese *kyais* who were Masyumi loyalists joined forces to establish an association of *pesantrens*, BKSPP (Badan Kerjasama Pondok *Pesantren*, 'Association for Co-operation between *Pesantrens*'), with which numerous *pesantrens* in West Java were to affiliate themselves. Most members of BKSPP were traditionalists in religious matters but had been active in Masyumi before it was banned, and the organisation was generally perceived as a Masyumi front organisation. Under Sholeh Iskandar's chairmanship, the BKSPP made efforts to modernise the management and didactic methods of its member *pesantrens* and to introduce useful modern subjects into the curriculum. Since his death (1992), the organisation has gradually drifted towards more puritan religious views and drawn attention with its anti-liberal pronouncements.[30]

The DDII also played an active role in the establishment of a few *pesantrens* that differed emphatically from the traditionalist institutions in their emphasis on reformist or Salafi religious thought. One of these was the *pesantren* Ulil Albab in Bogor (established in 1987), which catered especially to the students at that city's agricultural university and had the ambition of producing exemplary Muslim intellectuals. An earlier DDII initiative that targeted a less sophisticated public was established in the Central Javanese city of Solo, a bulwark of Javanese syncretism. The latter *pesantren*, Al-Mukmin, became better known by the name of the village on the edge of Solo to which it moved after some time, Ngruki.

The Pesantren of Ngruki

The *pesantren* Al-Mukmin (al-Mu'min) was established in 1972 by the chairman of the Central Java branch of the DDII, Abdullah Sungkar.[31] Among the co-founders was a Gontor graduate named Abu Bakar Ba'asyir, who was to remain Sungkar's closest collaborator for the next quarter century and his successor upon his death in 1999. Al-Mukmin aimed to combine the best aspects of two models, Gontor for the teaching of Arabic, and the *pesantren* of Persis in Bangil for the teaching of *shari'a*. Classical *fiqh*, the core of the traditional *pesantren* curriculum and also a major part of that at Gontor, was replaced by Qur'an and *hadith* studies in Ngruki as it had been in Bangil.[32] Sungkar, Ba'asyir and their colleagues were fiercely opposed to the Suharto regime, which they perceived as anti-Islamic, and they were strongly influenced by Muslim Brotherhood thought. This influence was to some extent reflected in the teaching of Islamic history and doctrine in the *pesantren*; the curriculum included some Salafi and Brotherhood-related materials.[33] The Brotherhood influence expressed itself mostly in ideological training and clandestine activism that they undertook in a network of contacts outside the *pesantren*.

Sungkar was an active member of a network of mosque-affiliated youth groups, the Badan Komunikasi Remaja Masjid (BKRM), in which some of the most radical preachers of those days were involved, many of them with Darul Islam contacts. In 1976, Sungkar and Ba'asyir joined the underground Darul Islam and became increasingly active in mobilising radicals outside the *pesantren*. Using the organisational model of the Egyptian Brotherhood, they set up an underground structure of cells (*usrah*), members of which were recruited among the most committed of radical mosque activists but also among ordinary neighbourhood toughs and petty criminals.[34] This underground organisation was also loosely referred to as 'Jama'ah Islamiyah', a name that was later to gain a certain notoriety. The relationship with the *pesantren* was a loose one; some of the more serious students at Ngruki were also recruited into the *usrah* movement, and some alumni played a part in extending the *usrah* network into other regions.

Sungkar and Ba'asyir openly opposed the state ideology of Pancasila and at the time of the 1977 elections they called for a boycott because the only good Muslim candidates (i.e., the former Masyumi politicians Natsir and Roem) were not allowed to participate. Arrested for their oppositional stand and their involvement in the Darul Islam movement, they spent four years in prison. After his release, Sungkar spent the next few years mostly in Jakarta, where he organised *usrah* groups that were part of the NII / Darul

Islam network. When in 1985 the police closed in on this network, he and Ba'asyir fled to Malaysia to avoid arrest.

It was around this time that Sungkar first sent a handful of followers to Pakistan in order to take part in the Afghan *jihad* and gain guerrilla experience. In the following years, a few hundred followers were to receive guerrilla training in Afghanistan and later, after the Afghan *jihad* was over, in the southern Philippines.[35] In the early 1990s, Sungkar and Ba'asyir broke with the Darul Islam leadership, partly because of personal rivalries and partly for religious reasons: their Salafi orientation and the mystical-magical practices in which the latter indulged were incompatible. The organisation that Sungkar consolidated under his own command became known as Jama'ah Islamiyah (JI) and, like the Darul Islam movement (DI), strove for the establishment of an Islamic state in Southeast Asia.

For most of the 15 years he spent in Malaysia, Ba'asyir lived a frugal life as an itinerant teacher and petty trader of medicinal herbs; in the 1990s, he established a modest *pesantren*, Luqmanul Hakiem, in Johor. By most accounts, Sungkar was always an activist and Ba'asyir the scholar and preacher (though one of radical convictions). Both returned to Indonesia after the fall of Suharto in 1998. Sungkar died in early 1999, and Ba'asyir succeeded him as the JI network's imam, although perhaps not in all respects as the leader. He returned to Ngruki and began teaching in the *pesantren* again. In August 2000, when various factions of the previous underground DI established a public association, the Majelis Mujahidin, Ba'asyir was selected as the *amir*, the political and religious leader of this organisation. Other DI factions declined joining the Majelis Mujahidin, preferring to remain underground. Ba'asyir's friends and associates have insisted that the terrorists who carried out the various violent actions attributed to the Jama'ah Islamiyah belonged to breakaway factions not under his command.[36]

Sungkar and Ba'asyir were both a source of pride and embarrassment for the *pesantren* at Ngruki. Their radical reputation was not good for the school's relations with local authorities and it inhibited the acquisition of students from outside the milieu that understood and supported the politics of these two teachers. Several of the teachers who stayed behind, however, shared their ideas, and the *pesantren* maintained contact with them over the years through visits by students and graduates. The ICG reports emphasise the centrality of Ngruki in the Jama'ah Islamiyah network, but many of the JI activists involved in violent acts, and in fact several of

Sungkar and Ba'asyir's oldest and most loyal associates, are not Ngruki alumni. There are indications that some JI activists were first recruited while studying in Ngruki, but it is not entirely clear what this recruitment meant.[37]

Compared to many other *pesantrens*, Al-Mukmin is poor and its teachers lead a precarious life, sometimes earning a little money on the side as preachers. Most of the students are from families that cannot afford high fees; the *pesantren* appears to have few prosperous supporters. Because of its radical reputation, few want to be seen financially supporting it. The *pesantren* carefully maintains its network of alumni, because it is through this network that new students are recruited. A few alumni have established, or joined, modest *pesantrens* themselves. There is a modest network of minor *pesantrens* that have a connection with Ngruki and appear to share its values and militant interpretation of Islam. One of these *pesantrens*, PP Al-Islam in Lamongan, East Java, acquired sudden notoriety because three of the Bali bombers were the brothers of the founder of this *pesantren*. One of the three, Mukhlas or Ali Gufron, was moreover a Ngruki graduate (unlike the brother who led the PP Al-Islam, in fact). However, it was probably more relevant that Mukhlas was also an Afghanistan veteran and had spent several years in Malaysia and taught in Ba'asyir's *pesantren* Luqmanul Hakiem alongside other Afghanistan veterans. The other two brothers had joined him in Malaysia as immigrant workers.

In an operation against a Jama'ah Islamiyah cell in Central Java, the police captured an interesting document that shows that this organisation was making efforts to establish contacts with *pesantrens* throughout the region for propaganda and recruitment purposes but had not been particularly successful. It is a long list of *pesantrens* and individual teachers of religion, with indications of their religious orientation and affiliation, number of followers, and whether or not JI had 'access' there in 1999 (i.e., before JI became associated with the subsequent wave of terrorist acts).[38] The contacts were mostly with individual teachers who did not have their own *pesantrens* or schools. *Pesantrens* affiliated with the NU or Muhammadiyah were mostly reported to be 'inaccessible'.

The Hidayatullah 'Network'

The 2003 ICG report implicates a number of other *pesantrens* in the Jama'ah Islamiyah, notably the 'Hidayatullah network'. Suspected JI activists spent brief periods in the *pesantrens* of this network.[39] The *pesantren* Hidayatullah of Balikpapan in East Kalimantan is no doubt an interesting and remarkably successful institution. The mother *pesantren* was officially established in 1973 by Abdullah Said, a former DI activist and associate of the leader of the Darul Islam movement in South Sulawesi, Kahar Muzakkar. It teaches a puritan, reformist Islam with a strong emphasis on the Qur'an and *hadith*.

Hidayatullah was soon much more than just another *pesantren*; it organised a wide range of social welfare and economic activities among the people living around the *pesantren*.[40] Its alumni established a rapidly growing number of dependencies of the Hidayatullah *pesantren* in various parts of the Archipelago. More recently the Hidayatullah network has transformed itself into a formal nation-wide association, with branches in almost 200 districts all over the country. This network is closely associated with the Bugis diaspora – the Bugis are a seafaring ethnic group originating from South Sulawesi, and there are Bugis communities throughout the Archipelago. 'Daughter' *pesantrens* or branches have been established wherever there is a Bugis diaspora community, from Acheh to Papua. The network also appears to have connections with what remains of the South Sulawesi Darul Islam network, but this is perhaps more a matter of sympathies than of actual organisational links.

The *pesantren* gained wide renown through a magazine it has published since 1988, *Suara Hidayatullah*, which at its peak achieved a circulation of 52,000. The magazine reads like a broadsheet of the Islamist International; it is militant, gives information on all the *jihads* being fought in the world, is fiercely anti-Jewish and anti-Christian, and has interviews with, and sympathetic articles on, all of the radical Islamic groups of the country. Hidayatullah has a strong sense of mission; it trains missionaries (*da'i*) to spread a reformist Islamic message to non-Muslims as well as nominal or traditionalist Muslims in the most distant corners of the Archipelago.

In spite of its DI origins and the militant Islamist tone of its publications, the Hidayatullah *pesantren* network has from the moment of its foundation made efforts to maintain excellent relations with the government, and it has consistently been the beneficiary of government favour. The mother *pesantren* in Balikpapan was officially opened by the then Minister of Religious Affairs, A, Mukti Ali. A decade later, the *pesantren* received a prestigious government award, the Kalpataru prize for environmental conservation, which was presented by President Suharto himself. Later, Suharto's first successor, president Habibie and Megawati's vice-president Hamzah Haz also made official visits to this *pesantren*. It frequently receives foreign visitors. In 1999, the *pesantren* was awarded an enormous forestry concession in East Kalimantan, as one of a very small number of *pesantrens* thus favoured.[41] In 2001, the Ministry of Religious Affairs designated Hidayatullah as one of the bodies authorised to collect and redistribute *zakat* on a nation-wide scale.

Pesantren Al-Zaytun

A survey of *pesantrens* with Islamist links is not complete without mentioning the *pesantren* Al-Zaytun in the district of Indramayu (West Java), which has been the object of many controversies over the past few years, because of the seemingly unlimited resources to which it has had access, because of allegations of heterodox beliefs and practices, and because of its alleged links with an underground DI network as well as the state intelligence organisation. The PP Al-Zaytun has drawn much attention because of its grand, modern and fashionable architecture and the megalomaniacal ambitions of its founder, a Gontor graduate and IAIN alumnus named AS (Abdussalam) Panji Gumilang. Construction was begun towards the end of the Suharto era, and the *pesantren* was officially opened by Suharto's successor Habibie in 1999. It has been receiving numerous dignitaries ever since, who usually praised it as a symbol of the progress of Indonesian Islam. It looks much more affluent and modern than most university campuses, with five-story dormitories housing 1500 students each (four of them built, six more planned), and a six-story mosque under construction that will have a capacity of 150,000 worshippers. The *pesantren* owns a considerable amount of land, raises cattle and fowl and organises various other economic activities, providing its students with on-the-job training.[42]

The extravagant style of this *pesantren* has led to much speculation regarding the sources of its affluence, and two seemingly incompatible sources have frequently been suggested: the Suharto family and the Darul

Islam movement. Strange though it may seem, the *pesantren* has enjoyed the warm sympathy and patronage of numerous members of the political elite, under Suharto as well as his successors, and it also appears to be very closely associated with one particular wing of the Darul Islam, the 'Regional Command IX' (KW9).

KW9 was a network active in the larger Jakarta and Banten districts and separate from the original DI, established by DI leaders who had surrendered to the army in 1962 and had later co-operated with state intelligence officers in various covert operations. KW9 was allowed to operate relatively freely, recruit new members, and raise money in various ways including – allegedly – through robbery and extortion. In the 1990s, a certain Abu Toto, who appears to be none other than Panji Gumilang, emerged as the commander of KW9 and put its organisation on more solid footing in terms of both membership and financing. Soon after the official opening of the *pesantren*, a flood of publications appeared, mostly by Islamist authors, denouncing Panji Gumilang for his dubious fund-raising activities, for his deviation from the original DI ideals, his collusion with shady elements in the state apparatus, and for promoting heterodox views and practices among his followers.[43] Some claim that KW9 members were taught quaint interpretations of the Qur'an and were not required to pray regularly or give up alcoholic beverages. At the same time, however, they allegedly declared the Muslims outside their own community to be unbelievers, taking whose property was legitimate. The community compared itself to the Prophet's followers in Mecca, before the establishment of the first Islamic state in Medina. In this phase, it was reasoned, the first Muslims faced a dominant heathen majority and their first objective was survival as a community. The canonical obligations and interdictions of the *shari'a* had not yet been implemented in Mecca, and KW9 similarly postponed imposing them until the Islamic state was actually established. Members, however, had to make sacrifices for the movement, and everyone was required to contribute a regular sum to the movement's treasury.[44]

Despite negative publicity, the *pesantren* Al-Zaytun continued to attract many students. Its founder and sheikh, Panji Gumilang, enjoyed such strong protection that he appeared immune to all criticism. The Ministry of Religious Affairs and the Indonesian Ulama Council (MUI) carried out investigations and found some truth to the allegations made by the *pesantren*'s critics. The MUI report found that many of the teachers and students probably have a DI background. Students are actively recruited by officers of KW9's regional structure, and large, not entirely voluntary contributions by DI families constitute a major source of the *pesantren*'s wealth, in addition to considerable grants received from members of the political elite. However, the report found no trace of the teaching of heterodox doctrines and practices in the PP Al-Zaytun. The curriculum is very similar to that of other Gontor-inspired *pesantren*, the report concluded.[45]

Instead of the *pesantren* being a hotbed of radical Islamist politics, then, it would appear that this *pesantren* effectively mobilises an existing Islamist network to collect funds and recruit students, who are given a mainstream religious and vocational training in a setting that radiates accommodation with the state and openness towards the outside world. Unlike the Hidayatullah network, Al-Zaytun shows no interest in international *jihadist* causes; its focus is on Indonesia, and its public discourse is a developmentalist one that is reminiscent of Suharto's New Order.

Conclusion

There is currently a wide range of *pesantrens* and madrasa in Indonesia, affiliated with all of the major currents in Indonesian Islam. What they have in common is that they teach Arabic religious texts, in most cases alongside a non-religious curriculum. Most of the *pesantrens*, and certainly most of the large ones, are affiliated with Nahdlatul Ulama or share its religious outlook. The core of their religious curriculum consists of Shafi'i *fiqh*, often complemented with Sufi ethics. Many of these *pesantrens* are led by charismatic teachers, who have considerable authority among the population at large. In election time they are therefore courted by politicians. Prior to the 2004 elections, for instance, leaders from most of the parties made high-profile visits to *pesantrens*, expecting their visits to influence voters. There have been times when the *pesantrens* jointly opposed government policies, for instance, over a proposed family law believed to be contrary to the *shari'a*, but most of the time these traditionalist *pesantrens* have accommodated themselves with the government and sought its patronage.

Reformist associations established their own *pesantrens*, offering curricula that corresponded to their reformist orientation, the study of *fiqh* being complemented or replaced by that of Qur'an and *hadith*. Gontor remains the model for most of the reformist *pesantrens*, some of which remain aloof from politics, whereas others court the government and yet others appear to perceive themselves as part of the international Islamic movement. A small number of *pesantrens* have aligned themselves with the ideas of the Muslim Brotherhood or the Salafi movement.[46]

Three distinct *pesantrens* or networks of related *pesantrens* have historical links with the underground Darul Islam movement: Ngruki, Hidayatullah and Al-Zaytun. Both Hidayatullah and Al-Zaytun appear to owe their success to pre-existing Darul Islam networks, the former also to the structure of the Bugis diaspora. Both have sought, and achieved, close and cordial relations with the government. Al-Zaytun appears even more accommodating with the government than the average NU *pesantren*. Hidayatullah has, it is true, adopted a militant and almost paranoid Islamist discourse, but its teachers and alumni have not been directly associated with any violent activities. This cannot be said of Ngruki; many people arrested in connection with terrorist violence in Indonesia or neighbour countries have either studied there or passed through the *pesantren* as visitors. What connects these men, however, is not Ngruki but their shared experience in Afghanistan, the southern Philippines or Malaysia; the same network includes many others who have never studied at Ngruki – in fact, the most prominent members of this terrorist network are *not* Ngruki alumni.

Notes

1 This *pesantren* was presented as the central hub in an Indonesian Al-Qaeda network in a report prepared by Sidney Jones of the International Crisis Group, 'Al-Qaeda in Southeast Asia: the case of the "Ngruki network" in Indonesia'. Jakarta and Brussels: International Crisis Group, August 2002. A later report by the same author, 'Jemaah Islamiyah in South East Asia: damaged but still dangerous', Jakarta: International Crisis Group, August 2003, lists a number of other *pesantrens* that appear to have a connection with the Jama'ah Islamiyah network.

2 The term 'modernist', as it is commonly used in Indonesia, may be somewhat misleading. It refers to all of the varieties of Muslim reformism, including the most literally scripturalist. The classic study is: Deliar Noer, *The Modernist Muslim Movement in Indonesia 1900-1940*, Kuala Lumpur, etc.: Oxford University Press, 1973.

3 Martin van Bruinessen, 'Muslims of the Dutch East Indies and the caliphate question', *Studia Islamika* (Jakarta) vol. 2 no. 3, 1995, 115-140.

4 Saiful Mujani and R. William Liddle, 'Indonesia's approaching elections: politics, Islam, and public opinion', *Journal of Democracy* 15(1), 2004, 109-123.

5 M.C. Ricklefs, *Mystic Synthesis in Java*, Norwalk, CT: EastBridge, 2006, p. 89.

6 Claude Guillot, 'Le role historique des perdikan ou "villages francs": le cas de Tegalsari', *Archipel* 30, 1985, 137-162.

7 J.A. van der Chys, 'Bijdragen tot de geschiedenis van het inlandsch onderwijs' ('Contributions to the history of indigenous education'), *Tijdschrift voor Indische Taal-, Land- en Volkenkunde* 14, 1864, 212-323; cf. M.C. Ricklefs, *Polarising Javanese society: Islamic and other visions (c.1830-1930)*, Singapore: NUS Press, 2007, pp. 49-52.

8 The historical evidence is surveyed in: Martin van Bruinessen, '*Pesantren* and kitab kuning: Continuity and change in a tradition of religious learning', in: W. Marschall (ed.), *Texts from the islands: Oral and written traditions of Indonesia and the Malay world* [Ethnologica Bernensia 4], Berne: University of Berne Institute of Ethnology, 1994, pp. 121-146. Available online at: http://www.let.uu.nl/~martin.vanbruinessen/personal/publications/*pesantren*_and_kitab_kuning.htm.

9 On the books studied in the *pesantren*, and the shifts in the curriculum see: Martin van Bruinessen, 'Kitab kuning: books in Arabic script used in the *pesantren* milieu', *Bijdragen tot de Taal-, Land- en Volkenkunde* 146, 1990, 226-269 (available online at: http://www.let.uu.nl/~martin.vanbruinessen/personal/publications/kitab_kuning.htm). There is a striking similarity to the curriculum in Kurdish madrasas, as described in: Zeynelabidin Zinar, 'Medrese education in Kurdistan', *Les annales de l'autre Islam* 5, 1998, 39-58 (available online at: http://www.let.uu.nl/~martin.vanbruinessen/personal/publications/medrese_education_kurdistan.htm).

10 On these aspects of the *pesantren* tradition, see also: Martin van Bruinessen, 'Traditions for the future: the reconstruction of traditionalist discourse within NU', in: Greg Barton and Greg Fealy (eds), *Nahdlatul Ulama, traditional Islam and modernity in Indonesia*, Clayton: Monash Asia Institute, 1996, pp. 163-189.

11 The ICG report 'Jemaah Islamiyah in South East Asia' makes the mistake of attributing puritan ideas to traditionalist institutions, reporting that out of over 14,000 rural *pesantrens* in Indonesia, some 8,900 'teach *Salafi* principles' (p. 26). This should be 'use the traditional (*Salafiyah*) curriculum and teaching methods'. The report assumes a correlation between *jihad* movements and Salafi ideas, but rightly points out that only a handful of *pesantren* 'have anything to do with JI or radical jihadism' and that even among the latter, most of the students 'emerge as pious, law-abiding citizens.'

12 An earlier version of the following sections appeared in: Martin van Bruinessen, 'Divergent paths from Gontor: Muslim educational reform and the travails of pluralism in Indonesia', in: Freek L. Bakker and Jan S. Aritonang (eds.), *On the Edge of Many Worlds [Festschrift Karel A. Steenbrink]*, Zoetermeer: Meinema, 2006, pp. 152-162.

13 H. Mahmud Yunus, *Sejarah pendidikan Islam di Indonesia [The History of Islamic education in Indonesia]*, Jakarta: Mutiara, 1979, p. 271-7. The number of Muhammadiyah-affiliated madrasas and *pesantrens* has, however, continued to increase as the organisation felt the need for more educated people with a knowledge of Arabic and Islamic scripture.

14 Lance Castles, 'Notes on the Islamic school at Gontor', *Indonesia* 1, 1966, 30-45; Ali Saifullah HA, 'Daarussalaam, pondok modern Gontor', in: M. Dawam Rahardjo (ed.), *Pesantren dan pembaharuan [The pesantren and renewal]*, Jakarta: LP3ES, 1974, pp. 134-154; Mahrus As'ad, 'Ma'had al-Juntûr bayna'l-tajdîd wa'l-taqlîd' ['The school of Gontor between renewal and tradition'], *Studia Islamika* vol. 3, no. 4, 1996, 165-193.

15 Yunus, *Sejarah pendidikan Islam*, pp. 307-314. Al Irsyad's opting for Arabic as the medium of instruction made it dependent on textbooks from Egypt, so that for several decades its students read about the geography of the Arab world and nothing or little about Indonesia. After Indonesian independence, some subjects were taught in Indonesian. On Al Irsyad, see also the excellent study by Natalie Mobini-Kesheh, *The Hadrami Awakening: Community and Identity in the Netherlands East Indies, 1900-1942*, Ithaca, NY: Cornell University Southeast Asia Program, 1999.

16 On Persis and its *pesantren*, see: Howard M. Federspiel, *Islam and ideology in the emerging Indonesian state: the Persatuan Islam (PERSIS), 1923 to 1957*, Leiden: Brill, 2001. Cf. my review of this book in *International Journal of Middle East Studies* 35 (2003), 171-173.

17 Harry J. Benda, *The Crescent and the Rising Sun: Indonesian Islam under the Japanese Occupation 1942-1945*, The Hague: W. van Hoeve, 1958.

18 C. van Dijk, *Rebellion under the banner of Islam: the Darul Islam in Indonesia*, The

Hague: Martinus Nijhoff, 1981; Holk H. Dengel, *Darul-Islam. Kartosuwirjos Kampf um einen islamischen Staat in Indonesien*, Wiesbaden: Franz Steiner Verlag, 1986.

19 M. Saleh Widodo, '*Pesantren* Darul Fallah: eksperimen *pesantren* pertanian' ['The *pesantren* Darul Fallah: experiment of an agricultural *pesantren*', in: M. Dawam Rahardjo (ed.), *Pesantren dan pembaharuan [The pesantren and innovation]*, Jakarta: LP3ES, 1974, pp. 121-133.

20 M. Dawam Rahardjo, 'The life of santri youth: a view from the *pesantren* window at Pabelan', *Sojourn: social issues in Southeast Asia* 1, 1986, 32-56; M. Habib Chirzin, 'Impak dan pengaruh kegiatan pondok Pabelan sebagai lembaga pendidikan dan pengembangan masyarakat desa' ['The impact and influence of the activities of the *pesantren* of Pabelan as an institution of education and village-level social development'], in: *Pesantren: Profil kyai, pesantren dan madrasah* [Warta-PDIA no.2], Jakarta: Balai Penelitian dan Pengembangan Departemen Agama R.I., 1981, pp. 69-78.

21 V.S. Naipaul, *Among the Believers, an Islamic Journey*, New York: Knopf, 1981.

22 The initials LP3ES stand for 'Institute for Economic and Social Research, Education and Information'. Its founders were affiliated with Masyumi and the Socialist Party of Indonesia, two parties that had been banned during Sukarno's last years and initially welcomed the New Order and its pro-Western development policies.

23 M. Dawam Rahardjo (ed.), *Pergulatan dunia pesantren: membangun dari bawah [The struggle of the pesantren world: construction from below]*, Jakarta: P3M, 1985; Manfred Ziemek, *Pesantren dalam perubahan sosial [The pesantren in social change]*, Jakarta: P3M, 1986.

24 Martin van Bruinessen, *NU: tradisi, relasi-relasi kuasa, pencarian wacana baru [NU: tradition, power relations, and the search for a new discourse]*, Yogyakarta: LKiS, 1994.

25 For an assessment see: Martin van Bruinessen and Farid Wajidi, 'Syu'un ijtima'iyah and the kiai rakyat: traditionalist Islam, civil society and social concerns', in: H. Schulte Nordholt (ed.), *Indonesian Transitions*, Yogyakarta: Pustaka Pelajar, 2006, pp. 205-248.

26 Djohan Effendi, 'Progressive traditionalists: the emergence of a new discourse in Indonesia's Nahdlatul Ulama during the Abdurrahman Wahid era', Ph.D. thesis, Deakin University, Department of Religious Studies, 2000; Laode Ida, *Kaum progresif dan sekularisme baru NU [The progressives and the new secularism in the NU]*, Jakarta: Erlangga, 2004; Martin van Bruinessen, 'Liberal and progressive voices in Indonesian Islam', in: Shireen T. Hunter (ed.), *Reformist Voices of Islam: Mediating Religion and Modernity*, Armonk, NY: M.E. Sharpe, forthcoming (2008).

27 Asna Husin, 'Philosophical and sociological aspects of da'wah. A study of the Dewan Dakwah Islamiyah Indonesia', Ph.D. thesis, Columbia University, 1998; Lukman Hakiem and Tamsil Linrung, *Menunaikan panggilan risalah: dokumentasi perjalanan 30 tahun Dewan Dakwah Islamiyah Indonesia*, Jakarta: Dewan Dakwah Islamiyah Indonesia, 1997; Martin van Bruinessen, 'Genealogies of Islamic

radicalism in Indonesia', *South East Asia Research* 10 no.2, 2002, 117-154 (available online at: http://www.let.uu.nl/~martin.vanbruinessen/personal/publications/genealogies_islamic_radicalism.htm).

28 The Indonesian Salafi movement that emerged as a distinct current in the 1990s (and that is the subject of Noorhaidi's contribution in this volume), owed little to the DDII, however. Its founders had direct links with Salafi circles in Saudi Arabia and Kuwait.

29 See the comments to this effect in: Kamal Hassan, *Muslim intellectual response to New Order modernization in Indonesia*, Kuala Lumpur: Dewan Bahasa, 1980; cf. Anthony H. Johns, 'An Islamic system or Islamic values? Nucleus of a debate in contemporary Indonesia', in: William R. Roff (ed.), *Islam and the Political Economy of Meaning*, London: Croom Helm, 1987, pp. 254-280.

30 M. Syafii Anwar et al., 'The perception of *pesantren* communities in West Java towards secularism, pluralism and liberalism', Reseach report, Jakarta: ICIP, 2005.

31 The history of this *pesantren* is sketched in: Farha Abdul Kadir Assegaff, 'Peran perempuan Islam (penelitian di Pondok *Pesantren* Al Mukmin, Sukoharjo, Jawa Tengah)' ['The role of Muslim women: research in the *pesantren* Al Mukmin, Sukoharjo, Central Java], Tesis S-2, Universitas Gadjah Mada, Program Studi Sosiologi, Jurusan Ilmu-Ilmu Sosial, 1995; Zuly Qodir, *Ada apa dengan pesantren Ngruki? [What is the matter with the pesantren of Ngruki?]*, Bantul: Pondok Edukasi, 2003; ES. Soepriyadi, *Ngruki & jaringan terorisme: melacak jejak Abu Bakar Ba'asyir dan jaringannya dari Ngruki sampai bom Bali [Ngruki and the terrorist network: following the trail of Abu Bakar Ba'asyir and his network from Ngruki to the Bali bombing]*, Jakarta: P.T. Al-Mawardi Prima, 2003.

32 The curriculum included the *tafsîr* of the Egyptian reformist Maraghi and the works on *hadith* by Ibn Hajar al-'Asqalani and by M. b. 'Ali al-Shawkani (Qodir, *Ada apa dengan pesantren Ngruki*, p. 52-3). Though not part of the traditional *pesantren* curriculum, these works are taught in numerous more reformist-inspired *pesantren*.

33 A list of books taught in Ngruki in the mid-1990s (in Qodir, *Ada apa dengan pesantren Ngruki*, p. 52) mentions *Jundullah [Army of God]*, a book that argues it is an obligation for Muslims to establish a state based on the divine law by the Syrian Brotherhood leader Sa'id Hawwa as one of the textbooks for doctrine. Another important text was the Salafi scholar M. Sa'id al-Qahtani's *Al-walâ' wa-l-barâ' fi'l-islâm [Loyalty and avoidance in Islam]*, which warns the student not to befriend non-Muslims or even Muslims of different persuasions. A former student recalls the moral imperatives of *al-walâ' wa-l-barâ'* as constituting the core of the disciplining in Ngruki (Soepriyadi, *Ngruki*, p. 24-5). These texts would not be found in more traditional *pesantrens*, or in most of the reformist ones.

34 The best published study of this *Usrah* network is: Abdul Syukur, *Gerakan Usroh di Indonesia: peristiwa Lampung 1989 [The Usroh movement in Indonesia: the Lampung*

incident of 1989], Yogyakarta: Ombak, 2003. A good early overview, based on court documents of trials against arrested *Usrah* members, is: Tapol, *Indonesia: Muslims on trial*, London: Tapol and Indonesian Human Rights Campaign, 1987. There is much useful information in a thesis by a Ngruki graduate: Muh. Nursalim, 'Faksi Abdullah Sungkar dalam gerakan NII era Orde Baru (studi terhadap pemikiran dan harakah politik Abdullah Sungkar)', Tesis Magister, Universitas Muhammadiyah Surakarta, Program Pascasarjana, 2001. See also Bruinessen, 'Genealogies' and International Crisis Group, 'Al Qaeda'.

35 Nursalim, 'Faksi Abdullah Sungkar'. A detailed overview of Sungkar followers who went to Pakistan during the 1980s is given in: International Crisis Group, 'Jemaah Islamiyah in South East Asia: damaged but still dangerous', Jakarta: International Crisis Group, 2003.

36 One of Ba'asyir's spokespersons, Fauzan Al-Anshari, claimed that whereas Sungkar's followers had been bound to him by a vow of obedience (*bay'at*), no one had made such a vow to Ba'asyir (interview, Jakarta, 16 March 2004). There is little doubt that Ba'asyir approved of *jihad* in the Moluccas in defence of the local Muslims there, but his associates claim that a part of the Jama'ah Islamiyah, led by Hanbali, went its own way after a meeting in which Ba'asyir rejected violence against non-combatants (various interviews).

37 One of my informants is a former student in Al-Mukmin, who was recruited into the NII by an older peer – not by a teacher! – in 1993, when Sungkar and Ba'asyir were living in Malaysia. Another frequent visitor of the *pesantren* told me that promising students would be singled out for special treatment. They would be woken up in the middle of the night and told to perform nightly prayers, after which they would be given special instruction, presumably of a religious but secret nature.

38 'Daftar Kyai / Ulama / Tokoh Masyarakat di Wilayah Wakalah Jawa Wustho (Jawwus) Bulan Robi'ul Akhir 1420 H / Juli 1999' [List of Kyai, Ulama and Prominent Personalities in the Region of the Central Java Command, Juli 1999]. Copy acquired by International Crisis Group; part of a set of trial documents of which copies have been deposited in the libraries of Australian National University (Canberra) and the KITLV (Leiden).

39 International Crisis Group, 'Jemaah Islamiyah', p. 26-27, uncritically repeated in various other reports.

40 The following paragraphs owe much to Hidayatullah's self-representations in its journal and the websites www.hidayatullah.com/ and http://id.wikipedia.org/wiki/Hidayatullah.

41 Reported by Margot Cohen, 'Faith in the Forest', *Far Eastern Economic Review*, 27 January 2000.

42 See the self-representation at: www.tokohindonesia.com/ensiklopedi/a/abdussalam/index.shtml, where the modernity of the *pesantren* and its excellent relations with members of the Jakarta political elite are emphasised, mentioning especially New Order

politicos who survived into the post-Suharto era. Two major halls in the *pesantren* are named for Presidents Suharto and Sukarno (the latter was dedicated during Megawati's presidency); there are also buildings named after the Golkar politicians Akbar Tanjung and Agung Laksono, suggesting patronage and protection.

43 Al Chaidar, himself a former activist in the KW9 structure and later closer to another wing of DI, wrote the first denunciation: Al Chaidar, *Sepak terjang KW. IX Abu Toto Syech A.S. Panji Gumilang menyelewengkan NKA-ÑII pasca S.M. Kartosoewirjo [How the KW9 of Abu Toto Sheikh A.S. Panji Gumilang corrupted the post-Kartosoewirjo Darul Islam movement]*, Jakarta: Madani Press, 2000. The Islamist activist Umar Abduh published no less than three books against Panji Gumilang and his *pesantren*: Umar Abduh, *Membongkar gerakan sesat NII di balik pesantren mewah Al Zaytun [Uncovering the deviant NII movement behind the posh pesantren Al Zaytun]*, Jakarta: LPPI, 2001; idem, *Pesantren Al-Zaytun sesat? Investigasi mega proyek dalam Gerakan NII [Is the pesantren Al Zaytun misguided? Investigation of a mega-project within the Darul Islam movement]*, Jakarta: Darul Falah, 2001; idem, *Al Zaytun Gate. Investigasi mengungkap misteri. Dajjal Indonesia membangun negara impian Iblis [Al Zaytun-gate, investigation of a mystery: Indonesia's Dajjal builds a diabolical dream state]*, Jakarta: LPDI, 2002. Video footage of a visit to the *pesantren* by the head of Indonesia's state intelligence organisation BIN, Hendropriyono, was widely circulated on video discs. The intelligence chief's unusually cordial speech, in which he threatened people who dared to slander Al-Zaytun, was seen by many as confirmation of the intimate links between Panji Gumilang and the intelligence apparatus.

44 Al Chaidar, *Sepak terjang KW9 Abu Toto*, pp. 104-8; Majelis Ulama Indonesia Team Peneliti Ma'had Al-Zaytun, 'Laporan lengkap hasil penelitian Ma'had al-Zaytun Haurgeulis Indramayu' ['Full report on the research concerning the school Al-Zaytun in Haurgeulis, Indramayu'], Jakarta: Majelis Ulama Indonesia, 2002.

45 Majelis Ulama Indonesia, 'Laporan lengkap hasil penelitian Ma'had al-Zaytun Haurgeulis Indramayu'; interviews with KH. Ma'ruf Amin, head of the MUI's investigating committee and with Ahmad Syafi'i Mufid, who carried out a similar investigation for the Ministry of Religious Affairs, March 2004.

46 In the list of teachers in Central Java mentioned in note 32 above, which was compiled by an apparent JI cell in 1999, 23 out of 368 were identified as Muslim Brotherhood-affiliated, 7 as Salafi and 6 as Darul Islam; 143 were affiliated with NU and 141 with Muhammadiyah. Most of the Muslim Brothers were not teaching in *pesantren* but in universities and colleges.

9 The Salafi Madrasas of Indonesia

Noorhaidi Hasan

Introduction

Indonesia has long been familiar with that Islamic education institution called the *madrasa*.[1] In the contemporary Indonesian context, the term refers to primary and secondary Islamic schools adopting a modern system of education, in which Islamic subjects are taught alongside general subjects. The main aim of the madrasa is to produce graduates like those from modern-style 'secular' schools, called *sekolah*, but is distinguished by its having a better understanding of Islam. Today there are more than 37,000 madrasas scattered throughout Indonesia. Some of them belong to private Islamic organisations, and another important portion are controlled by the government's Department of Religious Affairs.[2] Another Islamic education institution which operates in Indonesia is the *pesantren*. Slightly different from the madrasa, the *pesantren* is a rural-based Islamic educational institution which teaches exclusively Islamic subjects, using *kitab kuning* (classical Arabic books), with the main aim of producing religious authorities.[3] This institution is overwhelmingly identified with the traditionalist Nahdlatul Ulama (NU). It is an exemplary Islamic teaching centre in which the *kyai*, the traditional Javanese *'alim*, serves as the central figure.[4] Spurred on by the emerging modernist discourse at the beginning of the twentieth-century, other Muslim organisations, including Muhammadiyah, Al Irsyad and Persis, have also developed their own *pesantrens*, which appear to be a strong embodiment of Islamic modernism, combining features of both the madrasa and *pesantren* systems.[5]

Besides these older madrasas and *pesantrens*, known for their relatively moderate understanding of Islam, there has more recently emerged a number of conservative, if not exclusivist, Islamic educational institutions of a new type. Some of these have been involved in providing breeding grounds for violent mobilisation conducted by militant Islamic groups that rose in the aftermath of the collapse of Suharto's New Order regime in May 1998. These institutions generally grew out of Indonesia's increasingly closer connections with the dynamics of transnational Muslim politics over the last 20 years. One such example is the Salafi madrasas, Islamic teaching centres associated with those who explicitly identify themselves as Salafis, literally meaning the followers of the pious forefathers, *al-salaf al-salih*. They believe that to follow the *salaf al-salih* means to submit to the absolute literal word of the Qur'an and the *sunna*, and that this submission will determine whether one can be called Muslim or not. Although these madrasas are in some ways similar to the (traditional) *pesantren*, they appear to challenge all of the aforementioned educational institutions, including the *sekolah*, madrasa and *pesantren*. The system adopted indicates a rejection of anything regarded as a corrupting influence of Western culture and, at the same time, shows a marked aversion to the traditional corpus of religious authority. Interestingly, they construct a particular system of authority directly connected to the religious authorities in the Middle East and other parts of the Muslim world.

The developments in the aftermath of the events of 9/11 brought all Islamic educational institutions into the spotlight. They received a considerable amount of attention from foreign observers and analysts as well as the Indonesian authorities. Despite this, Indonesia's Salafi madrasas remain virtually unknown. These madrasas have often been confused with other conservative *pesantrens*, such as the *pesantren* Al-Mukmin in Ngruki, Solo, in Central Java, which has been accused of being a central hub in the radical Jama'ah Islamiyah network. Activists in this network, which has been active all over Southeast Asia, were involved in various devastating bombing attacks in Indonesia and the Philippines. In spite of certain ideological similarities – the Ngruki *pesantren* also claims to be a legitimate representative of the Salafi path (*manhaj*) – however, the Salafi madrasas discussed here should be distinguished from the Ngruki *pesantren*. The latter, along with a handful of *pesantrens* affiliated with the Persis and Al Irsyad reformist movements, represents a home-grown variety of Salafism.[6]

Given their mounting significance, this chapter seeks to examine how the Salafi madrasas have developed in Indonesia and the factors that have contributed to their proliferation. In this respect, it takes into account developments that have occurred both at the domestic and the transnational levels. The chapter also analyses profiles of madrasas, focusing on their physical appearance, curriculum and the background of their students. These three aspects will shed light on the distinctiveness of these madrasas compared to similar puritan Islamic educational institutions. Finally, this chapter will scrutinise the madrasa network, placing an emphasis on their transnational linkages with the Middle East.

The Expansion of Salafism in Indonesia

The history of the Salafi madrasas in Indonesia can be traced back to the mid-1980s, when the first Salafi communities in the country were becoming visible and assertive. The first striking signs of the expansion of Salafism in Indonesia were the emergence of bearded males wearing long flowing robes (*jalabiyya*), turbans, and trousers to their ankles (*isbal*), and of women wearing a form of enveloping black veil (*niqab*). Their main concerns revolved around the question of the purity of the faith, *tawhid*, and a number of other issues centred on the call for a return to strict religious practice and the subsequent moral integrity of individuals. A commitment to wearing the *jalabiyya* by men and the *niqab* by women, for instance, has been viewed by these Salafis as much more important than taking part in political activities. They believe that Muslim society must first be Islamised through a gradual evolutionary process that includes *tarbiya* (education) and *tasfiyya* (purification) before the implementation of the *shari'a* can be realised. As a strategy to reach this end, they have been fervently committed to *da'wa* activities, participating in the establishment of *halqas* and *dauras*.[7]

The emergence of an Indonesian Salafi movement and a network of Salafi madrasas was part of the global expansion of the contemporary Salafi *da'wa*, closely allied with the Saudi state and its own sectarian brand of Islamic thought and practice, Wahhabism. Named for Muhammad ibn 'Abd al-Wahhab (1703-1792), who launched a violent campaign against existing religious practices, Wahhabism constitutes one particular trend in the Salafiyya (purification) movement. Its theological foundations were derived from a number of classical Salafi scholars, including Ahmad ibn Hanbal (780-855), Ahmad ibn Taymiyya (1263-1328), and Muhammad ibn Qayyim al-Jawziyya (1292-1350). Wahhabism should be sharply distinguished from another movement that is generally known as Salafism and that emerged about a century after the original Wahhabi movement. This is the modernist reformism associated with Jamal al-Din al-Afghani (1838-1898), Muhammad 'Abduh (1849-1905), and Muhammad Rashid Rida (1865-1935), who also preached a return to the Qur'an and *hadith* but insisted on their rational interpretation.[8]

Unlike other reformist, modernist Muslim organisations that emerged across the Muslim world, the contemporary Salafi movement is squarely within the puritanical Salafi-Wahhabi tradition. Its adherents prefer to call themselves Salafi primarily because of the pejorative connotations of the term Wahhabi. Their allegiance to the Wahhabi tradition, however, is clear from the frequent references the protagonists of this movement make to Ibn Taymiyya, Ibn Qayyim al-Jawziyya and Ibn 'Abd al-Wahhab, the three classics of Wahhabism. Another clue is their frequent citing of *fatwas* issued by contemporary Salafi-Wahhabi authorities such as the late 'Abd al-'Aziz bin Baz (d. 1999) and Muhammad Nasir al-Din al-Albani (d. 1999).[9]

The proliferation of the Salafi *da'wa* movement is inextricably associated with the rising influence of Saudi Arabia in the global politics of the Muslim world. It gained momentum in the 1970s, when the kingdom succeeded in gaining an increasingly crucial position in the Middle East in particular and the Muslim world in general as a consequence of the defeat of Egypt and Syria in the Arab-Israel Wars of 1967 and 1973.[10] This position was reinforced by the explosion in world oil prices. Since then, Saudi Arabia has launched an immensely ambitious global campaign for the 'Wahhabitisation' of the *umma*.[11] The Rabitat al-'Alam al-Islami, set up in 1962, is the organisation responsible for this campaign, functioning as the main philanthropic agent in the liberal distribution of money to Islamic organisations all over the world.[12]

The role of Saudi Arabia in global politics faced a serious challenge when the Iranian Revolution erupted in 1979 and brought Ayatollah Khomeini to power. The Saudi kingdom was haunted by the speculation that a similar revolution could possibly wipe out its own monarchy. This anxiety was to some extent justified by the rise of a revolutionary Islamic group within the border of the kingdom itself. Led by Juhayman al-'Utaybi, the group seized the Grand Mosque of Mecca in November 1979.[13] The challenge posed by the Iranian Revolution became more apparent when Saudi Arabia witnessed a series of Shi'i demonstrations and Khomeini proposed that Mecca and Medina be granted international status.[14] Saudi Arabia tried hard to limit the devastating effects of the revolution. At the domestic level, it sought to prove its commitment to Islam by imposing a stricter enforcement of religious laws. At the international level, it intensified the spread of Wahhabism, whose doctrines contain anti-Shi'i sentiments.[15]

The inflow of Saudi Arabian influence has come to Indonesia mainly through the Dewan Dakwah Islamiyah Indonesia (DDII, Indonesian Council for Islamic Propagation), a *da'wa* organisation set up in 1967 by Muhammad Natsir and other former leaders of the Masyumi, the first and largest Islamic party banned by Sukarno, Indonesia's first president, in 1960. Because of Natsir's close personal relationship with Saudi elites, the Dewan Dakwah enjoyed Saudi support for the development of *da'wa* activities, including construction of new mosques, the founding of madrasas, the distribution of free copies of the Qur'an and other Islamic literature, the training of preachers and related objectives. These activities, in turn, contributed to the spread of the spirit of Islamic resurgence. The impact of the intensification of Islamic revitalisation launched by the Dewan Dakwah was felt most strongly on university campuses, which witnessed the rapid expansion of Islamic activities, marked by the increase in students' readiness to observe Islamic obligations.

The preconditions that had been created by the Dewan Dakwah laid a foundation on which Saudi Arabia could develop its Wahhabi influence to a greater extent. Particularly disquieted by the widespread impact of the Iranian Revolution, Saudi Arabia attempted to reinforce its influence in Indonesia, for which purpose it set up the Lembaga Ilmu Pengetahuan Islam dan Bahasa Arab (LIPIA, Institute of Islamic and Arabic Studies) in Jakarta in 1980. This institute was initially established as the Lembaga Pengajaran Bahasa Arab (LPBA, Institute of Arabic Teaching), which concentrated on the development of the teaching of Arabic. The LIPIA has turned out hundreds of graduates, more than thirty of whom receive grants each year to continue their studies in Saudi Arabian universities. These are recruited from among the best students, accounting for 5 to 10% of all graduates.

The appeal for volunteers to wage jihad in Afghanistan presented the first serious challenge to the foreign students studying in Saudi Arabia with grants from the kingdom to prove their commitment to Islam. They were persuaded to participate in the campaign to assist Afghan Muslims to repel the attacks of their communist enemies. It is not surprising that after finishing their studies many of these students decided to take part in the Afghan War. This also holds true for students from Indonesia. Hundreds of them preferred to not return home to Indonesia immediately, preferring to spend time in Pakistan and Afghanistan. Participating in the jihad there turned out to be a strange kind of fieldwork for some of them. They stood shoulder-to-shoulder on the Afghan battlefields with volunteer soldiers from various radical organisations in the Muslim world, who found in the Afghan war an arena in which they could channel their enthusiasm for the defence of Islam.

The Spread of Salafi Madrasas across Indonesia

The return of the first LIPIA graduates who had completed their studies in Saudi Arabia and had undergone their baptism by fire in the Afghan War marked the birth of a new generation of Muslim reformists in Indonesia, who called themselves 'Salafis.' Prominent among this cohort were Chamsaha Sofwan *alias* Abu Nida, Ahmad Faiz Asifuddin, and Aunur Rafiq Ghufron. Before being recruited to undertake an Arabic training programme at the LIPIA as a preparation to study in Saudi universities, they had studied in the madrasa and *pesantren* system, especially from the modernist end of the spectrum. Given this background, it is not appropriate to characterise them as 'lumpen intelligentsia,' as Oliver Roy (alluding to Marx) called the new generation of Islamic activists. Roy was referring to people whose poor education had aroused career expectations that could only be disappointed, and whose knowledge of Islam was either self-taught or imparted by new institutions and who lacked the competence of independent reasoning.[16] The Indonesian Salafis are, in fact, quite well educated and enjoy a certain respect as preachers, because of their command of Arabic and their facility with Islamic sources. Many of them were originally trained by the Dewan Dakwah, which has invested much time and energy into the preparation of religious authorities who are able to speak Arabic and have read classical and modern Arabic texts, and who, in contrast to traditional ulama, adopt puritan views. As Dewan Dakwah cadres, they are well acquainted with the Islamist discourses on modern political Islamic movements. More than anyone else, they were committed to the spread of Wahhabism under the banner of the Salafi *da'wa* movement.

The political atmosphere in Saudi Arabia in the aftermath of the seizure of the Grand Mosque undoubtedly contributed to the emergence of this new reformist generation. Saudi policy, devised to demonstrate the state's commitment to Islam more clearly while suppressing radical expressions of political Islam, appeared to act as a catalyst for widespread manifestations of Wahhabi resurgence all over the Muslim world, particularly among the youth, university students and university staff. This phenomenon was visible in their enthusiasm for demonstrating their commitment to religious propagation and a puritanical lifestyle, while refraining from openly criticising the government.[17]

The Salafi *da'wa* movement in Indonesia began to develop on university campuses. In the early 1990s, the movement gained a new impetus with the arrival of other Middle Eastern graduates and Afghan War veterans.[18] A man with a slightly different profile who also returned around this time was Ja'far Umar Thalib, who was to become Indonesia's best known Salafi activist. Ja'far was not a graduate of a Middle Eastern university but he was well acquainted with the Salafi movement. Born into a Hadrami (Arab) family, he grew up in the puritanical atmosphere of Al Irsyad and studied at the *pesantren* of Persis before continuing his studies at the LIPIA. After a falling out with a member of the teaching staff, he dropped out of the LIPIA. In spite of this, the then LIPIA director, 'Abd al-'Aziz 'Abd Allah al-'Amr, gave him a grant to study at the Mawdudi Islamic Institute in Lahore, Pakistan, from where he was able to gain support for a trip to Afghanistan.

The efforts to develop the Salafi *da'wa* activities gave rise to Salafi communities in various cities in Indonesia. The proliferation of these local communities was followed by the birth of Salafi foundations bearing names such as As-Sunnah, Ihya al-Turath, al-Sofwa, al-Lajnah al-Khairiyyah, Lajnah al-Istiqamah, and Wahdah Islamiyyah. The increasing attention that funding agencies in Saudi Arabia and other Gulf countries paid to supporting the Salafi *da'wa* activities following the Gulf War in 1990 significantly facilitated this development.

Congruent with the efflorescence of the Salafi foundations, Salafi madrasas emerged in various Indonesian provinces, with names associated with the slogans or doctrines popular among the Salafis, which revolved around the call for the revival of the Sunna. The oldest of the Salafi madrasas is the madrasa Ihya al-Sunnah, which was established near Yogyakarta in 1994. At that time, Abu Nida, who had been concentrating his efforts on university campuses, was becoming quite successful in recruiting university students to the Salafi movement. Many students who had previously been Ikhwan-influenced shifted to the Salafi movement. A change of state policy towards political Islam enabled the Salafi movement to organise *halqas* and *dauras* (study groups) for students openly. In the late 1980s, Suharto began introducing an Islamisation strategy that focussed specifically on the accentuation of Islamic symbols in the Indonesian public sphere. Interest and participation in the Islamic activities developed by the Salafi *da'wa* movement and other Islamic movements spread among the students. They enjoyed a new freedom and were no longer forced to conceal their involvement in Islamic activism.

The madrasa Ihya al-Sunnah was intended to be the centre from which the Salafi movement co-ordinated all its *da'wa* activities. Ja'far Umar Thalib, who helped Abu Nida to establish it, made it his own base. It was soon followed by the madrasa al-Turath al-Islami, founded in the same city in 1995. Between 1995 and 2000, a dozen other madrasas were established, most of them by those loyal to Ja'far Umar Thalib.[19] When the movement split into a group loyal to Abu Nida and the followers of Ja'far, most of the madrasas remained under the control of Ja'far's faction and were led by people whom he had trained in the Ihya al-Sunnah; only three major madrasas belong to the Abu Nida faction.[20]

The madrasas and the support of their teachers (*ustad*) were crucial factors in Ja'far Umar Thalib's success in mobilising followers in a new organisation, the Forum Komunikasi Ahlus Sunnah Wal-Jama'ah (FKAWJ, the Forum of Communication for the Followers of the Sunna and the Prophet Muhammad's Community), after the fall of the Suharto regime in May 1998. Unlike the earlier Salafi groups, which had been very low-key in their public performance, the FKAWJ adopted a high public profile, with statements condemning Western democracy as 'un-Islamic' and as a source of trouble for contemporary Indonesia. The intensification of the Salafis' mobilisation and their shift towards political activism and militancy went hand-in-hand with the escalation of the communal conflict that pitted Christians against Muslims in the Moluccas during Abdurrahman Wahid's presidency (1999-2001). The Salafis began talking about the need to wage *jihad* in support of the

Moluccan Muslims, which in their view was the only solution to the conflict. Following a massacre in Tobelo, in which more than 500 Muslims were killed and hundreds more lost their homes, the Salafis proclaimed the establishment of a paramilitary force, the Laskar Jihad. Under the leadership of Ja'far Umar Thalib, they stated their determination to wage jihad and demanded that President Wahid step down. Wahid angrily refused and instructed the army to prevent the Laskar Jihad from departing for the Moluccas. However, the group eventually reached their destination. Supported by *fatwas* declared by various Arabian Salafi scholars, they claimed that the President's permission was no longer necessary, since his refusal to endorse the jihad had effectively placed him in the class of illegitimate and unjust rulers.[21] The existence of a network of Salafi madrasas closely linked to Ja'far Umar Thalib was of crucial importance to the Laskar Jihad's operations in the Moluccas. It was especially through these madrasas that aspiring *mujahidin* from the countryside were recruited.

Salafi Madrasas: Different Portraits

The rapid proliferation of Salafi madrasas coincided with increased tension among the protagonists of the movement, especially Ja'far Umar Thalib and Abu Nida, who were competing for recognition as the movement's legitimate representative, which involved financial backing from Middle Eastern funding foundations. Although Ja'far Umar Thalib succeeded in recruiting a loyal following that gave him the confidence to claim that he was the chief leader among Indonesian Salafis, the financial contributions from Gulf-based foundations continued to flow solely into the pockets of Abu Nida and his group. This inevitably caused increasing tension between the two, which Ja'far exacerbated by publicly accusing his rival of 'Sururi' tendencies, apparently in order to undermine his trustworthiness in the eyes of his Saudi sponsors. The term 'Sururi' refers to Muhammad ibn Surur al-Nayef Zayn al-'Abidin, a scholar of Syrian origin and early Muslim Brotherhood affiliations, who had spent years in Saudi Arabia as a political exile but had later become a fierce regime critic, especially after the kingdom invited US troops to protect its territory against the threat of invasion by Saddam Hussein.[22] By describing his rivals as 'Sururi', which implied that they were contesting the Islamic legitimacy of the Saudi regime, Ja'far Umar Thalib managed to present himself as a Saudi loyalist and an opponent of rebellion against established governments.

The upshot was a long-lasting conflict within the Indonesian Salafi movement over the Sururi issue. Ja'far Umar Thalib called upon Indonesian Salafis to remain consistent with the purity of the Salafi *da'wa* and not follow the path of his 'Sururi' rivals, whom he accused of only pretending to be Salafis while in reality practising *takfir*, i.e., declaring Muslim rulers to be apostates who should not be obeyed. The commotion did not stop there. The Sururi issue also generated tension between Ja'far's Salafi movement and various Islamist groups influenced by the Muslim Brotherhood as well as the locally rooted movement for an Islamic State of Indonesia (NII, Negara Islam Indonesia or Darul Islam). These Islamist movements had expanded their networks with renewed vigour during the 1990s, when the Suharto regime adopted a more accommodating attitude towards Islam. Not without reason, the Islamists perceived that Ja'far's sweeping denunciations of Muhammad Surur and his invectives against Sayyid Qutb and the *takfir* doctrine were also directed against themselves. They took strong objection to being branded as 'neo-Kharijites' who were leading Muslims astray and were the potential cause of disaster for the *umma*.

These polemics did not have the result that Ja'far Umar Thalib must have hoped for: His professed loyalty to the quietist Salafi da'wa did not persuade the most significant Gulf-based donor foundations to choose him over his alleged Sururi rivals. Instead, they seemed to consider his manoeuvres as divisive for the entire Salafi movement, as having a negative impact on the dissemination of the Salafi message. The Abu Nida group, on the other hand, continued receiving generous patronage, for Abu Nida was well-connected and enjoyed the trust of the donor foundations. He had as a student received a study grant from the Rabitat al-'Alam al-Islami on the recommendation of Mohammad Natsir, the then DDII chairman, and he had studied Islamic law at the Imam Muhammad ibn Sa'ud University in Riyadh. During his studies, he had also worked as a staff member at the DDII branch office in Riyadh, where he made contact with funding agencies. After his return to Indonesia, he cultivated these contacts and carefully managed the projects he received from the funding foundations.

In their rivalry with Abu Nida, Ja'far and his group also developed their own network of contacts in the Middle East, paying special attention to Yemen-based Salafi ulama, for which reason they became known as the

'Yemeni' Salafis. Ja'far's rivals came to be known more broadly as the 'Haraki,' i.e., politically involved Salafis – another negative label that was first applied to them by Ja'far's group to suggest that they were somehow associated with political activism against the Saudi regime. In order to prevent his rivals from gaining the upper hand in Indonesia, Ja'far increased his *da'wa* activities and encouraged his students to establish their own madrasas.

The conflict among Indonesian Salafis is reflected in the differences in the physical appearance of the madrasas. The Madrasah Bin Baz, for instance, is a prosperous-looking and quite large complex, with a number of permanent buildings containing study rooms, a prayer room (*musalla*), an office, dormitories, and teachers' living quarters. As demonstrated by the inscriptions on their walls, these buildings were donated by various personalities in the Middle East, particularly in Saudi Arabia and Kuwait. This madrasa is built on one hectare of land in Piyungan, Bantul, some 25 kilometres south of Yogyakarta, that was donated by Sultan Hamengkubowono of Yogyakarta. Here, nine teachers are responsible for approximately 300 (male and female) students, who are divided into three educational levels: kindergarten, primary and secondary. The majority of them live in a dormitory in which there is a strict separation between males and females.

The Imam al-Bukhari madrasa, which also belongs to Abu Nida's group, is located in Selokaton, Surakarta, 15 kilometres to the east of Solo, on the main road from Solo to Purwodadi and shares many features with the Madrasah Bin Baz. It is actually even larger and better appointed. It covers a plot of roughly two hectares, with a dozen permanent building units, consisting of study rooms, office, library, dormitory, teachers' houses, and a two-story mosque in front. As in the Madrasah Bin Baz, every building unit here bears inscriptions on its walls with the name of the major donors – mostly from Saudi Arabia and Kuwait – who financed its construction. The school has an enrolment of 400 students who study at three different levels: kindergarten, primary and secondary. The number of male students is four times that of female students. All of them live in the dormitory, which has a partition that divides the males from the females. They school has 19 teachers, all of whom live in the teachers' housing provided by the madrasa.

These madrasas have greatly benefited from the support of their wealthy international donors. This support appears to have been quite selective, however, because not every *ustad* received the necessary financial support to establish a madrasa upon completion of his studies in Saudi Arabia. Many recent graduates were basically instructed to support existing Salafi madrasas in Indonesia. This may help explain the striking difference between the relatively few, well-funded and large madrasas of the Abu Nida and Ahmad Faiz Asifuddin group, on the one hand, and the much more modest ones of Ja'far's 'Yemeni' Salafi network. It is precisely because the latter did not have access to the large funding agencies with their strict criteria for supporting a madrasa, that the *ustad*s in this group established their own small and extremely modest madrasas in the villages where they carried out their *da'wa* activities. Even the Ihya al-Sunnah madrasa, which had long served as Ja'far Umar Thalib's headquarters, is an unadorned and impoverished-looking place. It is located in the village of Degolan near Kaliurang, on the slopes of Mount Merapi, approximately 16 kilometres north of Yogyakarta. The entire madrasa, which has a modest mosque at its centre, covers a plot of no more than 300 square metres, rented for a period of 10 years There are two cramped dormitories with walls of simple bamboo matting and with dirt floors covered with mats and plastic located about 100 metres from this mosque. It houses some 70 students, aged 7 to 17, divided into three age groups. Some of them are 'day' students who commute home to nearby villages. The entire teaching staff consists of four teachers, who rent modest accommodations in the immediate area.

The case of the madrasa Minhaj al-Sunnah in Magelang is similar. This madrasa has 120 students, aged 7 to 17 years. They occupy a small space in the corner of a modest mosque built on former paddy fields. All of the instruction takes place in the mosque. A few teachers' accommodations and a small office are located some 100 metres from the mosque. This is similar to conditions at the Al-Madinah madrasa, located in a village in Boyolali, some 20 kilometres from Solo. Although this madrasa has more than 100 students, its facilities are extremely limited. A modest mosque serves as the centre of its activities as well as the dormitory of a dozen of its students. The madrasa As-Sunnah, at Baji Rupa in Makassar, is just as poorly equipped, with three small wooden houses that serve as dormitories for its students and a small, modest mosque that functions as the centre of all madrasa activities. Four teachers teach some 50 students here, some resident and some living in nearby villages.

Although these madrasas were generally established within existing villages, the teachers and students strictly separate themselves from their physical surroundings. The madrasas are considered enclaves of 'holier than thou' piety, that view their environments as being dangerously immoral and self-indulgent. This attitude is, in turn, mirrored by their neighbours: because of its air of exclusivity, the local villagers tend to view the madrasa community, the *pondok orang berjubah* (hostel of men in long robes) as it is often called with disdain, considering the inhabitants as alien and weird, and a little threatening. These madrasas indeed appear to be separate, independent villages that exist within real villages. Teachers, students and other members of the madrasas are bound together in tightly-knit communities that restrict their contacts with outsiders. With few exceptions, the students are not allowed to make contact with the locals. The students often appear to be suspicious of outsiders. Their life is monotonous. Their main activities consist of praying, studying and memorising the Qur'an. Students are also subject to certain bodily restrictions and are forced to conform to a homogenous norm.

A recent study by Almond, Appleby, and Sivan claims that an 'enclave mentality' constitutes the core of many contemporary religious fundamentalist movements. It is 'the primary impulse that lies behind the rise of the tradition so as to forestall the danger of being sucked into the vortex of modernity.'[23] Fundamentalists usually construct a 'wall of virtue' around themselves that is based on moral values. This wall separates the saved, free, and morally superior enclave from the hitherto corrupt, worldly, local community. The enclave sharply pits the oppressive and morally defiled general society against their own community of virtuous insiders. In contrast to the inside, anything outside is conceived as a polluted, contagious and dangerous area.[24]

An enclave sets itself apart through spatial relations that carry symbolic and social meanings. It is a separate space in which behaviour, language and dress codes are strictly regulated. The severe nature of the rules serves to emphasise the gravity of the danger posed by the world outside, a danger that can only be warded off by the imposition of order in all aspects of life.[25] Here lies the importance of authority, as a guide that steers the behaviour of individual members. The specific patterns of behaviour, language and dress serve as distinguishing marks setting the redeemed apart from the outside world. In the language of a Salafi teacher, the pattern of behaviour, language, and dress is a question of identity that cannot be negotiated:

> Whether someone is a true believer or not can be seen from his behaviour, language, and dress. A faithful Muslim must behave like *al-salaf al-salih*, speak in the language of the Qur'an and the Sunna, and wear Islamic dress such as the *jalabiyya*, in order to distinguish himself from the infidels. As the *hadith* states, *man tashabbaha bi qawmin fa huwa minhum*: 'whoever resembles a [infidel] group, belongs to that group'.[26]

Teaching Method and Curriculum of the Salafi Madrasas

The Salafi madrasas developed by Ja'far Umar Thalib and his network reject all non-religious subjects in their curriculum, and this clearly distinguishes them from the *pesantrens* established by reformist Muslim associations, including those affiliated with the most puritan movement, Persis. The latter encouraged the teaching of modern subjects, such as mathematics, geography, and English. Like Muhammadiyah and Al Irsyad, Persis, whose religious outlook is close to Wahhabism, has been perceived by the Salafi preachers as having lost its reformist spirit and inclining too much towards rationalism.

The reluctance to adopt a grading system and modern subjects also distinguishes the Salafi madrasa Ihya al-Sunnah from the *pesantren* Al-Mukmin in Ngruki, which has adopted many elements of Salafism in its teaching. Al-Mukmin consists of three separate school units, Kulliyat al-Mu'allimin (KMI) and Kulliyat al-Mu'allimat (KMA), for boys and girls respectively, and the Madrasah Aliyah Al-Mukmin (MAAM). The first two schools devote the largest portion of their curriculum to religious subjects, but also teach secular subjects such as mathematics. The Madrasah Aliyah follows the madrasa model developed by the Department of Religious Affairs, meaning that 70% of its curriculum consists of secular subjects. However, during religious instruction, students are introduced to puritan and militant ideas, using books by militant ideologues of both Ikhwani and Salafi persuasions, such as Abu Bakar Ba'asyir's *Aqidah Islamiyah*, Salim Sa'id al-Qahtani's *al-Wala wa-l-Bara*, and Sa'id Hawwa's *Jund Allah*. To further bolster their militancy, some of the students are encouraged to attend extra classes in which senior teachers voice animosity towards the government as well as the US and its allies. On certain occasions, they are taken into the jungle to undergo physical and mental training, including hiking, mountain climbing, and camping.[27]

The model of Al-Mukmin may have inspired Abu Nida, who was a teacher at the Madrasah Aliyah in the mid-1980s, to combine the primary and junior secondary schools with his Madrasah Bin Baz. These schools offer the ordinary curriculum as prescribed by the Ministry of National Education, and their students take part in the national final examinations and receive diplomas, which gives them access to state higher education. Besides the state curriculum, the students take additional classes in religious subjects in the afternoon and evening and attend *ta'lim* (short religious lectures) after collective prayer. The same occurs at the Imam al-Bukhari madrasa established by Ahmad Faiz Asifuddin.

The students in the madrasas of the 'Yemeni' Salafi network study only Islamic subjects. The teaching of general subjects and the adoption of a state curriculum has been rejected. The system of instruction is conventional in nature. Every morning the *ustads*, or teachers, come to the mosque and seat themselves on the floor to begin teaching. The most senior *ustad* usually takes up a position in the centre of the mosque while the other *ustads* occupy its wings. Groups of students gather around each *ustad*, with copies of the Arabic text to be studied in their hands. The *ustads* read aloud from the books and explain the meaning of each sentence while presenting illustrations and examples. Sometimes they use a small blackboard to further elaborate their explanations. Some students take notes; others simply listen.[28] In the case of Arabic language teaching, students are repeatedly tested to make sure they mimic as fluently as possible the examples of the sentences given by the *ustad*. After the *ustad* finishes his lesson, students are allowed to ask questions. This continues until it is the time for noon prayer. Between the noon prayer and afternoon prayer, students eat lunch and rest. After the afternoon prayer, they come back to the mosque for another reading session with the *ustad*, which continues until about an hour before the sunset prayer. Between the sunset prayer and the evening prayer, students read and memorise parts of the Qur'an, as prescribed by their *ustad*.

The main subject studied in the Salafi madrasas is not *fiqh*, which is the main fare in the traditional *pesantren*, but Islamic theology (*'aqida*), or more precisely Wahhabi doctrine. This entails reading such works as *al-Qawl al-Mufid fi Adillat al-Tawhid* by the Saudi scholar Muhammad bin Salih al-'Uthaymin, which is a summary of Muhammad ibn 'Abd al-Wahhab's *Kitab al-Tawhid.* In some madrasas, students are obliged to memorise the entire text before they are allowed to study other books. Having completed this book, they are usually obliged to study the *Kitab al-Tawhid* itself or annotated commentaries of it, such as *Al Qawl al-Shadid 'Ala Kitab al-Tawhid* by 'Abd al-Rahman al-Su'udi. This is followed by an entire series of other books dealing with doctrine.[29]

Because all of these books are in Arabic, students are first required to study Arabic. Various aspects of Arabic are taught separately, including *nahw* (basic grammar), *sarf* (morphology), *mutala'a* (reading), *imla'* (writing), *muhadatha* (conversation), and *balagha* (rhetoric). They use popular books taught in the traditional *pesantren* to study these aspects of Arabic.[30] In addition to these, they make use of *al-'Arabiyya li al-Nashi'in*, a new, comprehensive Arabic textbook distributed free of charge to various Islamic educational institutions by Saudi Arabian embassies.

Wahhabi doctrine provides the foundation from which the students move on to other subjects such as Qur'anic exegesis (*tafsir*), prophetic traditions (*hadith*), Islamic legal theory (*usul al-fiqh*), Islamic jurisprudence (*fiqh*), and *da'wa* methods. For Qur'anic exegesis, works by contemporary Salafi authorities are preferred.[31] The *hadith* works include both classical collections such as Nawawi's 'Forty Hadith' (*Arba'in*) and later Salafi commentaries.[32] The required reading materials for Islamic legal theory include both works by classical scholars such as Juwayni and modern Salafi texts by the Saudi authority al-'Uthaymin.[33] *Fiqh* is taught in accordance with the Hanbali school, using mostly works by contemporary Salafi authors, including the well-known *The Path of the Muslim* by Abu Bakr al-Jaza'iri.[34] Finally, students are also required to study a number of books on the methods of *da'wa*.[35] All of the books in this curriculum, with the exception of Nawawi's *Forty Hadith* and Juwayni's classical handbook of legal theory, are within the narrow constraints as dictated by official Saudi Wahhabi teachings, and their authors are well-known Wahhabi luminaries (or, in the case of Ibn Taymiyya and Ibn Qayyim al-Jawziyya, recognised by the Wahhabis as their precursors). Through these books, students are firmly indoctrinated in the Wahhabi doctrine and worldview.

Some of the madrasas offer special programmes for university students, called *Tadrib al-Du'at* (the training for preachers) and *Tarbiyat al-Nisa* (education for women). These programmes last for a certain period of time, ranging from three months to one year. The *Tadrib al-Du'at* is designed to produce preachers ready to conduct *da'wa* activities. The subjects taught include Islamic theology, *tafsir*, *hadith*, Islamic history, Islamic law, ethics, and Arabic. The *Tarbiyat al-Nisa* is addressed to women and is aimed at moulding their personality in accordance with Wahhabi teachings. In this programme, participants study Islamic theology and Islamic jurisprudence, besides engaging in a number of instructions on behaviour, fashion, gender relations and the methods of taking care of husbands and children.

Abangan Converts

Despite the poor conditions of many madrasas and a heavy curriculum, the students of the Salafi madrasas never seem to lose their courage and enthusiasm for their study of Islam. They realise that this is part of the struggle that should be endured by a Muslim to uphold the dignity of Islam. The majority want to become preachers and devote their lives to *da'wa* activities. Some of the students receive financial support from their own families to cover their living expenses and tuition fees. But the amounts they receive tend to be very modest: on average between 50,000 to 100,000 Rupiahs (US$6-12) per month. Nonetheless, many families are unable to even afford this much. Fortunately, there are some generous donors, according to one Salafi *ustad*, including a sympathetic restaurant owner in Magelang, who was willing to cover the costs for the poorest students.[36]

The social background of the students in these Salafi madrasas is not immediately obvious; there is not a self-evident constituency for Salafism. In my observations, many of the students are from poor rural backgrounds. Their parents are petty merchants, artisans, unskilled labourers, factory workers, peasants, and agricultural labourers, with many of them being *abangan* rather than *santri* in religious disposition. *Abangan* is the term introduced by the American anthropologist Clifford Geertz (1960) for nominal Muslims in Java whose religious beliefs and practices are influenced by animism, Hinduism and Buddhism besides Islam. They are distinct from the *santri*, who are committed to a more or less strict adherence to Islamic norms. It is the *santri*'s concern with the formal, orthodox variant of Islam, Geertz argues, that distinguishes them from the *abangan*. For the *santri*, the *abangan*'s belief in invisible beings represents the influences of animism, Hinduism, and Buddhism that should be assiduously expunged.[37]

The interest that *abangan* people have in Islam has developed apace with the intensification of *da'wa* activities pioneered by the Dewan Dakwah and other Muslim organisations in the last three decades. Although some *abangan* came into contact with orthodox Islam a little late, they did so with a vengeance and adopted the most puritan and radical versions available in late twentieth-century Indonesia. The Iranian revolution and the Saudi counteroffensive made various styles of Islamic radicalism available that had the added attraction of being global and thereby attractive to people whose villages were being uprooted and decimated by accelerated modernisation. Salafism, with its simple black-and-white message, must have offered to at least some of the *abangan* who had lost their bearings in life, the solace of moral security and a new anchor in their social lives.

Once the step to adopt orthodox Islam was taken, many former *abangan* make great efforts to quickly transform themselves into 'true' Muslims. Their eagerness to fully conform to their new identity and learn more about Islam is apparent from their dedicated participation in various *halqas* and *dauras* and their efforts to learn Arabic. Even though they find it very difficult, they are enthusiastic to learn how to correctly recite the Qur'an and properly perform the ablutions (*wudu'*) and prayers (*salat*). Those who can already recite the Qur'an often feel they need to learn to improve their performance style as well. Ashamed of the typical Javanese mispronunciations of Arabic consonants that are sometimes ridiculed – Javanese tend to pronounce the Arabic *'ayn* as *ngain*, for instance – they make great efforts to work on their pronunciation by listening to cassettes of Qur'an recitations (*murattal*) by well-known cantors from Saudi Arabia.

They often follow this up with the adoption of new, Arab-style dress and letting their beards grow. This move is usually accompanied by a commitment to distancing themselves from their current relationships and environments. By doing so, they feel they can more readily assert their claim to being true Muslims. They also often replace their *abangan* names, such as Sutarto, Hartono, Raharjo, Suryanto, Sumarjono and Wardoyo, with more Islamic-sounding Arabic ones like Ahmad Haris, Muhammad Khalid, Hamzah, Ibn Usman, and Ibn Rasyid. This process of disassociation from tradition occurs quickly.

It is obvious that the Salafi madrasas play a significant role in accelerating the process of *santri*nisation among the *abangan*. They serve as centres for the dissemination of the Salafi *da'wa* movement in regions known as bastions of *abangan* culture. The Madrasah al-Madinah located in Boyolali, for instance, recruited hundreds of *abangan* children, especially from the surrounding areas in Central Java. Some of the students whom I interviewed there said that they were very ashamed that both their families in their home villages and people living in the areas around their madrasa still believe in the spirits inhabiting the trees, in magical rings and belts, and that they even ask spirits to help track down thieves when they are robbed. The feeling of shame regarding these 'superstitions' has spurred them on to study the 'real Islam' of the madrasa and to detach themselves totally from what they now consider 'non-Islamic traditions.' Through their Salafi madrasa educations, these students will become *santris*, committed to the purification of Islamic belief and to the spread of the Salafi *da'wa*. They are, in turn, encouraged to set up similar madrasas and develop their own *da'wa* activities in newly-targeted *abangan* areas.

Yemen as a Model

Most Salafi madrasas in Indonesia, especially those affiliated with Ja'far Umar Thalib and his network, use the Islamic teaching centres of the late Muqbil ibn Hadi al-Wadi'i, as their model. He was one of the outstanding Salafi authorities in Yemen. The repudiation of anything influenced by the West, including the grading system and non-religious subjects, is characteristic of Muqbil's Islamic educational system. Ja'far Umar Thalib, Muqbil's first Indonesian student, claims that this system is ideally suited to the Indonesian situation.[38] Simplicity, another characteristic of Muqbil's Islamic teaching centres, also inspires the way that the Salafi *ustads* run their madrasas.[39] The *ustads* in these madrasas are indeed mostly graduates of Muqbil's teaching centres. Otherwise, they are graduates of Saudi universities or Islamic teaching centres controlled by Saudi religious authorities, such as Muhammad bin Salih al-'Uthaymin, who was also in close contact with Muqbil. The relations of these *ustads* with their Middle Eastern mentors are relatively close and sustained over time. They stay in contact with their teachers through letters, by telephone and by fax, and frequently request a *fatwa* or simply advice from them when faced with a delicate question. These close relations moreover enable them to send their best students directly to the Middle East to study.

Muqbil gained recognition as a leading Salafi authority in the early 1980s, as a result of his efforts to spread the Salafi *da'wa* movement in Yemen. He acquired his grasp of the Wahhabi scholarly tradition in the course of almost two decades of studies in Saudi Arabia. He first studied at an Islamic teaching centre in Najran, that was run by the leading Wahhabi scholar Muhammad bin Salih al-'Uthaymin, before enrolling at the Islamic University of Medina. During this period, he had the opportunity to attend the *halqas* of some prominent Salafi authorities, such as 'Abd al-'Aziz 'Abd Allah bin Baz and Muhammad Nasir al-Din al-Albani. (The latter had been invited by Bin Baz to teach *hadith* at Medina Islamic university in 1961, when Muqbil had just begun his studies there.) Following accusations of his involvement in Juhayman al-'Utaybi's uprising and seizure of the Grand Mosque of Mecca in 1979, Muqbil was arrested. Having languished in a Saudi prison for several months, he was expelled to his native land.[40]

Back in Yemen, Muqbil began to spread Wahhabism by establishing the Madrasa Dar al-Hadith al-Khayriyya in Dammaj, his native tribal region, east of Sa'da. In his efforts to spread Wahhabism, various challenges arose, particularly from foes of the Wahhabis, namely, the Shafi'is, Isma'ilis and Zaydis, who have traditionally dominated Sa'da. They did not appreciate the incursion of the doctrines taught by Muqbil and wanted to maintain their dominance of the region. In fact, he sensed the bitterness of his foes, particularly that of the Zaydi *sayyids*, even before his departure to Saudi Arabia. Nevertheless, he survived the attacks by his detractors because of the support of his fellow tribesmen, the Wadi'is. He even succeeded in developing his own school into one of the exemplary teaching centres for Salafis throughout the world. Tens of thousands of students have studied with him, a significant number of whom came from outside Yemen, from such diverse places as Algeria, Libya, Egypt, Lebanon, Saudi Arabia, Somalia, and Indonesia, as well as Belgium, the United States and the United Kingdom.[41]

Muqbil's relations with Saudi Arabia were complicated but also dynamic. His imprisonment in 1979 must have been an unforgettable nightmare. He was very critical of the Saudi royal family at the time and was at one point even ready to denounce them as infidels. At the same time, his interest in the dissemination of Wahhabism, however, allowed him to maintain his alliance with Saudi Arabia. The Holy Mosque Establishment, a charitable organisation sponsored by the Saudi government, has officially supported all institutions of learning associated with Muqbil, including the Dammaj Centre, the Ma'abir Centre, the Ma'rib Centre, the al-Hudayda Centre, and the al-Khayr Mosque.[42]

In many instances, Muqbil has adopted positions supportive of Saudi Arabian foreign policy. For instance, he was also fiercely critical of the Iranian Revolution, against which he wrote a polemical tract, *al-Ilhad al-Khumayni fi Ard al-Haramayn* ('Khomeinian Heresy in the Land of the Two Holy Mosques'), which served the global Wahhabi counter-offensive. Similarly, during Yemen's civil war in 1994, he mobilised his followers to join the battlefront, alongside various Islamist forces, against the Marxist-Leninists in the south. This involvement earned him his reputation on the political scene in Yemen. After the civil war was won, he remained actively involved in Yemeni politics, co-operating with the al-Islah party, whose chief mission was the destruction of what remained of the Marxist regime in the former South Yemen.[43] It should be noted that the Islah party was very active in providing sanctuary for Afghan war veterans.[44]

Muqbil's relations with Saudi Arabia received a further boost when he came out in defence of Bin Baz against Muhammad ibn Surur and like-minded people who had condemned the Saudi scholar for issuing a *fatwa* legitimising the stationing of US troops in the kingdom. Muqbil spoke out strongly against Muhammad ibn Surur, calling him a *takfiri* and thereby implicitly placing him outside the community of Salafi scholars. Muqbil's stand on this divisive issue brought him into an alliance with Bin Baz's other defenders in Saudi Arabia, including Muhammad Nasir al-Din al-Albani, Muhammad ibn Salih al-'Uthaymin, Rabi' ibn Hadi al-Madkhali and Zayd Muhammad ibn Hadi al-Madkhali. These were the most influential Saudi Salafi authorities, with whom the *ustads* of the Salafi madrasas in Indonesia have also established links.

Repercussions of the Afghan War

The central position of Yemen in the growth of the Salafi madrasas in Indonesia is indubitably related to the Afghan War. This war enabled *mujahidin* from across the world to come into contact with one another and exchange information and experiences in an environment based on the ethos of the jihad. Networks were formed and relationships established. Salafis from around the world were united because of this war. They became acquainted with the centres of the Salafi *da'wa* movement and the Salafi Islamic teaching centres which are located in various parts of the Muslim world.

One of the factions of the Afghan *mujahidin*, which became the main destination of Salafis from around the world was the Jama'at al-Da'wa ila al-Qur'an wa-l-Hadith. This was a strict Saudi Salafi faction led by Jamil al-Rahman. It had special relations with the Pakistani Ahl-i Hadith, a reformist movement founded on the Indian Sub-continent in the nineteenth century, which is similar to Wahhabism in many ways, particularly in terms of its rejection of traditional practices, such as visiting the Prophet's grave.[45] Jamil al-Rahman himself is a graduate of a religious school, the Ahl al-Hadith in Panjpir, which is sponsored by Saudi Arabia. Before establishing this faction he was a member of the Hekmatyar's Hizb-i Islami.[46]

The Jama'at al-Da'wa set up its base in the isolated Afghan province of Kunar, where the central authorities had no control. Because of the movement's relation to Wahhabism, many of the jihad volunteers from Saudi Arabia, Jordan, and Yemen preferred this group over other *mujahidin* factions. With strong financial backing from private sources in Saudi Arabia and Kuwait, it gained sufficient strength to seize control of Kunar and establish a *Shura* Council there. Surprisingly perhaps, considering its strong Saudi connections, the Jama'at al-Da'wa adopted the doctrine of *takfir*, declaring the Afghan government and all those who obeyed it to be apostates. It was their religious duty as believers to struggle against these forces. One consequence of the *takfir* doctrine was that the Afghans living in government-controlled areas were treated like infidels, subject to the rules of *futuhat* (conquest), including killing the men who resisted and taking women and children prisoners.[47]

The Jama'at al-Da'wa developed a more hostile attitude towards non-Muslims and the West in general than any of the other factions. They considered them the enemies of Islam. Members of this faction frequently attacked journalists and humanitarian workers, accusing them of being agents of the West. But the engagement of this faction on Afghanistan's political scene ended when the Soviet Union withdrew; it retreated from the political struggle for power that followed. Jamil al-Rahman himself then became the target of assassination attempts by his rivals. The veterans of the movement spent their time conducting what they believed were *da'wa* activities. Resorting to iconoclasm, they destroyed statues and monuments and attacked local religious practices they considered as anathema in Islam.[48]

The link between Indonesian Salafis and Muqbil's students probably began to develop during the Afghan war when they met as members of the Jama'at al-Da'wa faction. Indeed, proponents of the Salafi *da'wa* movement in Indonesia generally claim that they joined this faction during their engagement in the war. The importance of this faction among them is indicated by the fact that some of the mosques they built upon their return to Indonesia were named after Jamil al-Rahman.[49] However, this relation was not reinforced until Ja'far Umar Thalib decided to leave for Yemen to study directly under Muqbil, only one year after he returned to Indonesia, which reaffirmed the classical relationship between Yemen and Indonesia. It should be noted that Hadrami immigrants, who began to find their way to Indonesia in the fifteenth century, have had a great impact on the development of Islam in the Indonesian archipelago.[50] Yet, their roles had diminished significantly during the twentieth century in the wake of the emergence of indigenous religious authorities, who had no connection with the Hadramaut. The main success of Ja'far Umar Thalib as the first Indonesian student of Muqbil was to initiate the co-operation which has enabled hundreds of Indonesian Salafis to study there.

Epilogue

The mushrooming of Salafi madrasas stagnated in the aftermath of the 9/11 attacks; their networks have since then gone down hill. Several madrasas were simply abandoned by students and were forced to close down. Various factors contributed to this stagnation. Since the 9/11 tragedy and the US response, the stream of Indonesian students going to Yemen (or, for that matter, to Pakistan) has practically dried up. Hundreds of foreign students who were still living in Yemen in 2001 were hounded by the Yemeni police and intelligence agencies and because they were suspected of having links to Osama bin Laden and Al Qaeda. Many of them were indeed subjected to interrogation and arrest and most were ultimately forced to return home.

The 'war on terror' has also created problems for the Salafi madrasas in Indonesia. They came under the suspicion of the police and intelligence agencies as well as the media, and some *ustads* claim they were interrogated by intelligence officers soon after 9/11. Almost immediately after the Bali bombing of October 2002, the Laskar Jihad, with which at that time most of the Salafi madrasas were connected, suddenly issued a statement that it was dissolving itself. Although its leaders claimed that it was due to a *fatwa* issued by a Saudi scholar who objected to the movement's involvement in politics, it shook the followers' confidence in their leadership. Doubts about the ideological purity of Ja'far and other leaders were exacerbated by rumours about the involvement of certain members of Indonesia's military in both the formation and the dissolution of the Laskar Jihad. This paralysed the activities of at least some of the Salafi madrasas, including the Madrasah Ihya al-Sunnah, which Ja'far Umar Thalib had at that time begun to rebuild. More importantly perhaps, the rapid rise and even more sudden demise of Laskar Jihad seriously undermined Ja'far's credibility as a leader of the Salafi *da'wa* movement. Many *ustads* in the Salafi madrasas began to question the sincerity of Ja'far Umar Thalib's commitment to the Salafi path. As a result of this lack of trust amongst the chief protagonists of the Salafi *da'wa* and the general tendency towards fragmentation and conflict, the Indonesian Salafi movement has been seriously weakened.

Notes

1 In Indonesian, the word is spelled *madrasah*, but I prefer to use the more common international spelling, except where the word is part of the name of a particular school. The Indonesian madrasa is distinguished from the *pesantren*, the traditional Islamic school, by the fact that the madrasa has a mixed (religious and general) curriculum and a grading system. A *pesantren* may or may not be organised as a madrasa. To make things more complicated, the Salafi movement uses the same term now for its own teaching institutions, that are based on Middle Eastern models and do not include general subjects in their curricula.

2 This number is based on data compiled by the Information Centre of the Ministry of Religious Affairs (Pusat Data dan Informasi Departemen Agama) in 2002.

3 For a further account of the differences between these three educational institutions, see Karel A. Steenbrink, *Pesantren, Madrasah, Sekolah: Recente Ontwikkelingen in Indonesisch Islamonderricht*, Ph.D. Dissertation, Nijmegen Catholic University, 1974.

4 On the *kyai* and the *pesantren*, see Zamakhsyari Dhofier, *The Pesantren Tradition: The Role of the Kyai in the Maintenance of Traditional Islam in Java*,Tempe: Arizona State University, 1999.

5 On the establishment of the reformist, modernist Muslim organisations and the schools they developed, see, for instance, Deliar Noer, *The Modernist Muslim Movement in Indonesia 1900-1942*, Kuala Lumpur: Oxford University Press, 1973.

6 Persis (Persatuan Islam, Islamic Union) is the most strictly puritan of Indonesia's Muslim Reformist associations, known for its exclusive adherence to the Qur'an and *hadith* and for its uncompromising opposition to local beliefs and practices as well as the traditional schools of Islamic law. Al Irsyad represents the Reformist current within Indonesia's Arab community and has been more oriented towards developments in the Arab heartland.

7 *Halqa*, literally means 'circle' and is a forum for the study of Islamic sciences, in which an *ustad* (teacher or preacher) gives lessons based on certain books, and his participants gather around him to listen to his lessons. It is distinct from *daura*, literally meaning 'turn', which is a type of workshop held for a certain period of time, ranging from one week to a month, during which participants stay together in one place and follow specific programmes.

8 John O. Voll, *Islam: Continuity and Change in the Modern World*, Second Edition, Syracuse: Syracuse University Press, 1994, pp. 53-6.

9 Being firmly associated with the global Islamic resurgence, this movement also inherited some aspects of Salafism, notably its anti-West sentiments, which inspired the birth of the twentieth-century Islamist movements, such as the Ikhwan al-Muslimun (Muslim Brotherhood) and the Jama'at-i Islami (Islamic Community).

10 Gilles Kepel, *Jihad, the Trail of Political Islam*, London: I.B. Tauris, 2002, p. 69.

11 Cary Fraser, 'In Defence of Allah's Realm: Religion and Statecraft in Saudi Foreign Policy Strategy', in: Susanne Hoeber Rudolph and James Piscatori (eds.), *Transnational Religion and Fading States*, Oxford: Westview Press, 1997, p. 222.

12 Reinhard Schulze, *Islamischer Internationalismus im 20. Jahrhundert*, Leiden: Brill, 1990, pp. 215-216; see also Kepel, *Jihad*, p. 72.

13 Regarding opposition movements in Saudi Arabia, see Mamoun Fandy, *Saudi Arabia and the Politics of Dissent*, London: Macmillan, 1999.

14 On the conflict between Iran and Saudi Arabia after Khomeini's revolution, see Fraser, 'In Defense of Allah's Realm', pp. 226-234.

15 Dale Eickelman and James Piscatori, *Muslim Politics*, Princeton: Princeton University Press, 1996, p. 151.

16 See Oliver Roy, *The Failure of Political Islam*, Harvard: Harvard University Press, 1996, pp. 84-5.

17 R. Hrair Dekmejian, *Islam in Revolution*. Syracuse: Syracuse University Press, 1985, pp. 139-40.

18 The most prominent of these graduates from Saudi universities with war experience were Yazid Abdul Qadir Jawwas, Yusuf Usman Baisa, Muhammad Yusuf Harun, Ahmad Zawawi, and M. Zaitun Rasmin. They were among the early leaders of the Indonesian Salafi movement.

19 These include the madrasa al-Madinah and the Imam al-Bukhari in Solo, the Minhaj al-Sunnah in Magelang, the Lu'lu wa-l-Marjan in Semarang, the Ibn Taymiyya in Banyumas, the al-Furqan and the al-Manshurah in Kroya, the As-Sunnah in Cirebon and another madrasa of the same name in Makassar, the al-Athariyah in Temenggung, the Ittiba' al-Sunnah in Sukoharjo and its namesake in Magetan, the Al-Salafy in Jember, the Ta'zim al-Sunnah in Ngawi, the al-Bayyinah in Gresik, the al-Furqan in Cilacap and another al-Furqan in Pekanbaru, and the Ibn Qayyim in Balikpapan. More recent additions are the Madrasah Bin Baz, the Madrasah Al-Ansar, the Madrasah Difa' 'an al-Sunnah in Yogyakarta and the Madrasah Ibn Taymiyyah in Solo.

20 These exceptions are the madrasa Al-Turath al-Islami in Yogyakarta, the Imam al-Bukhari in Solo, and the As-Sunnah as in Cirebon.

21 For a detailed account of this issue, see Noorhaidi Hasan, *Laskar Jihad: Islam, Militancy, and the Quest for Militancy in Post-New Order Indonesia*, Ithaca, NY: Cornell University Southeast Asia Program, 2006.

22 In spite of Surur's importance among the 'political' Salafis, little has been written about him in English. The best information is in Madawi al-Rasheed, *Contesting the Saudi State: Islamic Voices from a New Generation*, Cambridge University Press, 2007, pp. 72-77.

23 Gabriel A. Almond, R. Scott Appleby, and Emmanuel Sivan, *Strong Religion: The Rise of Fundamentalism around the World*, Chicago and London: University of Chicago Press, 2003, p. 30.

24 Ibid., pp. 33-7.

25 Ibid., pp. 46-52.

26 Interview with Muhammad Ihsan, Yogyakarta, 30 December 2002.

27 Muhammad Wildan, 'Pondok Ngruki and its Alleged Linkage with Radical Islamism in Contemporary Indonesia', paper presented at the *International Convention of Asia Scholars* (ICAS V), UKM, Malaysia, 2-5 August 2007.

28 This method resembles the *bandongan* system popular in the traditional *pesantren*.

29 The following works are studied: *al-Usul al-Thalatha* by Muhammad ibn 'Abd al-Wahhab; *al-'Aqida al-Wasitiyya* by Ibn Taymiyya or its annotated commentary, *Sharh al-'Aqida al-Wasitiyya* by Salih ibn Fauzan 'Ali Fauzan. Other recommended books include *Nabdha fi al-'Aqida* by Muhammad bin Salih al-'Uthaymin, *Sharh al-'Aqida al-Tahawiyya al-Muyassar* by Muhammad ibn 'Abd al-Rahman al-Khamis, and *Kitab al-Firqa al-Najiya* by Muhammad bin Jamil Zayn.

30 These include *al-Nahw al-Wadih, al-Amthila al-Tasrifiyya, Qawa'id al-Sarf* and *al-Balagha al-Wadiha*.

31 Notably *Usul al-Tafsir* by Muhammad bin Salih al-'Uthaymin and *Aysir al-Tafasir li Kalam al-'Ali al-Kabir* by Abu Bakr Jabir al-Jaza'iri.

32 *al-Arba'in al-Nawawiyya* by Salih al-Shaykh, *Mudhakkirat al-Hadith al-Nabawi* by Rabi' ibn Hadi al-Madkhali, and *Darurat al-Ihtimam bi-l-Sunan al-Nabawiyya* by 'Abd al-Salam Abi Barjis ibn Nasir Abd al-Karim.

33 *al-Waraqat fi Usul al-Fiqh* by 'Abd al-Malik ibn Juwayni, and two works by Muhammad bin Salih al-'Uthaymin, *Usul al-Fiqh* and *al-Usul min 'Ilm al-Usul*.

34 *Minhaj al-Muslim* by Abu Bakr Jabir al-Jaza'iri. Other required reading in *fiqh* includes *Taysir al-Fiqh* by Salih bin Ghanim al-Sadlan and *al-Mulakhkhas al-Fiqhi* by Salih ibn Fauzan 'Ali Fauzan.

35 Notably *Da'wa al-Du'at* by Ibn Qayyim al-Jawziyya and *al-Da'wa ila Allah* by 'Ali Hasan al-Halabi al-Athari.

36 Interview with Abdurrahman Wonosari, Magelang, December 2002.

37 Clifford Geertz, *The Religion of Java*, Glencoe: Free Press, 1960, pp. 121-30. For a comparison, see Mark R. Woodward, *Islam in Java: Normative Piety and Mysticism in the Sultanate of Yogyakarta*, Tucson: Association for Asian Studies, 1989.

38 Interview with Ja'far Umar Thalib, Yogyakarta, December 2002.

39 Interview with Abdurrahman Wonosari, Magelang, December 2002.

40 Bernard Haykel, 'The Salafis in Yemen at a Crossroads: an obituary of Shaykh Muqbil al-Wadi'i of Dammaj (d. 1422/2001)', *Jemen Report*, no. 2 (October 2002).

41 Haykel, 'The Salafis in Yemen'.

42 See Quintan Wiktorowicz, 'The New Global Threat, Transnational Salafis and Jihad' *Middle East Policy*, vol. VIII, no. 4 (December 2001), p. 32.

43 On the link between the Yemeni Salafis and al-Islah, see Eric Watkins, 'Islamism and Tribalism in Yemen' in: Abdel Salam Sidahmed and Anoushiravan Ehteshami (eds.), *Islamic Fundamentalism*, Colorado and Oxford: Westview Press, 1996, pp. 215-225; see also Paul Dresch and Bernard Haykel, 'Stereotypes and Political Styles: Islamists and Tribesfolk in Yemen', in *International Journal of Middle East Studies* 27 (1995), 405-31.

44 See James Bruce, 'The Azzam Brigades: Arab Veterans of the Afghan War', *Jane's Intelligence Review*, 1 April, vol. 7, no. 4 (1995), pp. 178-180.

45 Concerning the Ahl al-Hadith, see Barbara D. Metcalf, 'Traditionalist Islamic Activism: Deoband, Tablighis, and Talibs', ISIM Paper no. 4, Leiden: ISIM, 2002, p. 6.

46 Roy, *The Failure of Political Islam*, p. 118.

47 Barnett R. Rubin, 'Arab Islamists in Afghanistan', in: John L. Esposito (ed.), *Political Islam, Revolution, Radicalism, or Reform?*, Boulder: Lynne Rienner Publishers, 1997, pp. 196-7.

48 Ibid., p. 167.

49 Abu Nida named the mosque he built in Wirokerten (Bantul, Yogyakarta) after Jamil al-Rahman and Ja'far Umar Thalib gave the same name to his mosque in Degolan (Kaliurang, Yogyakarta). Later, when tensions arose between these two Salafi leaders, Ja'far changed the name of his mosque into 'Uthman ibn 'Affan, thereby indicating his desire to distinguish himself from Abu Nida.

50 See Syed Farid Alatas, 'Hadhramaut and the Hadrami Diaspora: Problems in Theoretical History', in: Ulrike Freitag and William G. Clarence-Smith (eds.), *Hadhrami Traders, Scholars and Statesmen in the Indian Ocean, 1750s-1960s*, Leiden: Brill, 1997, pp. 29-34.

Contributors

Mariam Abou Zahab is a specialist on Pakistan, lecturing at the Institut d'Études Politiques (IEP) and the Institut National des Langues et Civilisations Orientales (INALCO), both in Paris. As a researcher, she is affiliated with the Centre d'Études et de Recherches Internationales (CERI) in Paris. She has carried out extensive fieldwork in Pakistan, with a focus on Shi'ism, sectarianism and jihadi groups. She has published articles in various journals as well as edited volumes. She is the co-author, with Olivier Roy, of *Islamist Networks: The Afghan-Pakistan Connection* (London: Hurst / New York: Columbia University Press, 2004).

Jacqueline Armijo is an associate professor at Zayed University in the United Arab Emirates. She lived in China for more than seven years (1981-1983 and 1993-1998, with annual visits since then), where she carried out research on both the early history of Islam in China as well as the present-day challenges facing China's large and diverse Muslim communities. She received her Ph.D. from Harvard University where she focused on *Chinese Studies and Islamic Studies.* Before teaching at Zayed University, she also taught at Stanford University, Cornell University, Clark Atlanta University and the Hong Kong University of Science and Technology. Her research interests include the recent revival of Islamic education in China, the role of international centres of Islamic learning, the history of Islam in China, comparative studies of gender and Islam, and comparative studies of Muslim minority communities.

Martin van Bruinessen is professor of comparative studies of contemporary Muslim societies at Utrecht University and the International Institute for the Study of Islam in the Modern World (ISIM). He had his initiation in anthropological fieldwork in the mid-1970s in Kurdistan, where he studied tribal organisation, political authority and identity politics and to which he frequently returned. In the 1980s and 1990s he lived for almost a decade in Indonesia, carrying out research on various aspects of Islam, training Indonesian researchers and lecturing at Yogyakarta's State Institute of Islamic Studies. Interactions between the Islamic learned tradition, Sufi movements and heterodox currents constitute one of his lasting research interests. He published numerous articles and books, most recently the edited volume *Sufism and the 'Modern' in Islam* (co-edited with Julia Day Howell, London: I.B.Tauris, 2007).

NOORHAIDI HASAN is an associate professor at the Sunan Kalijaga State Islamic University of Yogyakarta, Indonesia, and the director of the Centre for the Study of Islam and Social Transformation (CISFORM) at the same university. His area of expertise is political Islam. He obtained his Ph.D. from Utrecht University in 2005, and was a post-doctoral fellow at the Asia Research Institute (ARI), National University of Singapore (2006-7) and the Royal Netherlands Institute of Southeast Asian and Caribbean Studies (KITLV) in the Netherlands (2007-8). His research interests concern the various manifestations of political Islam in contemporary Indonesia and other Muslim-populated countries in Southeast Asia, on which he presented papers in numerous conferences in Indonesia and abroad. His publications include *Laskar Jihad: Islam, Militancy and the Quest for Identity in Post-New Order Indonesia* (Southeast Asia Program, Cornell University, 2006).

FARISH A. NOOR is a senior fellow at the S. Rajaratnam School of International Studies, Nanyang Technological University (NTU) of Singapore, where he is research director for the research project cluster "Transnational Religious Networks Across Contemporary Southeast Asia." Between 2002 to 2007, he was a researcher at the Zentrum Moderner Orient in Berlin, where he worked on the transnational transfer of education and ideas between the madrasas of South and Southeast Asia, focussing on India, Pakistan, Thailand, Indonesia and Malaysia. He is the author of *Islam Embedded: The Historical Development of the Pan-Malaysian Islamic Party PAS (1951-2003)* (Kuala Lumpur: Malaysian Sociological Research Institute, 2004).

DIETRICH REETZ is a senior research fellow at the Zentrum Moderner Orient in Berlin and teaches political science at the Free University in the same city. His research focus has been primarily on Islam in South Asia but not exclusively so. He currently heads a research group on "Muslims in Europe and their countries of origin in Asia and Africa." His latest publications include *Islam in the Public Sphere: Religious Groups in India 1900-1947* (Oxford: Oxford University Press, 2006) and edited a theme issue of the journal *Comparative Studies of South Asia, Africa and the Middle East* (vol. 27(1), 2007), on 'South-South Linkages in Islam'.

YOGINDER SIKAND, a sociologist by training, is a freelance writer based in Bangalore, India, working mainly on Indian Muslim-related issues. He obtained his doctorate from Royal Holloway, University of London, and was a postdoctoral fellow at ISIM, a lecturer at Hamdard University in Delhi and until recently a professor at the Jamia Millia Islamia, New Delhi. His chief concerns include inter-faith understanding, India's subaltern groups, especially the Dalits, Sufism and popular piety, and Muslim education. His numerous publications include *The Origins and Development of the Tablighi Jama'at (1920-2000): A Cross-Country Comparative Study* (New Delhi: Orient Longman, 2002), *Islam, Caste and Dalit-Muslim Relations in India* (New Delhi: Global Media Publications, 2004) and *Bastions of the Believers: Madrasas and Islamic Education in India* (New Delhi: Penguin India, 2005).

MAREIKE WINKELMANN is an anthropologist specialised in Islamic education from a gender perspective in India. She obtained her MA in theology from the University of Kampen (1999) and was a M.Phil. and Ph.D. fellow at ISIM, obtaining her doctorate in 2005 from the University of Amsterdam. Her dissertation, based on fieldwork in India, was titled *From Behind the Curtain: A Study of a Girls' Madrasa in India*. Following the completion of her thesis, she moved to India, where she worked as a freelance translator, intercultural trainer and freelance academic. She recently moved back to Germany.

Glossary

(A = Arabic; I = Indonesian; J = Javanese; M = Malay; P = Persian; U = Urdu)

abangan (J)	nominal Muslims adhering to Javanese syncretistic beliefs
ahl al-bayt (A), *ahl-i bayt* (P)	the family of the Prophet: primarily his daughter Fatima, son-in-law Ali and their children, by extension including all the Prophet's descendants
akhlāq (A)	morals, ethics, proper behaviour
ʿālim pl. *ʿulamā*	scholar
amīr	leader, commander
ʿaqīda, pl. *ʿaqāʾid*	creed, doctrine; articles of faith
ʿaql	reason, ratio
ʿaqlī	rational; the rational sciences (also *maʿqūlāt*), which include philosophy but also *fiqh*, are distinguished from the traditional (*naql*) sciences or *manqūlāt*, notably *hadīth*
ʿazādārī (P)	mourning ritual, especially the crying for the martyrdom of Husayn
bidʿa, pl. *bidaʿ*	'innovation': a belief or devotional practice that was not present in pristine Islam and therefore must have been adopted from alien religious or cultural practices or have been more recently invented
daʿī, pl. *duʿāt*	preacher, missionary (literally, someone engaging in *daʿwa*, propagation of the faith)
dār al-iftā	the office of the chief *muftī*, the official institution where one can request a *fatwā*
dār al-ʿulūm	lit. 'house of sciences': higher religious school (especially in South Asia)
dars-i nizāmī (P, U)	the traditional curriculum of South Asian madrasas, named after the 18th-century scholar Mulla Nizamuddin of Farangi Mahall in Lucknow

daurah (I), *dawra* (A)	lit. 'circle': a series of religious lessons or training sessions, as given by Islamist or Salafi movements to their recruits
da'wa	lit. 'invitation [to Islam]': propagation of the faith
dhikr (A), *zikr* (P, U)	lit. 'remembering': reciting the name(s) of God or certain pious formulas as a spiritual exercise
fahm-i dīn (P, U)	'understanding of religion': the most basic course of religious knowledge in the South Asian madrasa curriculum
fazā'il (U), *faḍā'il* (A) (pl. of *faḍīla*)	excellent qualities
fāzil (U), *fāḍil* (A)	graduate of higher madrasa course (in South Asia)
fatwā, pl. *fatāwā*	opinion on a matter of religious importance, given in response to a question
fiqh	Islamic jurisprudence; Sunni Islam recognises four *fiqh* schools (*madhhab*), the Hanafi, Shafi'i, Maliki and Hanbali school. Shi'i *fiqh* or the Ja'fari *madhhab* is sometimes considered a fifth orthodox school
hadīth	'Prophetic tradition': a report on what the Prophet said or how he acted in a specific situation
hāfiz	'memoriser': a person who knows the Qur'an by heart
hajj	the pilgrimage to Mecca in the month of Dhu'l-hijja
halqa	study circle: traditionally consisting of the students seated around a teacher in a mosque or madrasa; in modern Islamist movements a closed group of followers being indoctrinated in the movement's understanding of Islam
hifz	memorisation; esp. learning the Qur'an by heart
'ibāda, pl. *'ibādāt*	obligation of humans towards God (as opposed to fellow humans), worship
'īd al-fitr	the feast ending the fasting month of Ramadan
ijtihād	solving a problem of Islamic law, for which no immediate scriptural answer is available, by individual reasoning
ikhtilāf	difference of opinion; especially the points of difference between the various schools of jurisprudence
'ilm-i kalām	theology
imāmbargāh (U)	congregation hall for Shi'a ritual ceremonies, especially those for mourning the martyrdom of Husayn
islāh	reform

ithnā'asharī	'Twelver': the Shi'a mainstream, which recognises twelve imams
jāhiliyya	the age of ignorance, i.e., the pre-Islamic period
jamā'a (A), *jamā'at* (P, U)	congregation
jāmi'a	university, centre of higher education
jam'iyya (A), *jam'iyyat* (P, U)	association
jihād	exertion, struggle, 'holy war'
kenduri (M)	ritual feast with a sacrificial meal
khurāfāt	superstitions
kitab kuning (M, I)	'yellow books': classical texts in the Arabic script studied in the *pesantren* and *pondok* (term used in Indonesia and Malaysia)
kyai (J)	religious teacher, especially the head of a *pesantren*
lebai (M)	a lower-level functionary of a mosque or *surau*, whose tasks include social functions such as presiding over weddings and funerals
madhhab (A), *mazhab* (P, U)	school of Islamic jurisprudence (the four Sunni schools are Hanafi, Shafi'i, Maliki and Hanbali)
madrasa, pl. *madāris*	school
ma'had	institute; in Southeast Asia, the term also denotes madrasas of a higher level (the *ma'had 'ālī* is usually of university level)
mahram	a woman's close male relatives, who can serve as her chaperone (i.e., those with whom marriage would constitute incest)
majlis, pl. *majālis*	gathering, council
manqūlāt	'traditional sciences': i.e., those based on handed down knowledge, such as Qur'an and hadīth
ma'qūlāt	'rational sciences': i.e., those based on reasoning, *'aql*
marsiya (P, U), *marthiyya* (A)	poem/song of mourning, especially for the martyrs of Karbala
maslak	denomination, 'sect' (lit.: way, road, method)
masā'ib (pl. of *masība*)	catastrophes, misfortunes (especially those befalling the Shi'i imams)
maulvī (U)	cleric, divine (term commonly used in South Asia)

mazhab (P, U), *madhhab* (A)	school of Islamic jurisprudence
mu'azzin (P, U), *mu'adhdhin* (A)	the person who gives the call to prayer (*azān/adhān*)
muballigh, muballigha	preacher (m/f)
muhājir	emigrant; in Pakistan, the citizens who came from India at the time of Partition
mujāhid, pl. *mujāhidūn, mujāhidīn*	fighter, participant in *jihād*
mujtahid, mujtahida	scholar (m/f) with the authority to deliver independent judgments on questions of Islamic law (*ijtihād*); in Iran, this title is bestowed upon the graduate who has completed the full curriculum of the *hawza*
munāzara	theological debate
nahw	Arabic grammar: morphology
naqlī	handed down, traditional (especially said of sciences of areas of knowledge, such as *hadīth* studies); cf. *manqūlāt*
nauha, noha (P, U)	lamentation, mourning
pesantren	the Javanese variety of madrasa, usually with resident students (*santri*)
pondok (M, J)	traditional Islamic school (especially in Malaysia); more specifically, the dormitory of a *pesantren* (from A *funduq*, 'hotel, inn'). The *pondok pesantren*, in Indonesia, is the entire school complex including classrooms and dormitories
qasīda	a metric poem, with a rigid rhyme scheme AA, BA, CA, DA
rūhānī, pl. *rūhānīyūn*	cleric, divine
sādāt (pl. of *sayyid*)	descendants of the Prophet Muhammad
al-salaf al-sālih	the pious predecessors: the first three generations of Islam
Salafism	puritan movement in Islam that calls for exclusive reliance on the Qur'an and *sunna*
salāt	the Muslim prayer (in P and U: *namāz*)
santri (J, I)	student in a *pesantren*; by extension, any strictly practising Muslim
sarf	Arabic grammar: verbal inflection
sayyid, pl. *sādāt*	descendant of the Prophet Muhammad
sesat (M)	deviant; '*ajaran sesat*' are deviant teachings

shirk	associating anything with God, 'polytheism;' to puritan Muslims, the belief in the possibility of mediation between humans and God, for instance, by saints, or in the effectiveness of magical cures constitutes *shirk*
sunna	the way of the Prophet, to be imitated by his faithful. The Prophet's *sunna* is primarily known through the *hadīths*, the reports on individual instances of his words or exemplary acts
surau (M)	a small prayer house, smaller than the congregational mosque (*masjid*)
tablīgh	propagation, predication
tafsīr	Qur'anic exegesis and commentary. A translation, because of the degree of interpretation and choice involved, is also referred to as a *tafsīr*
tajwīd	the proper articulation of Qur'anic Arabic
takfīr	declaring someone a *kāfir* or unbeliever; the term *takfīrī* refers to Islamist groups that declare nominally Muslim rulers de facto unbelievers for not ruling according to the *sharī'a*, implying these rulers should be fought
tanzīm	organisation
taqlīd	imitation, emulating a model; especially, following the rulings of scholars of one particular school of Islamic jurisprudence
tarbiya	education, training, disciplining
tarīqa	'the Sufi path': Sufi order
tasfiyya	purification
tawhīd	the absolute unity and uniqueness of God; for Salafis, this implies the rejection of all authority not derived from God or based on His will as expressed in the Qur'an and *sunna*
tibb	medicine, healing
'ulamā (pl. of *'ālim*)	scholars, divines
ūnānī tibb	'Greek medicine,' a traditional healing system based on the theory of four humours (known as Galenic medicine in the West); Ibn Sina's *al-Qānūn* is the most famous work in this discipline
usra (A), *usrah*, *usroh* (M, J, I)	lit. '[nuclear] family;' in the Muslim Brotherhood, the *usra* is a small group of members, who have intensive contact and are being trained / indoctrinated together

ustādh (A), *ustad* (I) *ustāz* (P, U)	teacher (term of address for a person of religious learning)
wifaq	pact, accord, agreement, unity; in the South Asian context an umbrella organization of religious schools
wā'iz	preacher
waqf, pl. *awqāf*	pious foundation
zakāt	obligatory alms 'tax,' consisting of a specified percentage of specific sources of income or wealth. The payment of *zakat* is one of the five 'pillars' of Islam
zākir, *zākira* (P, U), *dhākir* (A)	a person who performs the *dhikr (zikr)*, reciting God's name of certain pious formulas; in the South Asian Shi'a context, the person who recites the story of Husayn's martyrdom at Karbala

Acronyms and Names of Organisations, Movements and Institutions

ABIM	Angkatan Belia Islam Malaysia (Malaysian Islamic Youth Movement)
Ahl-i Hadith	South Asian puritan reform movement fiercely opposed to Sufi beliefs and practices as well as the traditional schools of Islamic jurisprudence; the study of *hadith* replaces most of the other traditional Islamic sciences
Al Irsyad	Reformist association active among Indonesia's Arab community
Barelvi	name given to the traditionalist mainstream in South Asian Islam, strongly oriented towards Sufism and the veneration of saints. Named after Bareilly, the residence of the leading nineteenth-century apologist of traditionalist Islam, Raza Ahmad Khan
BKSPP	Badan Kerjasama Pondok Pesantren (Association for Co operation between Pesantrens), a network of Islamic schools in West Java, Indonesia, previously affiliated with the Masyumi party
Darul Arqam	Sufi-inspired religious movement in Malaysia, with branches in Singapore and Indonesia. Transformed itself into the trading corporation Rufaqa' after it was banned in Malaysia
Darul Islam	Indonesian political movement struggling for the establishment of an Islamic state. First emerged during the struggle for independence in West Java; later joined by related movements in Aceh and South Sulawesi contesting the authority of the secular Indonesian Republic
DDII	see Dewan Dakwah Islamiyah Indonesia
Deobandi	one of the two mainstream movements of South Asian Islam, named after the moderately reformist madrasa of Deoband. Critical of Sufi orders and strongly opposed to saint worship and other 'popular' practices condoned by the more

	traditionalist Barelvi movement. An estimated 65% of the madrasas in Pakistan are Deobandi orientated
Dewan Dakwah Islamiyah Indonesia	'Indonesian Council for Islamic Predication,' organisation established in 1967 by former Masyumi political leaders
DI	see Darul Islam
FKAWJ	Forum Komunikasi Ahlus Sunnah Wal-Jama'ah, a Salafi group in Indonesia from which the militant Laskar Jihad emerged in 2000
Harkat-ul-Mujahidin	Pakistan-based armed militant group, primarily focused on the struggle in Kashmir
IAIN	Institut Agama Islam Negeri (State Institute of Islamic Studies), institutes for training religious teachers, judges of Islamic courts and other religious functionaries in Indonesia
IKIM	Institut Kefahaman Islam Malaysia (Malaysian Institute for Islamic Understanding), established in 1992 by Prime Minister Mahathir Mohamad to disseminate a modern understanding of Islam
ISTAC	International Institute of Islamic Thought and Civilisation, a research and postgraduate institute affiliated with the International Islamic University Malaysia
Jaish-i Muhammad	Pakistan-based militant group of Deobandi affiliation
Jama'ah Islamiyah	Radical underground Islamist network in Southeast Asia, members of which planned and carried out a series of spectacular terrorist actions
Jama'at al-Da'wa (Jama'at al-Da'wa ila al-Qur'an wa-l-Hadith)	Pakistan-based militant group, affiliated with the Ahl-i Hadith movement and connected with the Lashkar-i Tayyiba
Jama'at-i Islami	Islamist movement founded by Sayyid Abu'l A'la Mawdudi in late colonial India. After the partition of British India, the Pakistani and Indian branches operated largely independently of one another
Jami'a Millia Islamia	'Islamic National College', leading Muslim university in New Delhi
Jami'at al-Dirasat al-Islamiyya	'College of Islamic Studies', a radical madrasa in Karachi, Pakistan
Jami'at al-Zahra	women's college in the Shi'i seminary of Qom, Iran

Jam'iyat-i Talaba-i Islam (also: Islami Jamiat-e Talaba)	students' association affiliated with the Jama'at-i Islami
Jam'iyat-ul-Ulama-i Hind	association of scholars of Deobandi orientation in India, established in 1919
Jam'iyat-ul-Ulama-i Islam	association of Pakistani *ulama* of Deobandi orientation, established at the birth of Pakistan in 1948. Currently split into three factions, the militant Fazlur Rahman wing, the Samiul Haq faction and the Ajmal Qadri faction
Jam'iyat-ul-Ulama-i Pakistan	association of Pakistani *ulama* of Barelvi orientation
JI	see Jama'ah Islamiyah and Jama'at-i Islami
JTI	see Jam'iyat-i Talaba-i Islam
JUH	see Jam'iyat-ul-Ulama-i Hind
JUI	see Jam'iyat-ul-Ulama-i Islam
kaum muda	'the young people': general term for Muslim reformist groups in the Malay-speaking regions of Southeast Asia
kaum tua	'the old people': general term for traditionalist Muslims in the Malay-speaking regions of Southeast Asia
Kumpulan Mujahidin Malaysia (KMM)	'Malaysian Mujahidin Group,' obscure militant movement involved in a number of violent incidents
KW9	Komado Wilayah 9 (9th Regional Command), regional branch of the Darul Islam movement, covering Jakarta and adjacent districts
Lashkar-i Jhangvi	offshoot of the Sipah-i Sahaba-i Pakistan, even more militantly anti-Shi'a
Lashkar-i Tayyiba	Ahl-i Hadith affiliated militant organization, considered as the armed wing of the Markaz al-Da'wa wa l-Irshad, based in Murdike, Panjab, Pakistan
Laskar Jihad	armed Salafi movement that took part in regional conflicts in Indonesia during the years 2000-02
LIPIA	Lembaga Ilmu Pengetahuan Islam dan Bahasa Arab (Institute of Islamic and Arabic Studies), Saudi-funded teaching institution in Jakarta
Majlis-i Tahaffuz-i Khatm-i Nabuwwat	Deoband-affiliated association 'for the defence of the finality of Prophethood', i.e., primarily an anti-Ahmadiyya association
Masyumi	Indonesia's largest Muslim party, dissolved in 1960

Muhammadiyah	Indonesian reformist association, especially active in education and da'wa, the second largest Muslim association in the country
MATA	Majlis Agama Tertinggi (Supreme Council of Religious Affairs), Malaysia
MUI	Majelis Ulama Indonesia (Indonesian Council of Ulama), established by the government to explain government policy to the Muslim population and advise the government
Mutahhida Majlis-i Amal (MMA)	six-party religious coalition, including Jama'at-i Islami and Fazlur Rahman's JUI
Nadwat ul-'Ulama	Madrasa and association based in Lucknow, India
Nahdlatul Ulama	Traditionalist Muslim association in Indonesia, the country's largest association
NII /TII	Negara Islam Indonesia / Tentara Islam Indonesia (Islamic State of Indonesia / Islamic Army of Indonesia), alternative name of the Darul Islam movement
NU	see Nahdlatul Ulama
PAS	Parti Islam Se-Malaysia (Pan-Malaysian Islamic Party)
Persis	Persatuan Islam, Indonesian puritan reformist association
PKMM	Partai Kebangsaan Melayu Malaya (Malay National Party of Malaya)
PKS	Partai Keadilan Sejahtera (Prosperous Justice Party), Indonesian political party inspired by Muslim Brotherhood ideology
PP	Pondok Pesantren (in Indonesia)
Rabita Madaris Arabiya	association of Deobandi madrasas (in India)
Rabitat al-'Alam al-Islamiyya	Muslim World League
RMA	see Rabita Madaris Arabiya
Sipah-i Sahaba-i Pakistan	'Army of the Prophet's Companions in Pakistan', the first militant movement, emerged as an offshoot of the Deobandi JUI
SMII	Syed Maudoodi International Islamic Educational Institute, the Jama'at-i Islami's most important school
Tablighi Jama'at	originally Indian missionary movement; at present probably the largest transnational Islamic movement

Tahrik-i Nifaz-i Fiqh-i Ja'fariya	Pakistan's major Shi'i political organisation (later renamed as: Tahrik-i Ja'fariya Pakistan)
Tanzim al-Madaris al-Arabiya	'Organisation of Arabic Schools': the association of Barelvi (traditionalist) madrasas in Pakistan
Tanzim-i Abna-i Qadim	'Old Boys' Organisation', Deobandi alumni association (in India)
UMNO	United Malays National Organisation, Malaysia's ruling party
Wifaq al-Madaris	federation or union of madrasas. There are five such unions in Pakistan. For political lobbying they are united under the Ittihad Tanzimat Madaris Diniya (Union of Organisations of Religious Schools)
Wifaq al-Madaris al-Arabiya	the union of Deobandi madrasas in Pakistan
Wifaq al-Madaris al-Shi'a	the union of Shi'a madrasas in Pakistan
Wifaq al-Madaris al-Salafiya	the union of Ahl-i Hadith affiliated madrasas in Pakistan

Maps

1. India

2. Pakistan

3. China

4. Malaysia (& Southern Thailand)

5. Java (Indonesia)

India

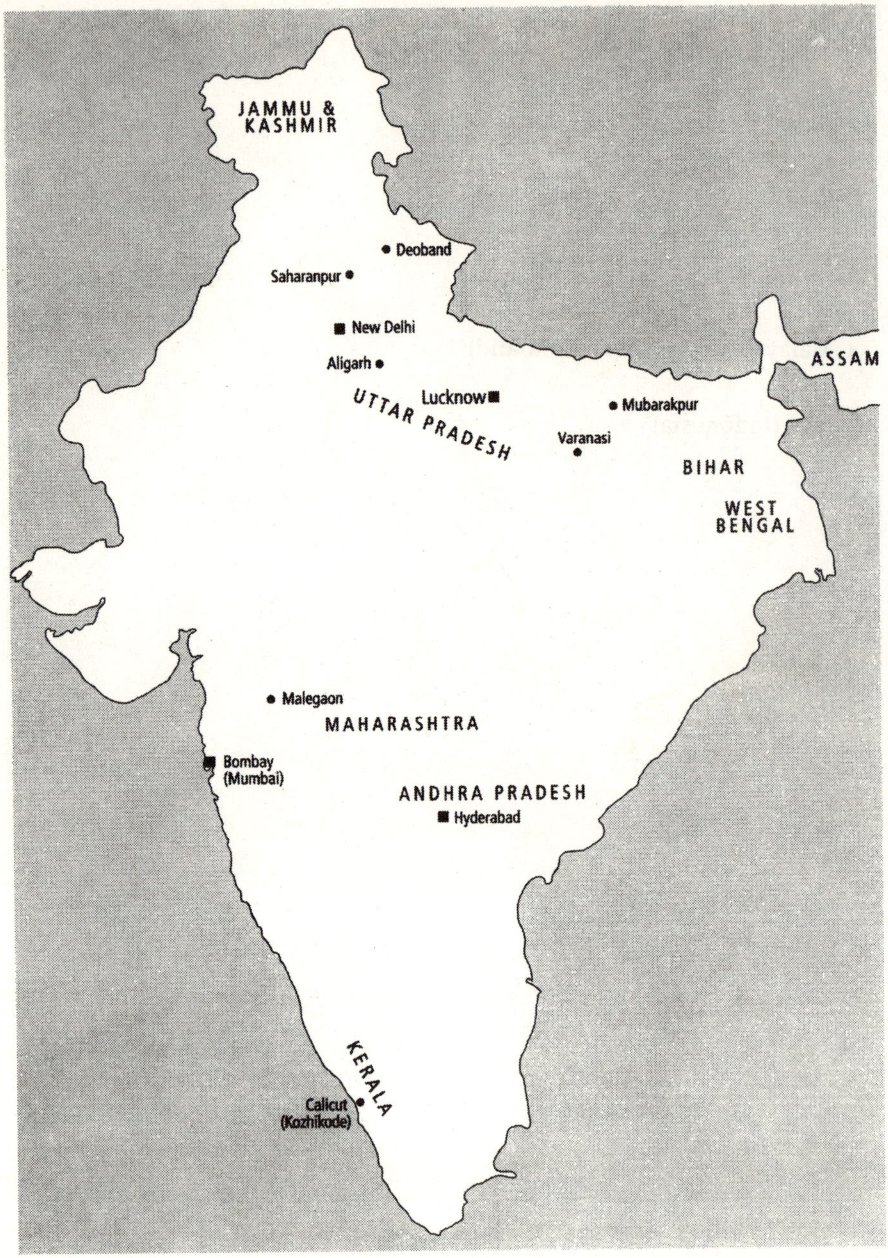
JAMMU &
KASHMIR
Deoband
Saharanpur
New Delhi
Aligarh
Lucknow
UTTAR PRADESH
Mubarakpur
Varanasi
ASSAM
BIHAR
WEST
BENGAL
Malegaon
MAHARASHTRA
Bombay
(Mumbai)
ANDHRA PRADESH
Hyderabad
KERALA
Calicut
(Kozhikode)

Pakistan

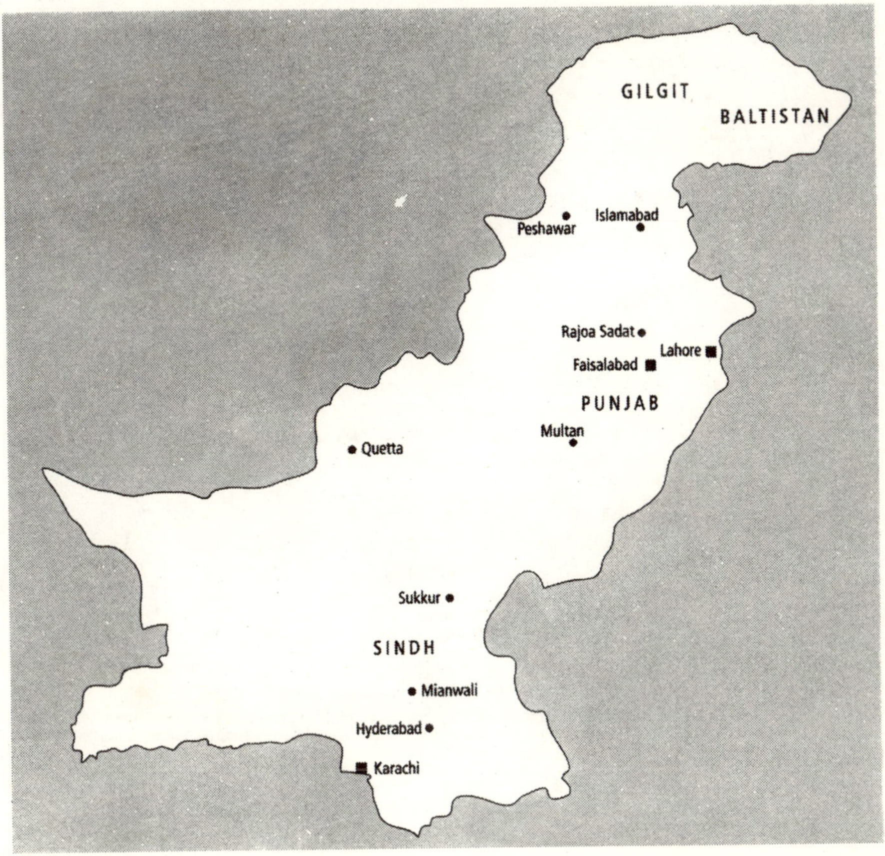
GILGIT
BALTISTAN
Peshawar
Islamabad
Rajoa Sadat
Lahore
Faisalabad
PUNJAB
Multan
Quetta
Sukkur
SINDH
Mianwali
Hyderabad
Karachi

China

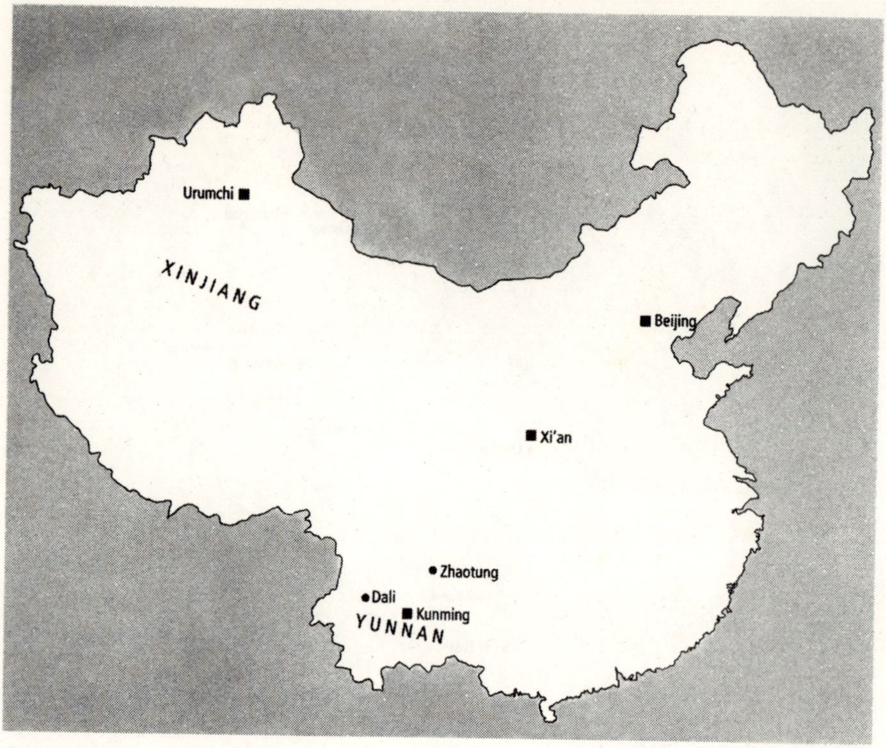
Urumchi
XINJIANG
Beijing
Xi'an
Zhaotung
Dali
Kunming
YUNNAN

Malaysia (& Southern Thailand)

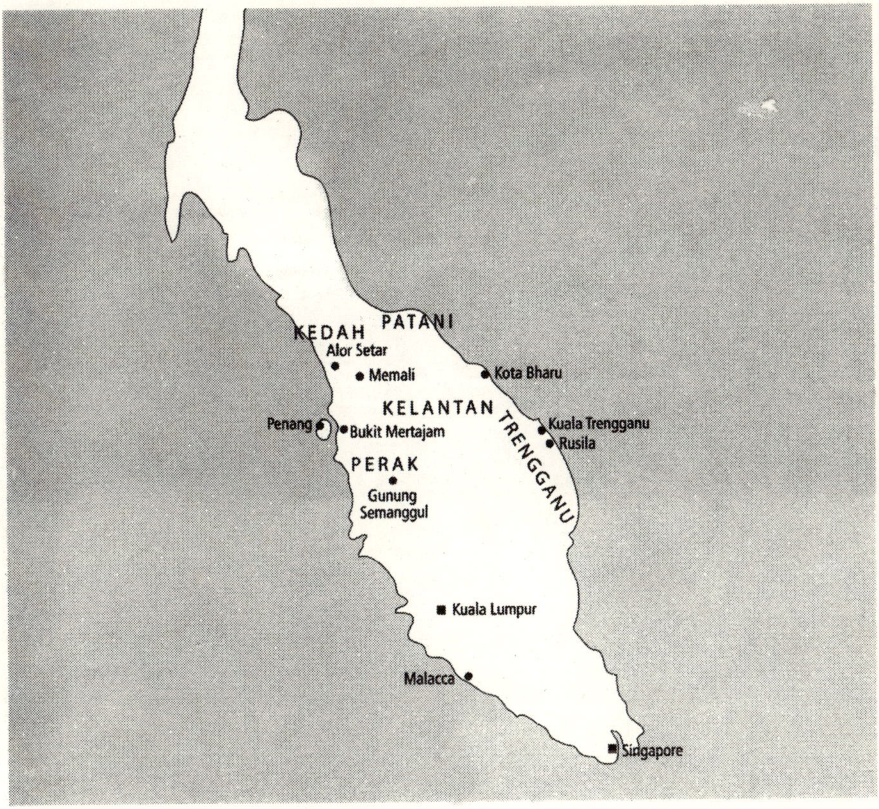

Java (Indonesia)

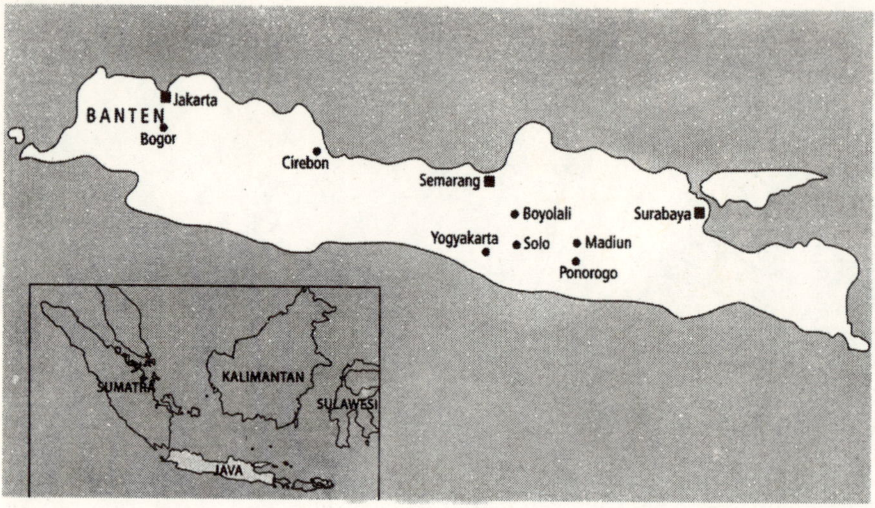

Index